Ghost of Our Grandfather

Geraldine (Schroder) Perry
Donna Schroder & Ken Fousek

With Research Assistance from Diana (Schroder) Spragg
& Sandy (Schroder) Frigo

Ghost of Our Grandfather

by Geraldine Perry, Donna Schroder, and Ken Fousek

Copyright © 2022 by Geraldine Perry

ALL RIGHTS RESERVED

ISBN; 978--1-66786-080-0

Cover by Jefferry Purnawan

Book Layout ©2017 BookDesignTemplates.com

Printed in the U.S.A.

To the grandfather we never knew
and to our late sister Diana (Schroder) Spragg and our beloved cousin Ken Fousek, who
passed away just weeks before this book went to print

Acknowledgements

This book originally began several years ago as part of a family history project spearheaded by Donna Schroder and initially involving the four Schroder sisters which included Donna, Diana, Sandy and myself, Geri. Sadly, Donna's identical twin sister Diana (Schroder) Spragg died a few months after our first, very fruitful road trip to our ancestral roots in South Dakota. Our youngest sister Sandy (Schroder) Frigo managed to join Donna and myself for most of our remaining road trips, providing not only good company but hundreds of photos and almost as many pages of research notes. Sandy's job prevented her from assisting us in the writing of the initial drafts of our maternal grandfather's life, so we recruited our cousin and long-time local historian Ken Fousek to help fill in details and overall content as we struggled our way through countless additional drafts. It was during this somewhat tedious process that the story of our grandfather and that of the Northern Plains unfolded in ways we never could have imagined.

Invaluable assistance was also provided by the entire team at the South Dakota Archives in Pierre, South Dakota, especially Virginia Hanson and Ken Stewart. We would be remiss if we did not include the many local historians we met or talked with on the phone in the Brule County and Charles Mix areas, especially Doris Ann Chemla from the Brule County Historical Society who met us twice to show us the materials the Society has been collecting and assembling in the basement of the old Catholic Church moved in from Bendon to the outskirts of Kimball. Similar thanks are in order for the many libraries, court houses and registrar offices who assisted us in our collection of original documents. We also want to thank the land patent researcher Don Smith whom we hired through Time Passages Genealogy to help us clear up some of the nagging questions surrounding our grandfather's early land acquisitions.

Last but certainly not least we must thank the many Fousek relatives (some of whom we met for the first time) for very generously giving us their time and sharing with us information they had acquired over the years.

Preface

This book began as a short sketch about our grandfather Vaclav James Fousek who died more than twenty years before any of us were born. It became, out of necessity, as much an historical account of a remarkable, often mis-represented and poorly understood period in American history as it was a story about our grandfather. It is, in essence, an historical biography of a man whose life and legacy were made all the more compelling by the era that shaped him. The essential elements of that era still reverberate today, hence the title *Ghost of Our Grandfather*.

In political, economic and personal terms our grandfather's challenging and multifaceted life was in many ways a composite representation of life on the Northern Plains. It was in fact the unexpectedly rich tapestry of our grandfather's life that led us to expand our research, which soon set forth roots into a surprisingly enlightening study of the old American West and the western frontier. Moreover, the key events in Vaclav's life, including why and how he and his extended family integrated themselves with the fearsome Dakota Sioux and the way economic and monetary matters impacted all of them, revealed our grandfather to be not just a man of his time but a man whose life circumstances provide important lessons for all of us today.

My sister Donna had been steadily working on our family history for several years before she managed to get myself, Donna's twin sister Diana, our sister Sandy and our cousin Ken Fousek involved. As we delved into the facts and details of our grandfather's life, we found his story to be unexpectedly captivating and far more gratifying than what tiny bits of family lore had been able to provide. The strangely enigmatic, yet supposedly well-known and widely respected individual whom we never met eventually emerged as a caring, highly intelligent, hard-working, family-oriented person who had managed to engage himself in an impressive array of political, social and business activities during the explosive westward expansion, often referred to as the Great Dakota Boom, that took place after the Civil War.

Like that of so many other pioneers of the Great Dakota Boom, our grandfather's hopes and dreams were severely constrained and otherwise burdened by the incredible hardships that came with carving out a new life in the wilderness. But perhaps even more importantly and certainly more germane to this story is that our grandfather's life was, like that of countless others, also defined and seriously impacted by seemingly inexplicable financial loss and tragedy stemming, as the Populists of the late nineteenth century so articulately charged, from the monetary system being incrementally foisted upon America.

Our grandfather died in 1923, in Dante, South Dakota more than two decades before any of us were born, and just seven years after he married our grandmother. Our mother Elsie, the eldest of their three children, was not quite six years old and Ken's father Clarence was not quite five years old at the time of their father's death. It was the second marriage for both, with our grandmother contributing three older children from a previous marriage and our grandfather contributing seven living children, plus seven grandchildren. Matters were made more complicated for us because our grandmother had married a third time, some five years after our grandfather's death, thereby acquiring seven additional stepchildren. It was by all standards a large, complicated family.

It may seem strange to some but it is true that we, together with all of our surviving cousins, knew very little about our shared grandfather. This was partly due to the fact that our grandfather died decades before any of us were born, precluding any chance of our meeting him or hearing all the wonderful tales he might have told about his life. Added to this was the fact that our elders, for the most part, neglected to share their own memories or tales they might have heard. Our own childhood memories consisted only of fleeting mentions of him that often seemed oddly shrouded in mystery. Discussions concerning him were even whispered in Czech by our elders to each other, obviously meant to be kept secret.

Photos we had of our grandfather were few, letters non-existent. The most important document in our possession was our grandfather's Will. This Will would eventually motivate us to unravel the primary cause of the financial disaster that befell him as well as his entire family beginning in 1920. This catastrophe in fact gripped all rural America, eventually spreading to urban America and the world by 1929.

As we began the difficult process of putting together all the myriad bits and pieces of information we were gathering about our grandfather's life, we discovered that we had precious few family tales or memories we could draw upon. The most vivid among the stories we had were provided by the youngest of us, Ken Fousek. One of these involved the time Ken happened to see a short clip on a local TV station, probably around 1953, discussing our grandfather as he stood next to the new buggy that he had purchased during a visit to Sioux City, Iowa in 1903. The only other story we had was when one of our much older mutual cousins told Ken about how our grandfather sold pots and pans in Iowa during winter to make extra money for the family. Only after carefully piecing together widely scattered documents and news articles were we able to reasonably conjecture where this story fit in the timeline of our grandfather's life.

The most vivid memory Donna, our two sisters and I have is that of visiting the Vega Cemetery where our grandfather is buried. We were taken to that cemetery numerous times throughout our childhood by our mother, who, during these visits, never told us any stories about her father or the cemetery in which he is buried, perhaps because she had few stories to tell, and perhaps also because the memories were, even then, too painful and too intertwined with confusing family stories. She never even mentioned that the farm just across the road from the cemetery had been homesteaded by her father and that the Crow Creek (Dakota Sioux) Indians would regularly camp there. Nor did she mention that the town of Vega, which her father, grandfather and uncle had built, once stood there, or that the cemetery itself was on the farm her grandparents, and our great-grandparents, had homesteaded.

Many, if not most, of our grandfather's descendants still live in South Dakota, the state that he came to call home. As my sisters and I crisscrossed the state visiting our cousins, the most striking discovery we made was that the sum total of information collected from all of these South Dakota cousins was very nearly as limited as our own. This information did of course add to our minuscule collection, but not by an amount large enough to unravel the mysteries that shrouded our grandfather's memory or, for that matter, enough to allow us to pull together in an understandable way all the disparate bits of factual detail we were slowly gathering.

Our quest began in 2009, insofar as our maternal grandfather Vaclav Fousek is concerned, and ended in 2017. Our yearly road trips found us visiting multiple courthouses multiple times, multiple registrars of deeds multiple times, multiple recorders of deeds multiple times, and multiple libraries in multiple states multiple times. We visited countless museums and met with local historians, primarily in Brule County, multiple times and last but not least, on each and every trip we spent several days diving into the various materials at the Archives at Pierre. Two years running we made the trek to Iowa to find out more about where our grandfather lived before coming to South Dakota.

At home, we would make phone calls to various government agencies, speak with local historians and librarians, review and organize the material we had collected during our trips and do online research. While we were in fact researching both sides of our family during this time, most of our time was spent trying to unravel the complicated and seemingly well-hidden story of our maternal grandfather and his family.

For entertainment as much as for edification, we spent countless hours readings stories of pioneer life and one would find me (Geri) reading aloud to my sisters the more salient parts of various books while en route from one South Dakota destination to another. These books included *Land of the Burnt Thigh* by Edith Kohl, *Frontier Woman* by Walter D. Wyman, *Nothing But Prairie and Blue Sky*, also by Wyman, and *Brule County History*, which was compiled by the Brule County Historical Society.

Donna belongs to *Ancestry* and made liberal use of that resource. Similarly, she subscribed to *Newspapers.com* and spent many hours combing through that resource. All of us made use of the digitized newspaper resource at *Chronicling America*. As a former HUD loan specialist and as a volunteer for her local VFW, Donna was thankfully familiar with spreadsheets and began compiling a number of these to facilitate and streamline our research efforts.

About four or five years ago Donna and I began to write up what we thought would be our grandfather's story. The first two or three versions were only a few pages long and, as we would soon find out, riddled with mistakes. We hired a land patent researcher to help us fill in some missing details concerning our grandfather's early whereabouts as a "Pioneer of the Great Dakota Boom" and dragged in our cousin Ken Fousek, who has been a local historian in his state of Missouri for many years (and who was a co-author of a book he and I wrote together on the monetary system), for council on where and how to go about digging up more material and to further verify to the extent possible what we had found.

Finally, as an author of two previous books, I began writing a more complete version of our grandfather's story with my sister Donna and cousin Ken serving as my proof-readers and content contributors. The inclusion of considerable historical context helped explain some of the more contradictory details of our grandfather's life. For example, life among the Sioux was not nearly as treacherous as we had originally imagined. We now know why. Also, the mysterious disappearance of the sizable estate left by our grandfather within a few short years after his death was at long last understood when we grasped the way the money system had worked against the farmer from the Populist period forward, and which in fact had been a main concern for farmers during that entire period.

For many reasons, including a paucity of family information about our grandfather, our journey has been long and arduous. We discovered that in order to fit together the tiny but enticing bits and pieces of information we found on our grandfather, we needed to learn more about the context of his life and that of his friends and family. We can say with conviction that our journey has been incredibly rewarding and enjoyable for all of us, in no small part because it forced us to explore subjects and issues in far more depth than we otherwise would have.

We delved deep into the Populist movement, particularly as it affected South Dakota, because we discovered that our grandfather was a Populist. There is a particularly poignant irony here because the main objective of the Populists was government issuance of money in amounts adequate enough to carry on rural business without crushing debt. Unfortunately, the Populists were outspent and outmaneuvered, not by William McKinley himself, but by those who backed him for President, an unhappy circumstance that would, mere decades later, rain down misery not only on our grandfather and his family but all of farm country.

We also explored agrarianism on the Plains, because our grandfather was, in addition to other vocations, a farmer who practiced diversified farming techniques more or less in the mode of Tama Jim Wilson of Iowa who was later to become U.S. Secretary of Agriculture. We similarly examined the complicated relationship between the Native American Indian and the pioneers, because both family lore and supporting details showed that our grandfather helped start a town where the Dakota Sioux Indians from the Crow Creek Reservation would trade and set up camp as a resting place while en route to destinations in the southern part of the state. And we looked into the Freethinker movement because we discovered that our grandfather was a Freethinker.

Almost as if some mysterious force were propelling us forward, we slowly began to solve a number of seemingly unsolvable puzzles. For example, we explained the riddle of why, as the online Lyman-Brule Genealogical Society states, there are "two unknown Negroes" among the seventeen unknown burials in the Vega Cemetery - this during a time when the "Jim Crow" period was rampant. We also were able to determine why the little of town of Vega, which our grandfather helped build, was considered the "trade center" of the area, while the nearby railroad town of Kimball was considered the "market center." And, perhaps most important of all, we solved the thorny enigma surrounding the catastrophic financial ruin that befell not only our grandfather and his entire family, but most of rural America in the 1920's. This particularly vexing mystery and the multiple tragedies that ensued would never have been unraveled had it not been for the fact that we serendipitously discovered that our grandfather had been not just a Populist, but a *South Dakota* Populist, and later had become a major shareholder of a small rural bank under odd circumstances.

The multiple financial losses and tragedies that occurred within our maternal grandfather's family following the 1920 farm depression similarly impacted our paternal grandparents' families a few years later during the better known and more widespread Great Depression. The almost unimaginable suffering and unspeakable tragedies that came out of these events helps us better understand why any mention of our pioneer ancestors was so infrequent and so muffled throughout our growing up years, despite the abundance of Wild West dramas then dominating American movies and TV.

The connection to the banking and monetary system also explained a lot about the real causes of the strange death of our grandfather's first son Charles, and the shocking suicide of my sisters' and my paternal grandfather not many years later. These kinds of episodes were hardly limited to our family; they occurred with vicious frequency all across the plains and were, as House Banking Chair Louis T. McFadden told the United States Congress in 1933, directly linked to the money system – just as the Populists had charged decades before.

In the end, all of this helps to explain how it was that the life of the person we know as our grandfather uniquely reveals the poorly understood role played by our monetary system in the westward expansion. For whatever reason we seem to have been chosen as the vehicle through which our grandfather's story would be told, and that is why we believe that the essence of his story lingers still on the Northern Plains

Contents

First Stop Iowa

Plat maps and census reports of the post-Civil War era reveal that many immigrant families, including both sets of our paternal great-grandparents and one set of maternal great-grandparents, farmed in Iowa before venturing forth into untamed Dakota Territory. Both sides of our paternal great-grandparents, for example, emigrated from Germany to northern Illinois where they lived for a few years before moving more or less in tandem to the same area in central Iowa to farm, and finally to Avon, South Dakota. Deviating from that pattern only slightly, the first home in America for our maternal great-grandparents and their young son was eastern Iowa.

So it happened that some one hundred and fifty-two years ago, when he was ten years old, our maternal grandfather Vaclav James Fousek traveled with his parents, our maternal great-grandparents, from what was then known as Bohemia in Central Europe to settle in Washington County, Iowa before moving west to Dakota Territory. The year was 1870, the same year that our paternal great-grandparents moved from the town of Shannon in Carroll County, Illinois to Grundy County, in central Iowa.

While both sets of our paternal great-grandparents rented small farms in Iowa before moving to Dakota Territory, the Fousek family was able to purchase, free and clear, a forty-acre farm near the little town of Ainsworth, Iowa about fifty or so miles west of the Mississippi River. The parents of our grandfather's first wife Barbara Havlik had already settled near Ainsworth, and it was on that farm that Barbara and most of her siblings were born.

Our maternal grandfather was born on September 1, 1860 in Mlada Boleslav, Central Bohemia (later the Czech Republic) as the only child of Stephen Fousek and Elizabeth (Alzbeta) Ceckova. The 1900 and 1910 U.S. Census Reports told us that he emigrated to the U.S. in 1870 with his parents. The 1880 U.S. Census shows that our grandfather was living in Highland Township, Washington County, Iowa with his parents, and at this point our grandfather's 90-year-old paternal grandfather George was also living with the family. Our grandfather's occupation was listed as that of farmer. He was 19 years old at the time.

By the time our ancestors arrived in Iowa, one-room log cabins, common to the early pioneers who settled in the more forested areas of eastern and central Iowa, had been replaced with frame houses. As such, our ancestors were able to enjoy, relatively speaking, a more comfortable lifestyle than the pioneers who had come before them. From what we have been able to gather from historians at the Living History Farm in the Des Moines suburb of Urbandale, it was a frame house that our ancestors would most likely have lived in when they came to Iowa, not a log cabin. In short, the Iowa frontier had all but vanished by the time our ancestors arrived in Iowa, which meant that newcomers like themselves were settlers rather than pioneers.

By 1870, countless farms and small towns blanketed the whole state, replacing all but a very tiny portion of the Iowa frontier. In a mutually beneficial, interdependent economic and social relationship, small towns served as the supply centers for the farmers in the surrounding area. In addition, stagecoaches and steamboats, those signature icons of the frontier, were giving way to the five railroad lines that already crisscrossed the state. Thanks to the railroad system then in place in Iowa, transportation was possible year-round instead of only during the warmer months.

Covered wagons still provided transportation for those venturing forth into Dakota Territory especially for those traveling to locations not served by a railroad. We were quite excited (and impressed) when we discovered that in the mid-1880s our paternal grandmother had traveled from Iowa in a covered wagon with her parents, siblings and identical twin sister to what is now Avon, South Dakota where her parents staked their homestead claim. The same mode of travel may not have been used by our maternal grandfather Vaclav and his parents because by 1880 the Milwaukee & St. Paul Railroad had made it as far west as Kimball, which was a railroad town within fifteen or so miles south of where they settled.

Earning a Living on Forty Acres

Land records show that our great-grandparents Stephen and Alzbeta (Vaclav's parents) purchased their first forty-acre parcel in 1871 outside of Ainsworth, Iowa for $250 cash, and their second forty-acre parcel, which was contiguous with the first, in 1875 for $900 with a $250 mortgage.

In contrast, our paternal great-grandfather, John T. Schroder, accompanied by his new bride and his mother-in-law, seems to have rented a farm upon arrival in Grundy County, Iowa. We say this for two reasons. Firstly, we found a chattel mortgage, recorded in Illinois just before the group left for Iowa, which shows that John T. had borrowed $385 from a relative named John G. Schroder using his "chattel" as security. The chattel included two horses, two cows, a wagon and some farm equipment. Secondly, an 1880 U.S. Census shows that by the time of that census, John T. was renting fifty acres of tilled land, plus 10 acres that remained "as meadow or tree land." By 1888 he moved his family to what would become Avon, South Dakota where he purchased a quarter section of land (160 acres) which housed a very crude cabin. We do not know whether this farm was mortgaged or not, but we do know that the acquisition of another parcel some twelve years later, in 1901, would be accomplished by assuming someone else's mortgage.

Our grandfather (center) and his father Stephen and mother Alzbeta, probably around the time he married his first wife Barbara.

We have no idea what farming methods our ancestors might have brought with them from the "old country," but we do know that agriculture in Iowa underwent considerable change after the Civil War during which time Iowa farmers had raised prodigious amounts of wheat as a cash crop. After the Civil War, Iowa farmers began to diversify by producing a variety of crops and livestock, some of which produce they traded with one another for other farm products and for finished goods from local merchants. This system allowed farmers to be more self-sustaining and economically independent. From what we have been able to glean from will documents and contemporary newspapers, this was similar to the style of farming our maternal grandfather Vaclav Fousek practiced all his life, using prairie grass and winter hay to feed his cattle.

Despite these changed production methods, farm work was still dictated by the seasons. In spring, farmers prepared and planted their fields. In summer, there was sheep shearing, haying and threshing. In autumn farmers picked corn, which we understand was the hardest task of all. In the winter months there was butchering, ice cutting, fence mending and wood chopping to do. Farm life was, by any measure, hard and exhausting work all year round.

On October 27, 1883, when he was 23, our maternal grandfather Vaclav married his first wife Barbara Havlik in Washington County, Iowa. Barbara was one of ten children born to Vaclav Wencil Havlik and Veronika Houzner. Both of Barbara's parents were born in Bohemia and came to the United States in 1857, after their marriage. Their oldest child, a little girl, was born in Bohemia but died in infancy while the family was still in Bohemia. Like our grandfather's parents, Barbara's parents settled in Ainsworth, Iowa where Barbara and all the rest of her siblings were born.

Barbara passed away on November 3, 1915 in Vega, South Dakota which was the little prairie town that the Fousek/Havlik clan built after they emigrated to Dakota Territory in the 1880s. Barbara's death certificate says she died of cardiac asthma, which is not actually a form of asthma but rather a type of coughing or wheezing that occurs with congestive heart failure. Family records say that Barbara died forty minutes before dinner of a possible heart attack, and a death notice appearing in the Gann Valley Chief said she died of enlargement of the heart. She was 55 years old.

It seems that the autumn of 1915 was a time of considerable loss for Vaclav because his father Stephen had died just a few weeks before Barbara, on September 28, 1915. It may be that both Stephen and Barbara had been ill for some time before they died. Evidence for this is provided by a bit of family lore as related by our mother, who said that Barbara had spent some time at what was then the very prestigious Sanitarium in Chamberlain for what our mother described as tuberculosis. In addition, a mere three days before his death, Stephen sold one of his two Vega, South Dakota farm parcels to his son Vaclav, while also providing a duly recorded deed for the other to his wife Alzbeta (who was also known as Elizabeth).

These small details taken together tell us that the last few months of 1915 must have been a very emotionally trying time for the entire family. Facing a future without his partner of thirty-two years and his father who had always been an integral part of his life must have looked very bleak and empty for our grandfather, especially so since his children had for the most part already entered adulthood.

Enter Our Grandmother

Burdened as he must have been by these losses, Vaclav nevertheless soon entered yet another event-filled chapter of his life when he met and soon married our grandmother Stephanie. By piecing together information provided in *Brule County History* together with our own family lore, we have surmised that our grandfather Vaclav met our grandmother, who also had been born in Bohemia, a few months after Barbara and Stephen's deaths, perhaps as early as February of 1916 when he took some hogs to Chicago. It is quite likely that he brought his hogs to the meat packing district in Chicago, known as the Union Stock Yards.

These stock yards had by then become the center of the American meatpacking industry and helped Chicago become known as "hog butcher of the world." Alternately known as the Back of the Yards and immortalized by Upton Sinclair's 1906 book *The Jungle*, the Union Stock Yards were not far from the Pilsen neighborhood where our grandmother Stephanie lived with her three young children. Pilsen itself, being dominated by lumberyards, factories, stockyards and breweries was the hub where workers would transform raw materials pouring in from the countryside into manufactured products that would be shipped east or sold inside the rapidly growing city.

Family lore has it that our grandmother Stephanie and grandfather Vaclav were introduced through a priest. This time at least family lore might be right. We say this because of the 1902 marriage certificate we managed to secure from St. Procopius Catholic Church in Chicago. This document shows the marriage of our grandmother Stephanie to her first husband Joseph Veselak but what was most interesting was that one of the witnesses listed on that document was one Fr. J. Beranek, whom we assume was a priest at the parish. We have managed to connect this clue to another bit of information gathered through South Dakota historical plat maps circa 1911. These maps show that a James Beranek, who was married to a sister of Vaclav's first wife Barbara, owned a farm about a mile from our grandfather's farm in Vega and as revealed by a number of newspaper clippings, had regular business and social dealings with the Fousek family. It seems entirely possible, even likely, that this James Beranek was in some way related to Fr. J. Beranek of Chicago.

So it is that we believe, just as family lore says, that a priestly introduction was how it came to be that, when he was 55, our newly widowed grandfather Vaclav Fousek married our grandmother Stephanie (Panovec) Veselak, herself already a widow at the tender age of 34 with three young children under the age of 11 to care for. They were married on July 9 of 1916 in Chicago, Illinois by a pastor of a Freethinker Congregation, which will be discussed in a later chapter.

Our grandfather, around the time he and our grandmother were married.

That summer of 1916 our grandfather Vaclav moved our grandmother Stephanie and her three young children to his home in Vega, South Dakota. Sadly, less than seven years after their marriage, our grandmother was again left a widow, this time with an additional three children under the age of six, when Vaclav died on March 1, 1923. According to his death certificate, the cause of death was Carcinoma of Sigmoid, or cancer of the sigmoid colon. An obituary in the Kimball Graphic said he had been ill for about six months before his death and will documents show that he had been operated on in Sioux City, Iowa on November 23, 1922. Interestingly, Vaclav's Death Certificate states that his birthplace was Crosnovsy, Czechoslovakia not "Mlada Boleslav, Central Bohemia," thus acknowledging the creation of the First Republic of Czechoslovakia in 1918.

Final Resting Place, Vega

Our grandfather and his first wife Barbara are buried in the Vega Cemetery, located on property that had been carved out of Stephen's homestead which was directly across from Barbara and Vaclav's homestead and much of the town of Vega in Brule County, South Dakota. Tiny slivers of evidence, carefully woven together, tell us that the town of Vega was, up until the mid 1930s, a tiny but thriving prairie town that Vaclav, together with Barbara's brother Wencil and his father Stephen, built.

Our grandfather's barn, partially rebuilt, and the Vega Cemetery are all that is left of Vega, with that cemetery having been deeded over to Camp Dakota Osveta (Dakota Enlightenment) No. 184 of Z.C.B.J. in 1926. According to online records, which are as of this writing still incomplete, the last burials took place in 2000. On April 28 of that year thirteen-year-old Ben Rank was buried in the cemetery, near his sister Jolene Marie who died at birth in 1989. 103-year-old Anna Kovanda was buried in the cemetery one month later, on May 28, 2000. However, during our own visit to the cemetery in 2017, we found three more burials that took place after 2000. Ben and Jolene's grandmother Elizabeth Lucille DuVall Rank was buried there in 2006; Richard C. Kotilinex was buried there in 2012 and George Havlik was buried there in 2016.

There are just under one and a half dozen unmarked graves in the cemetery which we assume were placed there before it was decided that the Vega Cemetery would become a bonafide cemetery in 1904. It is our belief that Vaclav and Barbara's daughter Libby, who died of diphtheria in 1903 just shy of her ninth birthday, is buried in one of these unmarked graves.

According to the online Lyman-Brule Genealogical Society there are "two unknown negroes" buried in the cemetery which would make them part of the fifteen unmarked burials. In an era when even cemeteries were often segregated by law, the mere fact that "two unknown negroes" appear on the Vega Cemetery roles speaks volumes about the Vega community and fit perfectly with what we were soon to discover about our grandfather's early religious and political activities.

On our 2017 visit, Ed Piskule who is the great-grandson of Barbara and Vaclav's youngest daughter Emma, said that Emma had told him that she had been present at the birth of three little babies of a black family named Houston who lived north of our grandfather's farm. We made the trek back to the cemetery and managed to find the headstone for these babies, which appears to be a newer-looking granite slab upon which the names Sidney, Loetta and Rosetta Houston are inscribed. Emma had told her great-grandson that the triplets died soon after birth and so we conjecture that they probably died around 1910 when Emma would have entered her teen years. Just who put the newer-looking granite headstone there is an unsolved mystery.

There is no indication that any Native American Indians were buried in this cemetery but that more than likely is because Native Americans had their own long-established rituals honoring the newly departed, part of which included sacred burial grounds.

The Vega Cemetery as it appears today. Photo taken by our sister Sandy in 2011.

CHAPTER 2

The West Beckons

Dakota Territory was officially opened for settlement in 1861 when out-going President James Buchanan signed the Organic Act. Per procedures laid out in the Northwest Ordinance of 1787, this Act essentially provided the framework for the administration and structure of the territory, conforming to the structure of state government and thereby preparing for the future formation and legal recognition of new states. William Jayne was appointed the Territory's first governor by President Lincoln. Jayne arrived in the designated capital of Yankton located in present day South Dakota on May 17, 1861.

Because it is relevant to our story, we mention here that the Dakota Land Company of St. Paul, Minnesota, which like other land companies was composed of land speculators and the politically well-connected, was involved in the founding of two of South Dakota's largest present-day cities. Sioux Falls was established in 1856, and Yankton in 1859, two and five years respectively *before* the territory was opened for settlement. As we were to learn, land speculation was a major force behind rapid and often irresponsible westward expansion, enabled as it usually was by "sham" treaties with the Native American Indians and financed by Eastern financiers and European syndicates.

The western United States was at this time a conglomeration of territories whose boundaries were in a continual state of flux both before and as new states were admitted to the union. Thus, as you can see from the accompanying map, Dakota Territory itself had been formed out of a leftover portion of the Minnesota Territory, after Minnesota became a state in 1858, together with a portion of Nebraska Territory. By 1863 part of that Nebraska Territory went to Idaho Territory with a portion of that taken from Idaho Territory in 1864. Nebraska achieved statehood in 1867 and a year later, in 1868, a portion of Dakota Territory was given to Wyoming Territory. By 1889 South and North Dakota along with Montana and Washington had achieved statehood, and by 1890 both Idaho and Wyoming had become states.

One year after the Organic Act was signed into law, the Homestead Act of 1862 was passed. Through this act ordinary citizens willing to move west were given the opportunity to acquire "free" land. However, the going was slow for the first fifteen years. According to John D. Hicks of *The Populist Revolt,* it was only after the hard times following the Panic of 1873 that a westward migration of any substance took place, this beginning in the late 1870s. Be that as it may, Bohemians were the first ethnic group to start filing claims in 1869 as a result of the 1862 Homestead Act. These Bohemians were followed several years later by Germans, Swedes, Norwegians, Poles and other Europeans who had been fleeing war and the relatively poorer social and economic conditions of Europe.

From what we have been able to glean from official records and documents, it appears that our grandfather and his first wife Barbara began exploring the Vega area sometime around 1883, during the period that became known as the Great Dakota Boom. Aided by increased rain levels, diminishing grasshopper plagues, the discovery of gold in the Black Hills, railroad expansion, and an endless supply of books and promotional materials replete with exaggerated claims of opportunity and success, some say this boom marked the end of the last frontier. Further assisting in the demise of the last frontier, according to John D. Hicks in his classic book *The Populist Revolt*, was the fact that "information that might deter settlers from coming was rigorously suppressed."

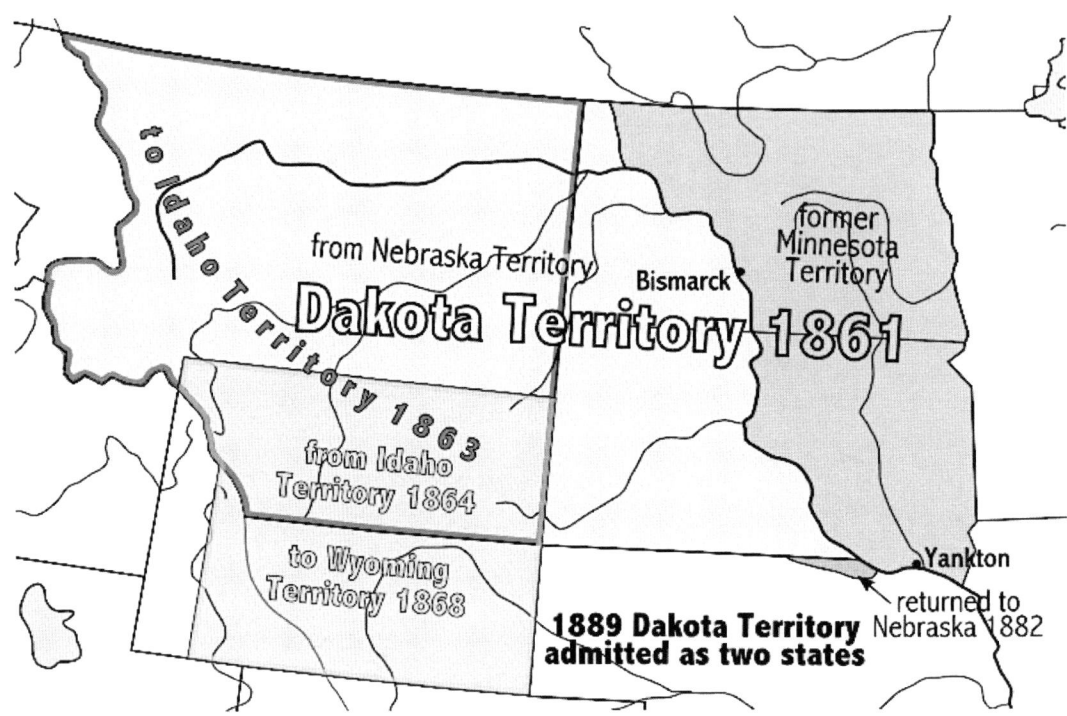

Dakota Territory 1861. Note the changes in 1863, 1864, 1868, 1882, and finally 1889 when North and South Dakota become states. A portion of the former Minnesota Territory makes up the newly formed Dakota Territory and will become part of the two newly formed states. The Missouri River runs from Bismarck south through Yankton with Yankton being the southernmost city of South Dakota. Our grandfather and his extended family settled about fifty miles east of the Missouri and one hundred miles northwest of Yankton. (The dark line running north to south through the middle of the territory is the western most boundary of the new states.)

As R. Alton Lee writes in *Principle Over Party*:

> The events of the Great Dakota Boom were duplicated throughout the Great Plains during this time, from Texas to Saskatchewan, stimulated by the transportation revolution. . . Land speculators, railroad promoters, and town builders fed the desire. Land and railroad agents shamelessly promoted the area as a farmer's utopia in order to entice land-hungry pioneers, even though average rainfall got progressively lower the farther west the railroad extended into the Great Plains. In fact, the region had been previously known as the Great American Desert, and the region had previously lived up to this reputation. . .By 1878, however, promoters were trumpeting the idea that "rain follows plow," spreading the popular theory that breaking sod facilitated a change in climate.

The Great Dakota Boom was the first of two Dakota booms. It took place in those counties east of the Missouri River, where the climate was somewhat more forgiving than lands that lay west of the river. This boom began roughly around the mid-1870s and ended in the late 1880s as dropping wheat and livestock prices, rising costs for machinery and transportation, and drought and grasshoppers once again became formidable challenges.

Amazingly, in just ten years, between 1878 and 1888, the population of the Dakota Territory had increased from 80,000 to 328,000, and the wheat crop grew from just under 3 million bushels in 1880 to over 60 million bushels in 1887. As a testament to homesteaders determined to do what it took to survive in this harsh new land, wheat production figures like these were not just impressive, they were without historical precedent. By way of comparison, it had taken fifty years for the prairie-grass states of Indiana and Illinois *together* to reach the level of wheat production Dakota had achieved in seven. Production figures like these also led to charges of overproduction, even though there could be no such thing when children and adults alike went hungry on a daily basis.

Untangling Confusing Details about Our Grandfather's Early Life in Dakota Territory

As mentioned, we have done our best to lay out the facts as established by official records and documents, but in some instances, we have been compelled to fill in gaps with a certain amount of conjecture, even as we continued to try to make sense of some accounts that appeared to us to be in error.

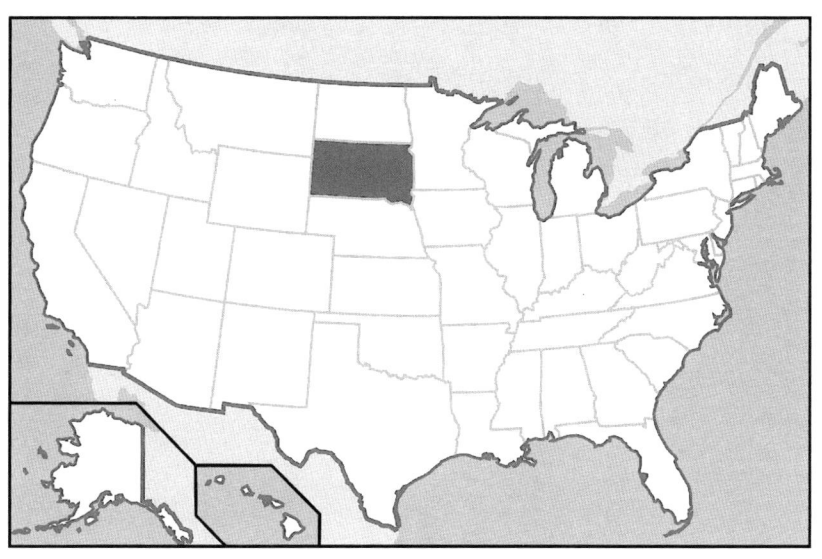

United States today. South Dakota is in shaded area. North Dakota is to the north, Montana and Wyoming to the west, Minnesota and Iowa to the east and Nebraska to the south.

For example, according to *Brule County History*, our grandfather and his first wife Barbara lived in Vega when they were first married, when the official records we were finding show they were married in Iowa in 1883 and census data shows they were living in Iowa two years later. In addition, *Brule County History* says that Vaclav traveled to Sioux Falls, South Dakota from Vega in winters to make money for the family.

To add to our confusion, an obituary appearing in the *Kimball Graphic* said that our grandfather first came to Brule County in 1883 and in 1886 settled on the reservation near Smith Creek with his wife and son. We later were able to sort out some of these puzzling details after a surprise discovery of a previously unknown "Preemption" claim filed by our grandfather in 1883 (which will be discussed in more detail in Chapter 4). For example, our eventual discovery of the "Pre" claim made it clear that our grandfather may have indeed adopted a common pattern of traveling back and forth to Iowa, both as a means of escaping the harsh Dakota winters and also to make money for the family, as early as 1883, suggested in *Brule County History*.

Prior to our discovery of the "Pre" claim, official records we had gathered told us that not only were Vaclav and Barbara married in 1883 in Iowa - *not* Vega - but they did not file their homestead claim on Smith Creek until 1890 where the town of Vega would be built. We also knew from official records that their son Charles was born on May 28, 1885 in Highland Township, Washington County, Iowa and that the June 1, 1885 Iowa Agricultural Census has our grandfather living in Iowa (explainable, as mentioned, by our later surprise discovery of the "Pre" claim to be discussed later).

As we sought to make sense of these details, we learned that "Vega" did not even exist until 1886 when a U.S. Post Office named Vega was created in Buffalo County, not Brule County. The Vega post office was moved to Brule County four years later, in 1890, at which point it may have developed into a quasi-town contained within one building that housed the Post Office, plus a store and a dance hall. The actual town of Vega came into its own ten years later, when the Post Office was moved to the farm of our grandfather's brother-in-law, which was directly across from our grandfather's farm. Interestingly, Vega ceased to exist as a full-fledged town sometime in the mid 1930's when we believe it was destroyed by fire, an all-too-common occurrence in the region. All that remains is the Vega Cemetery which still bears the name Vega on the cemetery gate. (See photo in Chapter 1)

Trew Hayes was the first Vega postmaster, and it is likely that the original post office was located on Trew Hayes' property in Buffalo County, just north of the Brule County line. Four years later, the post office was moved to a Brule County parcel owned by Abraham A. Meyers who became "Vega's" second postmaster on July 30, 1890. Meyers' tenure as post-master lasted 10 years.

Historical plat maps show that Smith Creek ran through Meyers' quarter section of land. The Meyers' parcel was slightly north and west of our grandfather's Brule County property, which family members referred to as "the Homestead" and on which both the Post Office and much of the town of Vega would eventually be located. Perhaps not surprisingly, A. A. Meyers was listed as one of the four witnesses that our grandfather recruited in order to secure the land patent for his Homestead property, through which small portions of Smith Creek also ran.

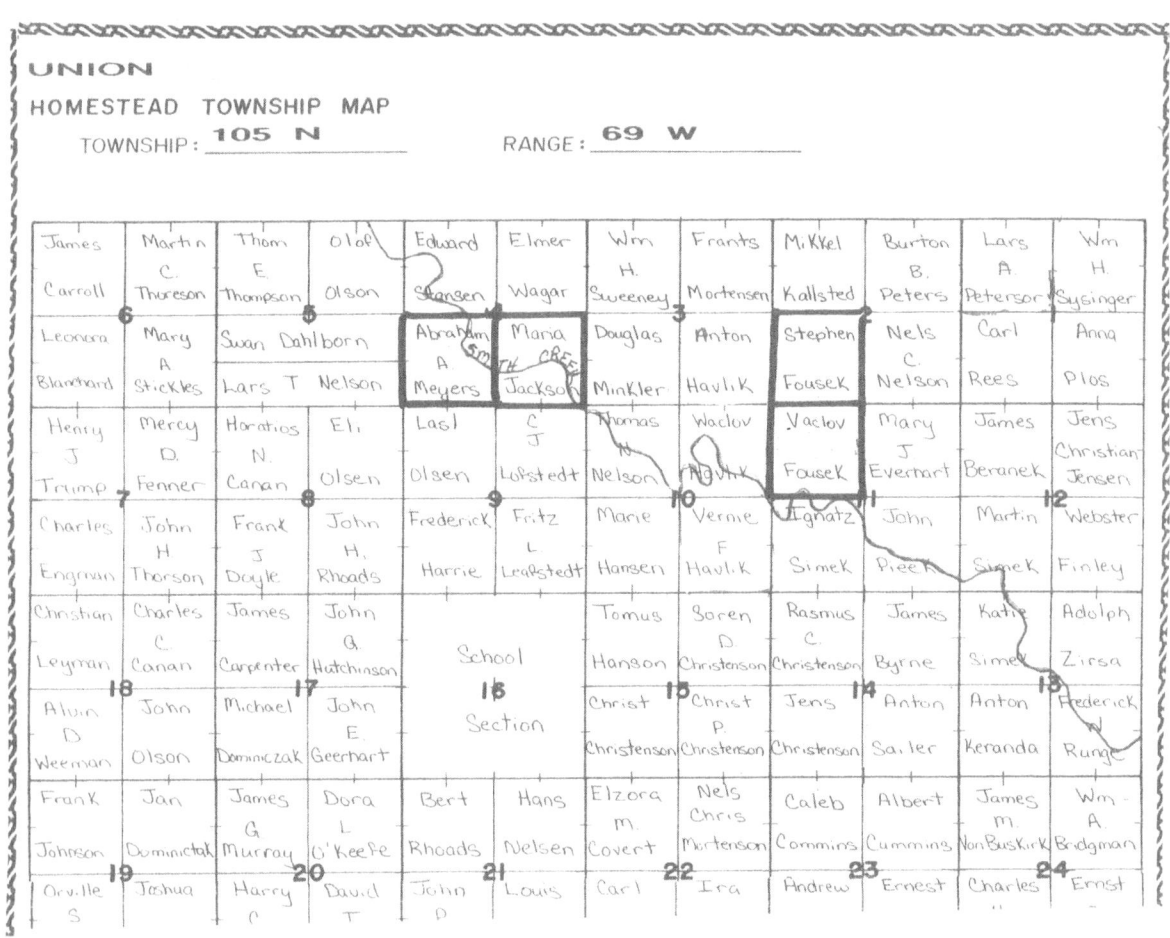

Plat map circa 1890 or 1900 showing the homesteads of Abraham Meyers and Maria Jackson, which are due west of Stephen Fousek's homestead. Our grandfather's homestead was due south of his father's. Union Township is on the northern edge of Brule County; the Missouri River is about fifty miles to the west..

According to *Brule County History*, "Meyers had obtained a post office for the neighborhood [and] he had built a frame building two stories high, the lower story wherein he kept the Post Office and a store, and the upper story was made into a dance hall." At some point Tom E.

Thompson bought the Meyers property, and converted the building known simply as "Vega" into a home. We know that towns were often built around post offices but Vega, as a post office/trading post or perhaps even as a sort of quasi-town, did not exist until 1886. This left us with the question concerning the whereabouts of our grandfather and his first wife Barbara between the time they were married in October of 1883 and 1888 when land patent application documents we had obtained for 1888 show our grandfather living in Lyonville, a town southeast of the future town of Vega.

Shifting Federal Policy Adds More Confusion

Curiously, *Brule County History* says that our grandfather obtained a patent for a section of land (section 33) in Kimball Township, for which the Registrar of Deeds at Chamberlain has no record. Based on his known land acquisitions and historical events that were then playing out in the area, it is perhaps possible that Vaclav and Barbara tried to stake out a homestead claim in Kimball Township. This is especially true if it can ever be established that Kimball Township, like Union Township, was part of the Crow Creek Indian Reservation that had been opened for settlement in 1885 and then closed a few months later. If this was the case, then our grandfather may indeed have staked a claim for a parcel in Kimball township but relinquished it because of a shift in federal law.

This shift in federal law occurred after Grover Cleveland, as the newly elected President of the United States, closed the Crow Creek Indian Reservation area that had four months earlier been opened to settlement by out-going President Chester A. Arthur. Although Presidential Proclamation 268, issued April 17, 1885 by President Cleveland indicates that only lands in Buffalo

THE GREAT RACE FOR THE WESTERN STAKES 1870

This period cartoon effectively conveys how and why the West was "won" as hastily, imperiously and inhumanely as it was.

County were affected, we are presently basing our scenario on information provided by the South Dakota Historical Collections, which says that at least Union and West Point Townships, both in Brule County, were "part of what had been the Crow Creek Indian Reservation, which took in, besides [Union] township, West Point Township as far south as American Creek. This reservation was opened for settlement in 1885 and after about four months it was closed by a newly elected President of the United States, but not until many settlers had moved onto claims and a great many of these never left even though they were repeatedly ordered to go and were threatened with being moved off by troops if they didn't go."

A first-hand account, based on the recollections of Nellie Louise Fuller Carey, provides some additional detail about what happened during this time period:

> I well remember when President Arthur opened the Government land for settlers and caused a lot of trouble. The people just rushed in from all directions to file on a claim. They could not touch any of the land where the agency was, but they came to look it over just the same. Then Cleveland was elected President of the United States. He recalled the Government land and held it until the Indians had first choice as they wanted to take land down on the [Missouri] river bottom so as to have plenty of water and fuel. People who had settled made trouble for the Indians, so the government sent men down on the river bottom right in front of the agency to build barracks for the soldiers. When finished there was a big army sent to take charge of the settlers and drive them off. The soldiers were stationed there about a year when all the barracks were taken down and moved away. The Indians took over the land they wanted, and the reservation was opened up again and the settlers had to take what was left and things became settled once more.

Kimball Township, like Union Township where Vega was located, is in Brule County. While many of the settlers stayed on their 1885 claims, many left and our grandfather may have been among those who chose to leave. This is of course provided the Kimball Township claim was indeed part of the closed portion of the reservation. The other more likely possibility, given other details we uncovered, is that our grandfather never obtained a claim in Kimball Township.

As it turned out, the reservation was reopened on April 30, 1888, and those who chose to ignore government orders were permitted to hold their claims. Given that our grandfather filed a Homestead affidavit for his Vega homestead in 1890, it is most likely that he and his young family settled "on the reservation near Smith Creek," as the *Kimball Graphic* obituary states, not in 1886 but rather sometime between in 1888 or 1890. But as we were to discover, the Fousek and Havlik families were indeed exploring and staking claims in the area as early as 1883.

CHAPTER 3

The Sioux

For several thousand years before the first "white man" ever set foot anywhere near Dakota Territory, a wide variety of peoples and Indian tribes inhabited the area. Among the most well-known of these people were the formidable Sioux, who it is said originally came to North America from the continent of Asia over the Bering Straits many thousands of years ago. The Great Sioux Nation was a broad alliance of many peoples united by a language that had three main dialects, Dakota, Nakota and Lakota. In their early history the Sioux were, generally speaking, nomadic hunter-gatherers, a lifestyle made easier when the Spanish introduced them to the horse in the 1500s. Like many other tribes, including the Mound Builders who lived in eastern and central South Dakota between 500 AD and 800 AD, and the Arikara (or Ree), that had settled in the Missouri Valley around 1500, many of the Sioux came to depend more and more upon agriculture for food.

By the early 1600s the Eastern Sioux, known as the Santee, who spoke in the Dakota dialect and who at the time lived in the Lake Superior area as hunter-gatherers, became increasingly involved in warfare with the Ojibwe or Chippewa, who lived to their east. The Ojibwe drove the Santee westward into what is today southern and western Minnesota which at that time was the agricultural territory of the Lakota (or Teton) Sioux and the Nakota (or Yankton) Sioux. The Santee, in turn, forced the Lakota and Nakota west into what is now South and North Dakota where these tribes abandoned agriculture in favor of a more nomadic lifestyle centered on hunting.

The largest of these three groups, the Lakota or Teton Sioux, ultimately located on lands west of the Missouri River, in the Black Hills area. By the early 19th century, the Lakota Sioux, who were bitter enemies of the afore-mentioned Arikara, had replaced the Arikara as the dominant native American group in the area. This was in part the result of the Arikara War of 1823, during which time several bands, or tribelets, of Lakota Sioux joined with the United States Army to defeat the Arikaras.

For this assistance the Lakota Sioux were awarded exclusive treaty rights over Black Hills lands in the Fort Laramie Treaty of 1851, despite the objections of the Cheyenne and Arapaho who also claimed rights by virtue of having occupied the area before the Sioux. The vision of the treaty was to provide safe passage for settlers travelling on the Oregon Trail and to make a lasting peace among the eight affected tribes who were often as not at war with one another. This treaty was broken almost immediately when the Lakota Sioux and Cheyenne began attacking the Crow over the following two years, setting off a long series of disputed claims over the Black Hills lands by various Indian tribes. Relations between the various camps were only made worse when the U.S. government proved unable or unwilling to slow the large increases in migration caused by the gold rush begun in 1848.

By the 1870s the Sioux had succeeded in forcing the Arikara entirely from their lands and into North Dakota where the Arikara joined the Hidasta and Mandan. Ironically, the Arikara – who had earlier been defeated by the Lakota and the U.S. Army, now began to scout for the U.S. Army stationed at nearby Fort Stevenson and in 1874 they guided George Armstrong Custer on his

Black Hills Expedition. Two years later a large group of Arikaran men fought alongside Custer against the Lakota Sioux, Arapaho and Northern Cheyenne at the Battle of the Little Bighorn.

Understanding the Sioux and how they peacefully coexisted with our grandfather and his family was a bit of a challenge because of many seemingly conflicting accounts. We were intensely interested however, due to some family lore that said that our mother's half-sister had been sweet on Sitting Bull's grandson, so a-searching we did go.

Starting with the basics, our research indicates that the term Sioux referred to any ethnic group or tribe belonging to what has been called the Great Sioux Nation, which itself was a confederacy of over a dozen tribes which were in turn split into three subgroups defined by dialect. As mentioned, by the time our grandfather had arrived in the area, the Lakota occupied territory that lay west of the Missouri River, while the Dakota and Nakota stayed east of the river.

The name Sioux is actually an abbreviation of Nadouessioux which was originally applied to them by the Ojibwe tribe of Minnesota. It meant "little snakes" or enemies. Meanwhile the Sioux would usually call themselves Dakota or Lakota, meaning "friends or allies, or to be friendly." However friendly they may have been, the Sioux were feared by virtually all Western tribes from the great lakes all the way to the Rockies.

Corporations, Not Settlers, Petition for Treaties as a Means of Obtaining New Land - to Sell

Into this complex and nuanced history stepped Homesteaders and settlers. Although it is true that squatters had for generations been moving farther and farther west well before the Homestead Act or the "opening" of the territories, neither squatters, nor settlers nor homesteaders ever purchased or otherwise legally acquired U.S. land directly from Native American nations.

This stemmed from the fact that Article 1, Section 8 of the U.S. Constitution gave Congress the power to regulate commerce with the Indian Tribes (as well as with foreign nations and among the several states). In 1790 the first Congress under this new Constitution passed its first law exercising this power. That law essentially adopted Indian land policy that had been in place since 1763 when the United States was still under British control and it said that all sales of lands made by any Indians or any *nation* of Indian tribes must be "made and duly executed at some public treaty, held under the authority of the United States."

Just prior to this 1790 law, at the conclusion of the Revolutionary War in 1783, the British had ceded the Northwest Territory to the United States in the Treaty of Paris. As a result, the new American government formulated and adopted the Northwest Ordinance of 1787 as a means of laying out the procedures for admitting new states to the Union. Article 3 of Section 14 of the Northwest Ordinance asserted that "the utmost good faith shall always be observed towards the Indians; their lands and property shall never be taken from them without their consent; and, in their property, rights, and liberty, they shall never be invaded or disturbed..."

Consequently, part of the stipulations contained in treaties with the Native American Indians required the government to provide monetary and other types of compensation to the tribe in question. The U.S. government then was supposed to distribute this land to U.S. citizens for free or at very low prices. However, the vast bulk of land acquired through these treaties ended up going to corporations and business interests with political connections. Moreover, the terms of these treaties were often as not dictated by these same influential groups, even though the actual parties to the treaties were the U.S. Government, acting on behalf of *all* U.S. citizens, and Native Americans. Chief among these influence groups were fur trading companies, railroad land companies, and land speculation companies formed for example by state and local political leaders who used these companies to secure land titles from failed homesteaders as well as from the government. Even Indian Agents got into the land speculation business.

The rights of Native Americans were further curtailed by a series of Supreme Court decisions under Chief Justice John Marshall, beginning with the Johnson & Graham v M'Intosh decision in 1823. These decisions incorporated the Doctrine of Discovery (of new lands). Drawing upon relevant Papal Bulls of the 15th century, the Marshall Court used the Doctrine of Discovery as a way to support decisions which invalidated possession of land by native cultures, in part because of their supposedly inferior character, in favor of the "established" government.

Marshall wrote in 1823 that land grants from European governments not only conveyed ownership but also "have been understood by all to convey title to the grantees, subject only to the Indian right of occupancy." This assertion, while flawed on its face, to this day forms an important part of our legal foundation insofar as it concerns Native American possession of land, despite the fact that the Marshall decisions did not go without considerable criticism.

And so it was that as the Doctrine of Discovery became a "settled" part of American law, land became increasingly easier to obtain using treaties, even blatantly sham treaties as the vehicle. By the 1830's, under President Andrew Jackson, U.S. government policy supported the removal of western American Indian Tribes to make way for European immigrants. Discovery of gold in California a few years later, in 1848, only increased support of this policy, tacit and otherwise.

From that time forward treaties would result in the Dakota Sioux people losing large portions of their land. These treaties also meant that settlers typically purchased land from corporations, rather than from the U.S. Government. Obviously, these corporations and related business interests had ample incentive to lure settlers as well as homesteaders to the area. Homesteaders of course acquired land from the government by filing a claim and fulfilling certain legal requirements, as per the Homestead Act of 1862, the Timber Culture Act of 1873 and the Preemption Act of 1841.

So it came to pass that by 1890, our grandfather and nearly all his extended family had filed homestead claims on land that had been, until 1888, part of the Crow Creek (Dakota Sioux) Indian Reservation which itself was located on land that had originally been part of Minnesota Territory. This reservation had been established in 1862 following the Dakota War or Sioux Uprising in Minnesota. Located on the east side of the Missouri River, the reservation included bottom lands along the Missouri that had once been farmed by the Arikara (or Ree), who as mentioned earlier were by the 1870s forced by the Lakota Sioux to completely retreat to North Dakota where they joined the Hidatsa and Mandan. It needs to be said that inhabitants of the Crow Creek Reservation had no relationship to the more westerly Crow Tribe that was, together with the Lakota (or Teton) Sioux and six other tribes, part of the Fort Laramie Treaty of 1851 which, as mentioned earlier, involved land west of the Missouri.

The Sioux Uprising or Dakota War of 1862

We grew increasingly curious to find out just how it was that our grandfather and his entire extended family managed to not just come out alive, but to co-exist peacefully with the fearsome Sioux. To do that we needed to look at the Sioux Uprising or Dakota War of 1862 in a bit more detail. As we were to discover, this "Sioux Uprising" was actually the largest Indian war in American history even as it provided the incentive for atrocities to be waged on unrelated tribes in the West. Although an accurate count of the dead will never be known, it is estimated that one hundred fifty Sioux were killed, not counting the thirty-eight later executed. In addition, seventy-seven soldiers lost their lives along with as many as eight hundred unarmed, non-combatant settlers also losing their lives. All told, literally thousands were left dead, wounded, diseased, captured, and/or displaced. It was by all measures an incredibly brutal war, and even today the trauma caused by it haunts the descendants of those touched by the war.

The spark that started the war occurred on August 17, 1862 when four starving Dakota Sioux hunters stole food and killed five white settlers in the process. A band of about 100 to 150 young Dakota Sioux, under the influence of "white men's devil water" (rum), seized upon that event to declare war on the whites who would not keep their treaty promises and to reclaim their homeland.

Most of the approximately seven thousand Dakota Sioux living on two Minnesota Sioux Reservations that had been established by treaties in 1851 were opposed to the war and never participated. However, in the early morning hours of August 18 some sixteen hundred Dakota Sioux warriors on foot and on horseback went to war, fanning out across both sides of the Minnesota River, killing men, women and children in their beds and taking hundreds of others as captives. Raids, attacks and battles were carried out mostly against defenseless settlers for the next six weeks. Tragically, the Dakota Sioux warriors ended up attacking the wrong people as it was various elements and policies of the Federal government along with its agents and corporate sponsors who were the root cause of their troubles.

Painting of the Minnesota Massacre at the start of the Dakota War of 1862

By September 16, the federal army took control of Minnesota's military forces, and the battle was all but over. On September 26, six weeks after the war had started, the Dakota Sioux surrendered. A military tribunal was hastily set up, and after speedy trials, 303 Dakota men were sentenced to death. On December 26, 1862, a little more than four months after the first attack occurred, 38 Dakota men were hanged, making this, even to this day, the largest mass execution in U.S. history. And had President Lincoln not commuted their sentences, an additional 264 Dakota Sioux men would have been hanged.

The immediate trigger for the Dakota War could be found in the tremendous influx during the 1850s of white Americans and recent immigrants moving into what would soon be the state of Minnesota. The Dakota were forced to compete with these new settlers for dwindling game supplies - a situation made worse by the fact that the Dakota Sioux were not allowed to leave their reservation in search of game.

As mentioned earlier, this all was prompted by those corporations and businessmen whose political connections allowed them to successfully agitate for more Native American land to be acquired via treaties. For example, it was the fur traders who by the 1840s had seized upon the opportunity to ensnare the Dakota Sioux in debt so as to make them more "amenable" to the idea (and necessity) of selling their land which these traders and similar business interests then could sell to settlers at a handsome profit. As a result of two 1851 treaties with the Dakota Sioux, and the propaganda that accompanied "newly available" land, the population in the soon-to-be state of Minnesota surged from just 6,000 in 1850 to over 150,000 by 1857.

Those two treaties were the Traverse des Sioux and the Mendota, both signed in 1851, and through which the Dakota Sioux gave up about 98% of the land they called home and depended upon for food. Local Indian agents began to immediately violate the terms of these treaties, and the U.S. Senate eliminated Article 3 of one of the treaties without the knowledge or consent of the Dakota Sioux, an act that significantly reduced what the Dakota Sioux were to receive under the terms of the original agreements. By the time of the Dakota War, the Dakota Sioux were not only facing shortages of game but also storable food crops due to poor harvests from the year before. This situation was made worse by the fact that the payments to the Indians by the U.S. government were late, owing to the on-going Civil War. Traders then refused to extend credit to the Dakota Sioux with which they might purchase food, and one government agent in charge of a warehouse full of food simply refused to deliver it to the Dakota Sioux.

A shadowy, so-called Indian Ring thus added yet another unfortunate layer to this political, social and economic tapestry. Composed of unprincipled politicians, contractors and Indian agents, individuals in this group, separately and in concert, found ways to "capitalize" on the business transactions between the federal government and the Native Americans. Crimes included refusal to extend much-needed credit, supplying inferior goods at exorbitant prices and outright theft. Yet even in the face of overwhelming evidence, prosecutions were few. Many settlers were aware of these kinds of chicanery, as indicated by historian Alexandra E. Stern in her 2015 article titled *"War is Cruelty": The Civil War Lessons of the Dakota War of 1862*, when she writes:

> When blood first started to spill in August 1862, some Minnesotans were quick to see the war's beginnings "in the thievish and dishonest conduct of Government Agents, Officers, Traders, and the vile confederates that procure their appointment and share their plunder and then gloss over and hide their iniquity." The concurrent American Civil War played a part in delaying the payment of the Dakotas' annuities in 1862, as the federal government, waging a costly war against the Confederacy, was short on the hard currency required to pay the pensions. Already starving in the late summer of 1862, the Dakota could not afford to wait much longer for the money owed to them, particularly when local traders refused to extend additional lines of credit to the hungry Indians.

The Dakota War resulted in the imprisonment of about 1600 Dakota Sioux women, children and older men outside Fort Snelling in Minnesota. Ironically, Fort Snelling had been built in 1825 to try to keep peace between the Dakota Sioux, who had been fighting for decades to reclaim land from the Ojibwe, who themselves had much earlier been driven west into Dakota Sioux territory by the Iroquois. That winter of 1862-63, nearly 300 Dakota prisoners died at Fort Snelling, victims of soldier and settler reprisals and illness. Again, the innocent had been swept up with the guilty. By the Spring of 1863, the Dakota Sioux were banished from Minnesota to a new reservation, the Crow Creek Reservation, in Dakota Territory, which reservation originally included Brule County, South Dakota where our grandfather would eventually settle.

By April of 1863 the Dakota Expulsion Act was signed into law by President Lincoln. The federal government seized the remaining 10-mile-wide strip in Minnesota and exiled the Dakota Sioux from Minnesota whether they took part in the Uprising or not. Military expeditions were used to drive the Dakota Sioux and even the Navajo (Dine tribe), Winnebago (Ho Chunk tribe) and other tribes unconnected to the Sioux Uprising further and further west with disastrous results, including wholesale massacres, for the tribes involved. In addition, all treaties with the Dakota Sioux were abrogated and the Dakota were banned from residing in the state of Minnesota. Then, because not all of the Dakota Sioux had participated in the War, another treaty signed in 1863 with non-combatant Dakota Sioux created the Sisseton Reservation in present-day northeastern South Dakota in 1867. One year earlier, in 1866, the Santee Reservation had been established at the mouth of the Niobrara River in Nebraska for the Santee Dakota, who were facing starvation at the Crow Creek Reservation.

Alexandra E. Stern, mentioned above, points out that most Dakota Sioux never even participated in the Dakota War and adds critical context that informs us as to how our grandfather managed to co-exist peacefully among the Sioux:

> The waging of the Dakota War was a violent but conflicted affair. Most Dakota, particularly those engaged as farmers, never even participated in the destruction to persons or property in 1862. Many Dakota proved unwilling to forego all ties with Minnesotans with whom they had developed bonds of friendship and trust.

> While killings were largely arbitrary during the early hostilities, many Americans survived because Dakota fighters recognized various kinship bonds between the two peoples, forged through either marriage or friendship.

> Minnesotans found themselves woefully unprepared for the conflict since most "could not believe that the Indians were bent on anything as serious as murder."

Meanwhile, in 1858, in an action unrelated to the Sioux Uprising but perhaps eminently related to the speculators who had founded the city of Yankton, another treaty had been negotiated

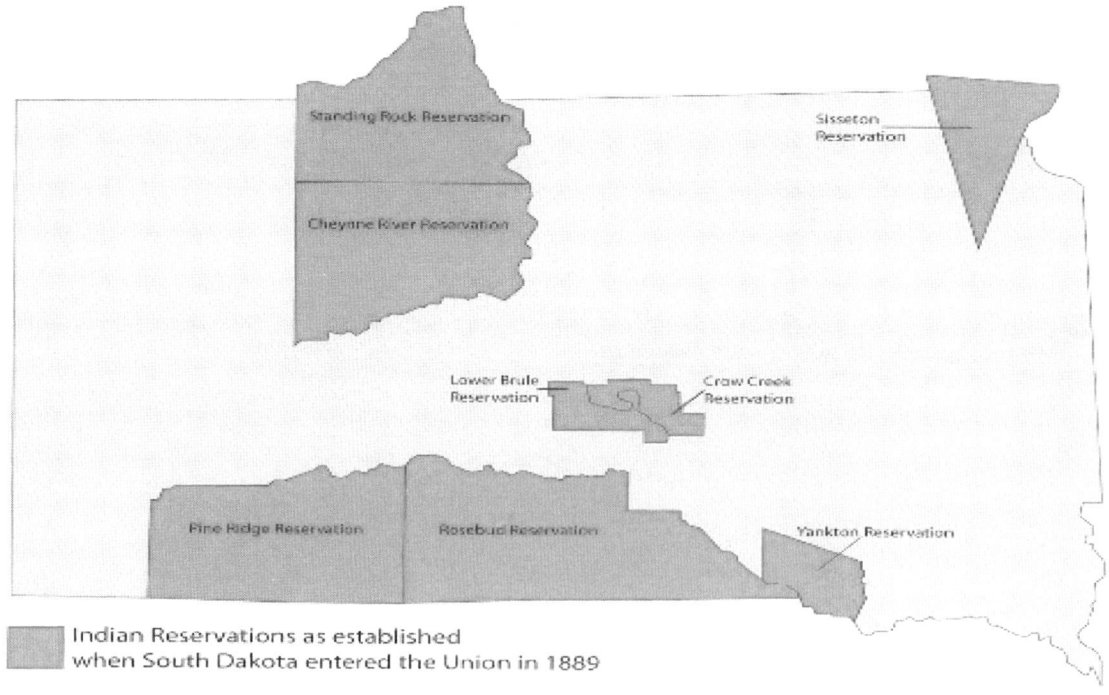

Map available at the South Dakota Historical Society website showing Indian Reservations in South Dakota in 1889. The Great Sioux Reservation west of the Missouri River had by that time been massively reduced. The Crow Creek Indian Reservation, whose western border is the Missouri River, was less aggressively reduced when its southernmost border was moved north to the Buffalo/Brule County line. Hence our grandfather and his contemporaries were able to file homestead claims in Brule County.

with the Nakota (or Yankton) Sioux. This treaty was peacefully negotiated under the leadership of Chief Struck-by-the-Ree, who had become a friend of the white man as well as a chief, and it created the first Indian Reservation in South Dakota known as the Yankton Agency. Chief Struck-by-the-Ree's name is interesting in that it harks back to the Arikara, sometimes referred to as Ree who some consider to be the state's first farmers. Also of note for our story is that the Yankton Agency reservation was located in Charles Mix County where our grandfather would spend the last two and a half years of his life.

In an odd twist of fate, it was the Mdewakantons together with another band called the Wahpekutes who were the main perpetrators of the Sioux Uprising, and it was the Mdewakantons who would be among the principal residents at the Crow Creek Reservation near where out grandfather settled. Importantly enough to our story is that it is often said that the Sioux Uprising set off a whole series of Indian wars on the northern plains that only ended with the battle of Wounded Knee in 1890. This is a claim that we feel might be somewhat over-generalized, at least insofar as eastern South Dakota is concerned.

The series of Indian wars typically referred to are collectively known as the Great Sioux War of 1876. They took place west of the Missouri, with the Battle of the Little Bighorn and the Wounded Knee Massacre being the most notable battles. This so-called Great Sioux War was due to yet another reneged treaty known as the Fort Laramie Treaty of 1851 having been replaced by the Treaty of Fort Laramie in 1868, in which lands west of the Missouri, including the Black Hills, were again awarded to the Lakota Sioux. Just two years after the Treaty of Fort Laramie of 1868 was signed, the Federal government withdrew the Black Hills lands from the Lakota that were part of the 1868 Treaty. This was unacceptable to the Lakota Sioux who believed the Black Hills to be sacred land and objected to the mining there for gold.

By way of contrast, relations between settlers and native Americans had settled down east of the Missouri, at least if we read South Dakota Historian Herbert Schell correctly when he wrote that the hostilities resulting from the Dakota War that had spilled over into Dakota Territory kept settlers in continual fear until 1867. In other words, per Herbert Schell, hostilities east of the Missouri River had for all intents and purposes ceased by 1867. This was at least fifteen years *before* our grandfather first began exploring the area.

Missouri River Divides Eastern Dakota from the West

This history suggests some of the differences between "East River" Sioux who were part of the Crow Creek Reservation near our grandfather and "West River" Sioux who made up the Great Sioux Reservation. As it happened, the vast lands that had been granted to the major Plains tribes by the Fort Laramie Treaty of 1851 were considerably reduced by the 1868 Treaty of Fort Laramie, which established the Great Sioux Reservation. This was five years after the Crow Creek Reservation had been established, and ten years after the Yankton Reservation had been established. The land of the Great Sioux Reservation took in all of South Dakota west of the Missouri River, plus one might say, purely for the sake of simplicity, that it also included the Crow Creek Reservation that had been created by treaty five years earlier in 1863.

A mere two years after the treaty of 1868, the Great Sioux Reservation was again reduced when the federal government withdrew the Black Hills lands, offering remuneration that has never been touched. One year later, Congress abandoned the treaty system when it passed the Indian Appropriation Act. Though Americans did continue to negotiate agreements with the Indians with the purported goal of creating millions of ranches and farms across the West, the Indian Appropriation Act ended official recognition of individual tribes within the U.S. as independent nations "with whom the United States may contract by treaty." (This policy changed again nearly one hundred years later, when the federal government began encouraging Native American tribes to exercise self-governance over tribal matters).

Custer's discovery of gold in the Black Hills during his 1874 Expedition lured hundreds of gold seekers into "west river" Sioux Territory. Even though all available soldiers were sent into the field to track down these "squatters" as these gold seekers were called, the lust for gold kept them coming and even enticed soldiers themselves to go AWOL while they too searched for gold.

Today the Crow Creek Agency is located in the western portion of Buffalo County as well as Hughes and Hyde Counties to the north. One can see from the names on old plat maps that many parcels in Pershing Township, Buffalo County where our grandfather would eventually acquire three parcels of land, were owned by Native Americans. Our grandfather had also acquired two parcels in El Dorado Township, Buffalo County in the 1880s and by 1890 had staked a homestead claim in Union Township, Brule County. The early plat maps we found showing El Dorado Township and Union Township have no indication of Native Americans having made claims there. In any case, the main point here is that the Crow Creek Reservation that our grandfather came to in order to stake out his Timber Claims and homestead claim was never truly a part of the original Great Sioux Reservation that lay west of the Missouri River. Nevertheless, both reservations were effectively dismantled by the Dawes Act of 1887 (also known as the Indian Allotment Act) and its successor law enacted in 1889, called the Sioux Act.

The object of the Dawes Act or the Indian Allotment Act of 1887 was to break up communal Indian lands, both east and west of the Missouri, into individual 160-acre farms with one family living on each farm. The act also granted U.S. citizenship to those Native Americans who stayed on the land for 25 years and "adopted the habits of civilized life." The whole plan met such resistance that it was abandoned by the federal government in 1934, but by then much of the damage to Indian culture had already been done.

The object of the Sioux Act of 1889, which was enacted the very same year South Dakota achieved statehood, was to create five smaller reservations out of the original Great Sioux Reservation located west of the Missouri. By the time of this 1889 Act, increasing numbers of Teton (Lakota) Sioux were already turning to reservation life as a way of avoiding starvation, since roaming buffalo herds had by then been almost completely decimated by the railroads, hide hunters and cattle barons, cutting off a critical food source for the nomadic Teton Sioux.

Once the boundaries of those five reservations were established, about 9 million acres representing one half of the former Great Sioux Reservation, were opened by the federal government for public purchase for ranching and homesteading purposes. Lakota tribes were to receive $1.25 an acre for these lands. However, a series of severe droughts dampened interest until more favorable weather conditions, together with a more developed railroad system and an improved economy, returned around 1900. Our grandmother's third husband had staked a homestead claim near what is now Midland, west of the river, in 1904 and lost it by 1910, no doubt due to the dry climate.

An education kit on homesteading put out by the South Dakota Historical Society says that the second Dakota boom that began around 1902 and ended in 1915 was in part due to the Dawes Act. And, according to South Dakota historian Herbert Schell, demand by the time of the second Dakota boom had increased to the point that the government was prompted to negotiate a new series of agreements with each of the five sub-tribes, which of course again reduced the size of the original Great Sioux Reservation. The government also resorted to the lottery system as a means by which to place land tracts on the market. The prices paid to the Sioux for this land generally ranged between $2.50 and $6 per acre, with these monies to be put in a government fund for the purpose of "educating and civilizing" the Native Americans.

Because most of the more desirable land east of the Missouri had already been claimed, nearly all of the land taken up in the second Dakota boom lay west of the Missouri River, where the population increased from 43,782 to 137,687 between 1900 and 1910. However, the drier climate west of the Missouri did not lend itself to traditional farming, and the size of the parcels did not lend themselves to grazing livestock. The Enlarged Homestead Act of 1910 recognized this by allowing homesteads to be increased from 160 to 320 acres in dryer states, but South Dakota did not adopt the act until 1915 because it didn't want to become known as a dry state. By 1916, the Stock-Raising Act allowed 640 acres to be homesteaded.

To make matters even worse for Native Americans than it was for new settlers was the fact that tribal members were prevented by law from selling their allotments for 20 years. All of this, together with the misguided establishment of boarding schools for Sioux children and other programs designed to "force-civilize" Native Americans meant that all tribal members, but particularly those west of the Missouri, did not fare well under these arrangements.

Fear Often Exaggerated and Sometimes Misplaced

Rumors and various forms of chicanery and intrigue further complicated things. One account in Brule County History provided by a man whose family had made the move to Brule County from Iowa by wagon in 1888 when he was young, said that "once we got to Dakota we heard tales of Indian trouble. The tales were so bad that we kids took turns standing on a hill south of our home to watch for Indians but they never came. . . White renegades dressed like Indians did steal and kill and Indians were sometimes blamed."

Such was the political and social environment that our grandfather and other settlers confronted when they came to this heavily promoted "land of promise." Yet, as we have been discovering through our own research, stories about atrocities and injustices committed by either Native Americans or settlers upon one another seem to have been greatly exaggerated, this fact notwithstanding various orchestrated genocides of Native American tribes carried out by some government officials and their allies in California and elsewhere. In fact, the kind of day-to-day interpersonal relationships between the Dakota settlers and the Sioux, especially those on the Crow Creek Reservation, that we have seen described were far more often cordial, even cooperative, than hostile.

We have for example, a story related by Pukwana pioneer Orah M. (Thompson) Glass in her small tome entitled "History of Pukwana and Vicinity" - Pukwana being a railroad town founded in 1881 in what was then Dakota Territory. Orah had come to Pukwana with her family when she was a young girl, somewhere around 1894, after South Dakota had become a state. Her story has to do with a Fourth of July celebration held soon after she and her family arrived. This celebration had been organized by Pukwana residents for the benefit of Native Americans living at Crow Creek, which she says was about twelve miles north of Pukwana and a long ride by horse and buggy from Pukwana. Interestingly, Orah's location puts Crow Creek not all that far from the Abraham Meyers' Vega post office and store. Part of her description of this celebration is as follows:

> On arriving at Crow Creek, a crude platform was erected with planks where we staged our program consisting of songs and "speeches." Among other numbers, Clarence Birchard sang "Molly and the Baby, Don't You Know." This was about your writer's (Orah Glass's) first introduction to Indians in their native state, and I marveled at how nicely some of the young girls looked in their vivid colored velvet on a hot day such as this was. They gathered round to hear our program.

Sitting Bull and His West River Lakota Sioux

With respect to our own grandfather's family and friends, we found accounts about Sitting Bull's tribe sometimes crossing the Missouri to terrorize settlers east of the river. According to Brule County History, these "East River" settlers however could be reassured by the fact that the Dakota peoples living on the Crow Creek Reservation would chase Sitting Bull's people back.

Sitting Bull, who is known for his role in the defeat of General George Armstrong Custer at the 1876 Battle of the Little Big Horn, had fled to Canada after that battle, giving his people a choice to join him or live on the Great Sioux Reservation. After several years in Canada and with his people on the brink of starvation, he finally surrendered to U.S. forces.

Following this surrender Sitting Bull and his dwindling band of about 158 followers were held at Fort Randall for twenty months. While there, they camped south of the fort and were kept under loose surveillance. Visitors flocked to the fort by the hundreds to see the famous chief and to have their pictures taken with him. Handling such large crowds of course became quite a problem for the soldiers, and so they were not at all sorry to see Sitting Bull removed to the Standing Rock Reservation, which straddles the border of North and South Dakota, in 1883.

Photo of Sitting Bull taken by D.F. Barry in Bismark

Sitting Bull was allowed to leave the Standing Rock Reservation only with permission of Indian Service agent James McLaughlin. Permission was granted for Sitting Bull to tour parts of Canada and the northern United States for a show that included Annie Oakley, who Sitting Bull admired for her shooting abilities. Despite the presence of Annie Oakley and other luminaries, the show was called the "Sitting Bull Connection." Sitting Bull again received permission to leave the reservation during the summer and early fall of 1885 when he toured the United States with Annie Oakley and others as part of the popular Buffalo Bill Cody Wild West Show. According to the book *Sitting Bull: His Life and Legacy* written by his great-grandson Ernie LaPointe, Sitting Bull was "introduced at every show as the 'killer of Custer' and he was greeted with disrespect at every stop. Yet, at every location, people lined up to meet him and paid to get autographs. He was a very popular attraction."

It has been said that Sitting Bull earned a small fortune by charging for his autograph and picture, but, according to LaPointe, he gave most of the money away to "the ragged little white children begging in the streets."

Sitting Bull was noted for his observation that the white man knew how to build things, but he didn't know how to share. While arguably true for the more urbanized society that Sitting Bull may have had contact with during his Wild West tours, our research tells us that this observation did not apply to settler society out on the prairie.

For example, one account, similar to many others we have come across, given by the wife of Barbara's brother Wencil in *Brule County History* describes how she and her husband Wencil took on the task in their later years of raising eight grandchildren, ages 1 to 16 years of age, on behalf of a daughter that had passed away at the age of 33. She goes on to say that many pioneers did this, and even took on the task of raising the orphaned children of neighbors. Unlike Sitting Bull's encounters with "the ragged little white children begging in the streets," Wencil's wife Stella says that "it was our job to see that these motherless children were fed and cared for – and that we did." Her account is not an isolated one.

Five years after Sitting Bull's last Wild West tour, in 1890, the rise of the Ghost Dance religion, termed "Dance in a Circle," swept through the five Sioux agencies west of the Missouri River, signaling their dissatisfaction with their situation. Although LaPointe tells us that this religion was resisted by Sitting Bull himself, the religion was embraced by other members of the tribe, creating a rift that led to the murder of Sitting Bull on December 15, 1890, just a few months after our grandfather had filed an affidavit on the Vega homestead, which was of course east of the river.

Two weeks later, on December 29, 1890, the Wounded Knee Massacre occurred. Described by Herbert Schell as a tragic battle between a body of Ghost Dancers under Big Foot and U.S. soldiers on Wounded Knee Creek, this battle resulted in the deaths of nearly 200 Native Americans, including women and children, and thirty-one soldiers. It must have been a gruesome scene, with bodies of Sioux women and children found scattered as far as 2 miles from Wounded Knee and "all kinds of scalps of the soldiers found upon the Indians who killed them."

Though Big Foot and his Ghost Dancers ultimately returned to their home thus averting a general uprising, one can only imagine the shock waves of terror that must have rippled through all of Dakota Territory, both east and west of the river, because of this tragic event. Yet as we have also learned from first-hand accounts, even Native Americans on the west side of the river would eventually be seen engaging in wholly voluntary and un-hostile, quite civilized acts of compassion that included hauling water to drought-stricken settlers.

It also seems that, by the time of the "Rosebud Opening" in 1909 during the second Dakota Boom, the West River Lakota Sioux had begun taking a cue from Sitting Bull. As Edith Kohl explains in *Land of the Burnt Thigh*, in the midst of the chaos that developed as a result of the land lottery in the tiny frontier town of Presho, through which the Milwaukee Railroad was bringing vast throngs of land seekers, Native Americans could be found mingling on the crowded station platform, "brave in paint and feathers and beads, offering to pose for 50 cents a picture."

A first-hand account, based on the memory of a young Nellie Louise Fuller Carey cited earlier, illustrates some of the ways the West River Sioux themselves were managing, and to an extent integrating, by the late 1880s and early 90s:

> There was a store there [at an agency on the Lower Brule], where the Indians could buy or trade for goods. Mostly they traded different kinds of animal hides.
>
> This small village had just one street. The man who had charge of the agency lived in the first house; the doctor lived in the next house, then we lived in the third house. Next to us were the two men who taught farming, then a small building like a restaurant for the people who traveled around sightseeing or cared to stay all night. Next was a blacksmith shop and last, the store.
>
> There was a big space between the town and the Missouri River where the men played ball or could camp. There was a nice little church as well. The minister was an Indian who was married to a white woman.
>
> When the Indians came in on Saturday and received their rations, they all drove out to a big corral about a mile from town. Here the officials would have some steers ready for the farmers to set in motion inside the corral. As the steers would begin to run around in circles, two men who were standing upon a platform in the center, would take turns shooting the steers as they passed by. When all were killed, the corral gate was opened and each Indian would bring in his Indian pony and drag out the steer that he wanted to butcher and take home for the family. Sometimes the squaws would help the Indian men as they were butchering their steers.

In similar fashion, the following portion of Iva King's haunting account of her Brule County childhood experiences, found in *Brule County History*, illustrates how settlers west of the river were learning to co-exist alongside the West River Sioux. Although Iva had lived in Union Township, Brule County as a young girl, after marriage she and her husband moved across the river to the newly created Lyman County. The area that made up Lyman County had been part of Brule County for judicial purposes up until 1893 when it was split off as a separate county. Specifically recounted here is an Indian encounter occurring after Ida's marriage in 1895:

Every quarter section had a family on it so neighbors were close but many Indians roamed the country and the nights were long and lonesome with only the call of the coyotes or the hooting owl to break the silence.

It so happened one cold winter day in December of 1895 while I was busy washing baby clothes in the kitchen, leaving my baby girl of about six weeks asleep in the adjoining room, that my mother's intuition prompted me to look in and see how my baby was. Imagine my feelings when, on entering the room, I found four Indian braves warming themselves and one of them bent over my baby in her cradle. I tried to pick her up but before I could reach her, he had taken her up and wrapped her in his shawl. They seemed to consult with one another, but I could understand only one word they used, "papoose." I knew it was Indian custom to enter a home unannounced and ask for food or anything that struck their fancy. So I thought fast, "How could I reclaim my baby girl?" Spying an unopened plug of chewing tobacco my husband had placed on a corner bracket, within my reach, I took it and began trying by sign language to barter for my baby. After some very serious consultation on their part, the brave took the tobacco and gave my unharmed baby girl to me, with a big "Ugh". They left the house, and I was much relieved to see them go down across the meadow and disappear in the trees along the river. That evening when my husband came home, he told me how Flying Eagle and his three friends had crossed on the ferry (the river didn't freeze until January of that year) and Flying Eagle told him how they had held his pretty papoose and how he admired her.

Town of Oacoma Once a Gateway to the REALLY "Wild West"

Iva King cited above also paints a picture of living in the "Wild West" after she and her husband moved from Union Township, which is East of the River, to Lyman County which was west of the river, saying in part:

It seems, looking back, that those first years [after her marriage] were hot, dry, and windy. There were several electrical storms causing fires that burned the short, dry grass and oftentimes the timber as well. The ground was mostly gumbo and dried out leaving wide cracks in the earth where rattlesnakes often took shelter. It was soon discovered that this short, native Buffalo grass was the ideal feed for livestock and a few of the homesteaders rapidly developed into successful cattlemen, buying up the homesteads of their neighbors as fast as they received their patents from Uncle Sam. So the west river country became the land of the cattlemen and the cattle rustler, where both thrived for a time.

I had pioneered in Union Township but this was different, this was Lyman County. This was the Wild West, the land where the cowboys rode their horses into saloons in Oacoma and shot the glasses off the bar and the flies off the ceiling. The land where great herds of cattle roamed the hills and plains. . .The river was a barrier, every family had a skiff with oars and would row across to Chamberlain for mail, groceries, the doctor or whatever the case may be.

Iva's daughter Ozitte, who grew up west of the river, recounts her impressions of the Indians, which she says became permanent:

The Indians were everywhere, but I had no fear of them, only pity and compassion. The braves had their long black hair in braids interwoven with gay ribbons or strips of cloth. The squaws with the papooses strapped to their backs with a shawl. The little boys and girls, the men and women, all with buckskin moccasins and their silent expressionless countenances. I wondered what was in their hearts. I remember one night when my parents awakened me and carried me out of the door saying, "Listen, you may never hear this again." In the distance, maybe many miles away could be heard the rhythmic beating on the tom-toms. My parents told me it was an Indian war-dance, that the Indians did this when they were unhappy, and that they wanted me to remember it.

Vega and the Crow Creek Sioux Indians

Both family lore and our research indicate that Native American Indians would often camp at Vega on their way from Fort Thompson to Wagner and the surrounding area to visit their friends and relatives. Apparently, these Native Americans would organize their caravans around the time that government annuities came in. Since the Native American attitude toward, and general understanding of money, differed markedly from that of settlers, they would often use a fair portion of their annuity money to buy trinkets they did not need, and had no use for at trading posts along their route – or they might gamble it away on improvised horse races. Their preferred method for securing the things they needed seemed to be through barter.

In the case of Vega, we are told by *Brule County History* that in the early years Crow Creek Sioux would simply set up camp at Vega and mind their own business, never bothering anyone. But as time went on, everyone became so well acquainted that Native American Indians always brought things to trade, including fur pelts, for things they needed. These dealings were still going on when our grandmother and her children moved to Vega in 1916.

When we were young, our Aunt Ann – who was our grandmother's daughter from her first marriage – used to take obvious delight in showing us photos of her teenage heart throb and the pony he gave her. Until very recently, when research proved us wrong, we firmly believed that this heart throb was Sitting Bull's grandson. Now we think he must have actually been a member of the Crow Creek Sioux tribe, perhaps the son of a chief, or perhaps our aunt's heartthrob had been a member of the Yankton Sioux whose reservation and farms were located near where the family later lived. It seemed clear to us at least that our aunt remained smitten with this young fellow to the end of her days.

Photo of an encampment of Crow Creek Sioux circa early 1900s. We are guessing this to be the type of camp the Crow Creek Sioux would have set up in Vega on their periodic pilgrimages to the southern part of the state.

CHAPTER 4

Staking a Claim in Dakota Territory

When he was just ten years old, our grandfather and his parents packed up and left behind everything and everyone they had ever known in their native Bohemia and crossed three thousand miles of ocean and another thousand miles of land in order to start a new life near the little town of Ainsworth, Iowa where they paid cash for a forty-acre farm. That was in 1870. Some twenty years later, on May 5, 1890, our grandfather filed a homestead claim for 160 acres in Brule County, South Dakota. He was 30 years old at the time. On that exact same day, May 5, 1890, his father Stephen, our great-grandfather, also filed a homestead claim just across the road from his son Vaclav.

Both these homestead claims were less than a mile south of the Buffalo/Brule County line and it was here that Vega would blossom into a thriving town rather than simply an outpost with a post office. Information we gleaned from the 1900 U.S. Census indicates that our grandfather's third child Tillie was born in Vega on May 8, 1890 – just three days after the homestead claims had been filed, with Vega at that time being a one-building post office/community center on Abraham Meyer's farm about one mile to the west of our grandfather's homestead. The Will we had obtained showed that this Vega homestead would form part of our grandfather's estate when he died at the age of 63, on March 1, 1923 at his home in Dante, a town located in Charles Mix County just south of Brule County.

Early in our search we had gleaned information from several obituaries as well as *Brule County History* indicating that Vaclav and his first wife Barbara had come to Dakota Territory between 1883 and 1886. This suggested that the couple had been in the area at least four years before filing a claim in 1890. Interestingly, the same 1900 U.S. Census from which we obtained information on Tillie's birth also indicated that Vaclav's second child, a daughter named Rosa (or Rosie), was born in Vega on April 29, 1889, or a little more than a year *before* Tillie was born and Vaclav had filed his homestead claim. At the top of the page of that 1900 U.S. Census was printed "Union Township, Brule County," indicating that the family was living in the immediate area even before the Vega Post Office was moved from Trew Hayes' property in Buffalo County to Abraham Meyers property in Brule County in 1890. But we still had no evidence that either Vaclav or Barbara - or both - had come to Dakota Territory as early as 1883.

It truly was through a combination of good fortune and continued digging that we were eventually able to find conclusive evidence of our grandfather's arrival in Dakota Territory in 1883. This evidence was tucked away in an old hand-written ledger kept under lock and key at the Pierre Archives and it was there that we found the very faded hand-written legal entries for Vaclav's and Stephen's separate but adjacent claims, both dated March 10, 1883, and located in what would become Buffalo County, South Dakota.

This evidence clearly showed that thirteen years after our grandfather and his parents had left their birthplace in Bohemia to come to Iowa, our then twenty-two-year-old grandfather, together with his parents, left the relative comfort of Iowa to embark on yet another remarkable journey, perhaps even riskier and more perilous than the first, this time into untamed Dakota Territory. Their obvious goal was to stake a claim for "free" land made possible by the Homestead Act of

1862. And as we discovered to our surprise, the Native American Sioux who lived near the place where Vaclav and his parents eventually settled, proved to be far more sociable and far less of a threat than we had previously imagined. Perhaps this was at least partly because our grandfather, his parents and their neighbors faced challenges that were strikingly similar to those faced by their Sioux neighbors – the most serious of which were food scarcity and abysmal economic conditions arising from inconsistent, poorly considered and poorly executed government policies.

These challenges were then magnified many times over by multi-year droughts and legendary winter blizzards, not to mention storied insect plagues and rattlesnake infestations along with the presence of other formidable vermin. This was bad enough, but fast-moving, spontaneous grassland fires could and often did wipe out whole communities in mere minutes leaving residents with the option of frequent rebuilding with scarce resources or simply giving up and moving elsewhere to try to start over. These fires are said to be the reason this area was called "the land of the burnt thigh" by the Sioux who lived there.

From this perspective it should come as no surprise that the sum of these challenges proved insurmountable to fully sixty percent of all homesteaders, along with countless settlers who had purchased land either from ubiquitous speculators or from each other. For their part, Native Americans hung on by a thread, with most by this time relegated to reservation living and government handouts.

The Disappearance of the Great American Buffalo

Rogues, chiselers and vagabonds seemed to come with the territory and were, of course, additional if somewhat ancillary challenges to be reckoned with. But one important and formidable resident of the old American West had already vanished from the Great Plains by the early 1880s when our grandfather ventured into Dakota Territory. We are referring here to the great Ameri-

can buffalo herds that once blanketed the plains.

Once numbering close to an estimated thirty to sixty million, these massive herds had dwindled to about ten million by 1870 and were split in two by the building of the Union Pacific Railroad which cut the Great Plains into two segments, one north and one south. As Christopher Knowlton writes in his fascinating book *Cattle Kingdom*, "the southern herd of some five million animals would disappear in a matter of four years, from 1872 through 1875. The slightly smaller northern herd would survive longer, but facing similar assaults, it vanished by 1883."

Knowlton adds that in addition to the Union Pacific Railroad, another important factor that contributed to the demise of the buffalo was "the unwritten policy of the frontier military to deprive the Plains Indians of their most critical foodstuff – bison beef – thus ensuring their eventual dependence on the U.S. government for food rations." This unwritten policy was extended to include the building of spurs off the new railroad lines, thus providing commercial and recreational hunters easier access to the buffalo. In short, and through both written and unwritten policy, the region was effectively laid open for the unencumbered development of large cattle conglomerates through the partitioning off native Americans into specially designated areas and simultaneously eliminating the buffalo altogether.

The cattle industry (dominated by large cattle conglomerates) with which the buffalo were forced to compete, originated in Texas with the famous Longhorn cattle drives moving north to either railroad hubs or military posts. The industry grew quickly after the Civil War when investor capital from the East and from Europe became more readily available. The cattle barons competed directly with small cattle ranches in the area, prompting these small ranchers to form the Knights of Reliance in Lampasas, Texas in 1875. The Knights of Reliance were the Southern forerunners to what became known as the Populist movement, of which our grandfather was a part.

To achieve the kind of profits needed to pay investors, the cattle industry became a willing accomplice to the eradication of the bison. It was the pressure for profits together with the rapid decline of the buffalo that then allowed this budding new industry to grow rapidly into what became the driving force behind the greatest agricultural expansion the nation had ever seen. As Knowlton observed: "The two great bovine herds displaced each other. . . Cattle, the thinking went, functioned better than the wild bison as a machine for converting grass into hide and meat, and ultimately into profits."

By the late 1870s Knowlton remarks that there were worries that the cattle industry had overexpanded and overleveraged because "by some accounts, total investment in the cattle industry now exceeded the capitalization of the entire American banking system." He then adds that "by other accounts, Cheyenne, Wyoming, the epicenter of the boom, had the highest median per capita income in the world."

Among those running the burgeoning cattle industry, as Knowlton points out, were "many of the country's richest families and individuals – Marshall Field, the Rockefellers, the Vanderbuilts, the Flaglers, the Whitneys, the Seligmans, and the Ameses – [who all] were now cattle investors" even though they were not themselves cattlemen. The industry also attracted Scottish and English investors who were seeking better returns on their capital than they could find elsewhere. Even foreigners who aspired to become cattlemen though they knew nothing about cattle *or* the cattle business got into the act. One noteworthy example provided by Knowlton was an Englishmen by the name of Moreton Frewen, an English squire who founded the first joint stock cattle company registered in England, through which he started his own cattle operation near Cheyenne, Wyoming. Another was a Frenchman known as the Marquis de Mores.

According to Knowlton, Frewen acquired 160 acres through the Homestead Act and 640 acres through the Desert Act, in addition to making use of the open range for his cattle operations which itself was crowded with speculators, new money, and other giant cattle conglomerates. Although Knowlton says that the Marquis de Mores purchased a parcel of undetermined size, it is perhaps more likely that he was a squatter, just like his neighbor Theodore Roosevelt had been. The online Theodore Roosevelt Center says that "Theodore Roosevelt established two ranches in the badlands of western North Dakota: one called the Maltese Cross, seven miles south of the

Northern Pacific Railroad (1883), and the other called the Elkhorn, 35 miles north of the village of Medora, North Dakota (1884)." Interestingly, they assert that "Roosevelt never owned a single acre in North Dakota. Like most other ranchers in the badlands, he was a squatter on lands that still belonged to the public domain or the Northern Pacific Railway Company.

Roosevelt's cattle operations, like virtually all of the big cattle conglomerates, were located west of the Missouri. These massive operations did not materially affect our grandfather and his neighbors because even though the cattle in Vaclav's neighborhood were allowed to avail themselves of open fields, these cattle were just one part of small mixed farming operations, as opposed to the massive, single-product beef or sheep operations immediately to the west. Thus, when the shockingly brutal "Big Die-Up" winter of 1886-87 with its massive blizzards, ice storms and 50 degree-below zero temperatures came to cattle country - following on the heels of a scorching drought the previous summer, the cattle industry was brought to its knees, heralding the end of one of the greatest speculative bubbles of the Gilded Age.

According to an article titled *The Big Die-Up: The Death of the Old West?* appearing in the April 24, 2017 issue of the online *American Cowboy* magazine, author Ron Soodalter writes of the event:

> Hardly any of the cattlemen—many who were absentee owners, living as far away as Scotland and England—had possessed the foresight to put in a store of hay against such a disaster [because of over-reliance on the open range]. It has been estimated that at least 90 percent of the cattle on the Northern Ranges perished. When spring brought the thaw, it revealed millions of dead cows, dotting the plains to the horizon, damming the rivers and streams, and raising a stench that wafted over thousands of square miles, with an unimaginable throat-closing intensity.

Soodalter concludes that the Big Die-up finished a majority of the cattle barons and related stock growers outright and pushed those who did manage to continue raising cattle to do so with smaller herds, while at the same time and of necessity forcing them to become farmers in order to grow their own fodder with which to feed their cattle. Theodore Roosevelt, as one of these stock growers, had himself lost two-thirds of his herd to the Big Die Up, causing him to write to his sister that he was getting out of the cattle business.

Knowlton asserts that although the Big Die Up badly staggered the industry, "the true end of the era is better signposted, according to most historians, by the most famous of the range wars that followed; the murderous and controversial crossroads known as the Johnson County War" Also known as the Wyoming Range War and the War on Powder River, this conflict began in 1889, just two years after the Big Die-up had left its mark on the area, and did not end until 1893.

Coming to a head in Wyoming, which was the epicenter of the cattle industry, in 1892, this particular range war was waged by small ranchers and big cattle barons in a truly epic struggle for land and water rights. It all began when the surviving large cattle operations began to ferociously persecute alleged rustlers. However, most of these so-called rustlers were settlers who were competing for land, livestock and water rights. When the big cattle operators hired gunmen to invade the county, the small farmers and ranchers got together with the state lawmen and formed a posse of 200 men, leading to a grueling stand-off that was ended only after President Benjamin Harrison sent in the United States Calvary to keep the two factions at bay. Nevertheless, fighting continued for several months afterwards.

The Johnson County War was - luckily for our grandfather - a war he did not have to fight; he had plenty to contend with as it was.

Twists and Turns in Our Grandfather's Early Land Acquisition Attempts in the Wild West

As we have previously laid out, tracing the pre-1890 whereabouts of our grandfather and his first wife Barbara proved to be a far more difficult task than we had originally anticipated. Our journey began, logically enough we thought, with our grandfather's Will. This Will included seven quarter sections of land, all located in South Dakota, that formed part of his estate in 1923. Three of these properties were in Union Township, Brule County with one of those three properties being his original homestead. Three of the remaining quarter sections were in Pershing Township, Buffalo County, which was not all that odd when one understands that the Brule/Buffalo County line was less than a mile to the north of Vega. The seventh parcel was in Meade County on gently rolling land at the far northern edge of the Black Hills.

We soon realized however, that the information in our grandfather's Will did not provide any promising details concerning exactly when, or where, it was that our grandfather first came to Dakota Territory. Indeed, owing to the complicated nature of land transfers between family members that characterized our grandfather's later holdings - which will be explained in more detail in later chapters, our grandfather's Will was of no help to us at all in learning his earliest whereabouts.

Fortunately, and at the suggestion of historians at the South Dakota Archives in Pierre, we searched through federal land patent records. This resource provides information showing who had obtained "first title deeds" or land patents to specified parcels of land and when they obtained them. These records are primarily available at the Bureau of Land Management, General Land Office (GLO) Records Automation website, which informs visitors to that website that "Federal Land Patents offer researchers a source of information on the initial transfer of land titles from the Federal government to individuals."

We quickly found the land patent record for our grandfather's homestead located in Brule County, mentioned earlier. We also found what would turn out to be an *eighth* parcel recorded as a "Timber Culture" patent for a quarter section of land located in Buffalo County. For quite a while we assumed that this Timber Culture property was one of the seven parcels listed in Vaclav's Will. *It was not.*

As we eventually realized, this eighth parcel was *not* in Pershing Township, Buffalo County, as were the three Buffalo County properties listed in our grandfather's Will, but rather this particular property was in *El Dorado Township*, Buffalo County. It wasn't until much later that we realized that in 1904 our grandfather had swapped this eighth parcel for one owned by his brother-in-law that was located kitty-corner from our grandfather's homestead.

Continued digging led to the discovery of a *second* property in El Dorado Township. This was in addition to the Timber Culture land just mentioned, making it the *ninth* parcel that had, at one time, belonged to our grandfather. Close attention to detail helped us determine that, like the first El Dorado Township property for which we easily found a Timber Patent (awarded in 1898), this second property in El Dorado Township had also been awarded a Timber Patent (this one in 1892) - a highly unusual and irregular happenstance since two of the same type of patent were not typically awarded to the same individual. Some historical background together with a bit of deeper sleuthing helped us find an explanation for how this might have happened.

Pioneers, Propaganda, and the Law

New settlers were being incessantly schooled, mostly by railroad companies, about the fact that three types of land acquisition rights could be exercised by the same individual – unless that individual already owned land, in which case he could only file for a homestead claim. That exception aside, one individual could obtain a total of 480 acres of land by filing for three types of claims on three different quarter sections of land, with each quarter section equaling 160 acres. When averaged out, the total cost for the whole 480 acres could be as little as 50 cents an acre. Four hundred and eighty acres was a lot of land, being the equivalent of a square that was one and a half miles wide and one and a half miles long.

The average farm in the United States at the time was under 150 acres and many farmers actually earned a living on 40 or 80 acres, as was the case of Vaclav's father Stephen. So, as you might well imagine, the idea of obtaining so much land at such a low cost had immense appeal not just for those desperate to escape city slums but for anyone desiring a better life for themselves and their families. To be sure, this "free" or very cheap land offered young men such as our grandfather an opportunity to establish his own farming operation and raise a family.

Most of these homesteaders risked everything in honest pursuit of the American Dream. As we shall see, they not only left behind everything that was familiar to them only to face an extremely hostile and unforgiving environment, but they were forced to compete with a multitude of speculators, land barons and even those who were willing to move outside the bounds of the law as a means of securing cheap land for themselves.

Three pieces of Congressional legislation were the basis for obtaining these 160-acre parcels with each of these undergoing revisions over the years. Each state not only handled these land acquisitions differently but to complicate matters even more for us, some records may have been misplaced or lost when Dakota Territory transitioned into the states of North and South Dakota in 1889.

The first and most well-known of these laws was the Homestead Act of 1862. This Act enabled an individual, male or female, to obtain 160 acres of land basically free (outside of a small filing fee) after he or she had lived on the land for five years and improved it with buildings, fences and a home. Said individual also had to be at least 21 years of age and show proof of citizenship or declaration of intent to become a citizen. An interesting if less well known and less used feature of the Homestead Act was that it allowed a claimant the ability to obtain a "first title deed" by purchasing his homestead for a minimum of $1.25 an acre after six months of residency, which was a feature similar to the requirements of the Preemption Act of 1841 discussed later.

Native Americans were not left out entirely because on March 3, 1875 the Indian Homestead Act was passed as a means of encouraging Native American Indians to engage in farming. As discussed in the previous chapter, many tribes had already been farming for centuries, so in that sense this inclusion of Native Americans was, perhaps, not a completely unrealistic idea. Like the Homestead Act, claims could be filed for 160 acres by Native Americans who were 21 years of age and the head of a household, and in a manner paralleling the Homestead Act regarding non-citizen immigrants, this Act required the individual to "abandon his tribal relations and adopt the habits and pursuits of civilized life." Of course, as discussed in the previous chapter, the Dawes Act of 1887 and the Sioux Act of 1889 provided additional "incentives" to Native Americans to take up farming.

One of many threats faced by homesteaders came from claim jumpers, who wittingly or otherwise tried to expropriate claims officially staked out by homesteaders. This typically happened when a homesteader moved to a nearby town or even out of the territory during the winter months in order to take up jobs to earn extra money, which seems to be what our grandfather did, at least according to family lore. People known as claim jumpers would see a vacant homestead and simply move in. Some of these claim jumpers might have mistakenly assumed that the homestead had been abandoned and thus ripe for the taking. More often, clam jumpers simply saw opportunity. In all cases, neighbors and relatives generally acted on their absent neighbor's behalf by doing whatever it took to get rid of the trespasser, whether by summoning the law or even by taking matters into their own hands.

Another threat to homesteaders came from the ubiquitous speculators, who according to the online South Dakota history website, "moved in" with the homesteaders by acquiring large amounts of land. These speculators would actually pay other individuals to settle on a claim for 6 months and then have those individuals buy up the property with the speculator's money. This process created an artificial land squeeze that pushed up prices and allowed the speculator to reap tidy profits by selling off parcels when prices rose sufficiently.

The second piece of legislation that could be used in conjunction with the Homestead Act was the Timber Culture Act of 1873. This law was designed to encourage the planting of trees and homesteading in the West. Initially, a patent (which was a first title deed) could be obtained once a claimant planted 40 acres of trees and maintained them for 10 years. This 40-acre requirement was reduced to 10 acres just five years later, in 1878, since trying to make trees grow in a semi-arid region was a "mockery of nature" as one US Congressman put it.

According to the online Minnesota Legal History Project, most timber culture claimants were not interested in planting trees, but merely wanted to add another quarter section to their hold-ings or, more commonly, sell the parcel to an interested party "at an advance" - before actually obtaining a patent. The Timber Culture Act did not have requirements either for residency or improvements made to the land. Partly because of this the Timber Culture Act was often abused, primarily by the big cattlemen. Professor Everett Dick, cited by the Minnesota History Project, described how and why this was so:

> The Timber Culture Act lent itself to the rancher more readily than the Homestead Act be-cause residency and improvements were not required; it was necessary only for the cowman to have his cowboys allow their names to be used and for them to perjure themselves at the appropriate moment. There was no building of cabins, even fragile shacks, and no anxiety that someone might be watching to see that the entryman spent a night on the claim now and then. Many tree claims were entered, relinquished after three years, and re-entered by another em-ployee.....In 1888 the land officer at Sidney, Nebraska, stated that there had never been a final proof for a timber-culture claim in that district. The routine he said, was enter, hold, relin-quish, change claims; enter, hold, relinquish, and so on; indefinitely holding and keeping quan-tities of the public domain from the newcomers until the claims became valuable.

> . . . In the eyes of the land officers, [the Timber Culture Act was more harmful than either the Homestead or the Pre-emption act because it permitted the manipulations that kept large are-as tied up, and it played into the hands of the big interests. Thousands of settlers were pre-vented from exercising their legal right to acquire homes. On the other hand, it was a godsend to the rancher, who could not legally secure the land he needed.

> Cattlemen, however, were not the only ones who misused the Timber Culture Act. The pur-pose of the law, of course, was to encourage the growing of trees, and the statute stated that land, to be admissible for taking under the act, had to be "devoid of timber." But by means of the ever useful, ever pliable frontier oath, valuable coal lands—and incredible as it may seem, even timberlands—were separated from the government by the use of this [Timber Culture] act.

The last piece of legislation that could be used by an individual to legally acquire a total of 480 acres was the Preemption Act of 1841. This Act proved to be the biggest source of confusion for us as we attempted to trace our grandfather's earliest whereabouts.

As originally drawn up, this Act gave squatters who had been living on federal land the right to purchase up to 160 acres for $1.25 an acre before the land was offered for sale to the general public. A claimant also had to show proof of a dwelling and improvements to the land. In one of several iterations of the law, the claimant was required to be a resident of the land for at least 14 months. At its inception the law was vigorously opposed by Eastern business interests who be-lieved that such easy access to land would drain them of their labor supply. But it was mostly speculators and their allies in government who offered the strongest opposition, primarily by working to create laws that impeded a squatter's utilization of first right of purchase of the land they occupied.

Like the Timber Culture Act (and the Desert Land Act which applied to land west of the Missouri and which was utilized by Moreton Frewen mentioned earlier to secure for himself an additional 640 acres), the Preemption law led to considerable amounts of corruption by enabling non-settlers a method by which to acquire large tracts of land illegally. Speculators for instance would coerce accomplices, including hired hands, to falsely claim that they were living on the land that the speculators wanted, thus keeping land away from ordinary settlers. Speculators also sometimes went into the money lending business which further enhanced their ability to take advantage of cash-strapped settlers inasmuch as lenders dictate the terms and to whom a loan is made.

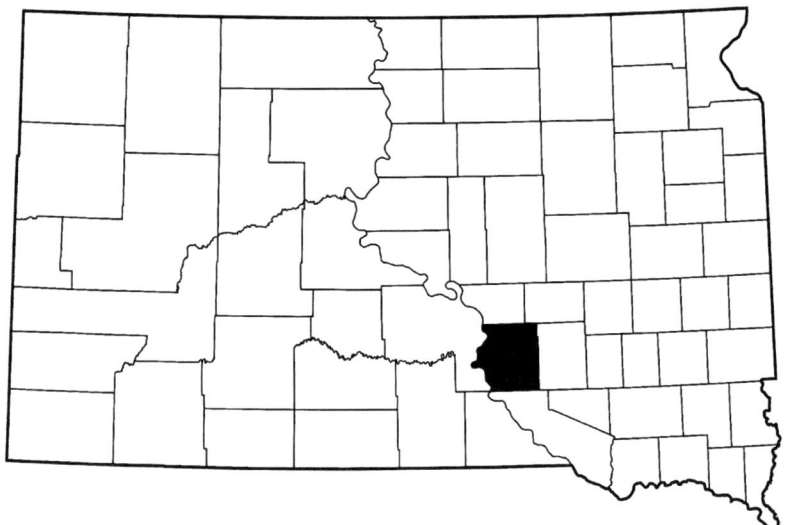

Brule County is in the shaded area, and Union Township, where Vaclav settled is on the northern border of Brule County. Buffalo County is directly north and Charles Mix County, where our grandfather would later live, is directly south of Brule County. The western boudary of all three counties is the Missouri River.

Land patents, or "first title deeds", were awarded for both Timber Culture claims and Homestead claims once all specified legal requirements had been met and a small filing fee had been paid. As mentioned, the Homestead Act included a purchase option similar to that of the Preemption Act, but a Preemption claim was slightly different. While the Homestead Act allowed the individual a choice of either purchasing his claim for $1.25 an acre from the federal government or getting it at no cost so long as residency and improvement requirements were met, the Preemption Act only gave individuals an opportunity to purchase a claimed parcel from the federal government at $1.25 an acre, before said land was made available to the general public and so long as other requirements were met. Teddy Roosevelt for example might have filed a Pre-Emption claim for 160 acres of the land his ranches occupied by exercising his right to pay the going rate of $1.25 an acre prior to the land being offered for sale to the public. Instead, Roosevelt chose to remain a squatter.

It turns out that our grandfather had indeed filed for land under all three of these pieces of legislation available to him at the time. This came as quite a surprise when we found this out since the records we had previously acquired told us only that our grandfather obtained one homestead patent and two Timber Culture patents – one patent having been awarded in 1898 and the other in 1892. One of the biggest sources of confusion for us stemmed from the fact that only those who owned no other land were able to file for a Preemption claim. Thus, if Vaclav's goal was to acquire the full 480 acres as allowed by law, then he had to file for a "Pre" claim first, before he filed for either a Timber Culture Claim or a Homestead Claim. Stephen meanwhile could not file a Preemption claim since he owned land in Iowa.

Our Grandfather's Tangle with the Law

As it turned out our dogged efforts to uncover the illusive details surrounding our grandfather's earliest ventures into Dakota Territory soon led us on an unexpected journey into the chaotic and often unruly ways of the "Wild West".

Although we had hired a land patent researcher and made two separate visits to the Gann Valley Registrar of Deeds, we initially failed to find any concrete information regarding the fact that our grandfather had indeed filed a Pre-emption claim on March 10, 1883, in El Dorado Township, Buffalo County. This of course was the same township and county where we had already found a Timber Patent that had been awarded in 1898. Neither of these parcels had been itemized in our grandfather's will, which it may be recalled included *three* parcels in Pershing Township, Buffalo County and *none* in El Dorado Township. As mentioned earlier we eventually found, almost serendipitously, concrete evidence of this "Pre" claim in a handwritten ledger tucked away under lock and key at the Pierre Archives.

However, our first clue that our grandfather had indeed filed a pre-emption claim came when we found an article from December of 1891 that appeared in both the *Mitchell Daily Republican* and the *Mitchell Capital.* The article in both newspapers read:

> J. C. Marshall vs Vaclav Fousek, Buffalo County. Contestant filed contest against claimant's final proof in May, 1887. The former register and receiver held that the law had not been complied with by Fousek, which decision was affirmed by the Commissioner. The Secretary now reverses both decisions and states that it is not clearly shown that Fousek acted in bad faith or that he failed to comply substantially with the law.

Although we are left to conjecture as to exact details, it is clear that our grandfather had been involved in a legal battle with J.C. Marshall, who is described in another article cited below as probate judge of Buffalo County. From the scant details of the above article, it appears that an unnamed "contestant" filed a legal challenge against our grandfather in May of 1887 when our grandfather went to "prove up" his claim, which for a Pre-emption claim meant choosing to take the purchase option prior to the land being offered for sale to the general public. It seems that Marshall, as the "former registrar and receiver" ruled that our grandfather had "not complied with the law" and ruled against our grandfather who then took his case to the Commissioner who in turn upheld Marshall's decision.

Not to be deterred, our grandfather then appealed to the Secretary (perhaps the Secretary of State, since South Dakota was by this time a state) who reversed both of the earlier decisions, stating that it was not made clear in the earlier rulings that our grandfather "acted in bad faith or that he failed to comply substantially with the law." The time that had elapsed during this legal wrangling appears to have been four years, from the time of the first challenge in May of 1887 to the date the article reported the final ruling in December of 1891.

A bit of intrigue was added to this story in an article we found through a further search of *Chronicling America,* available online. Note that this article appeared *two years earlier* than the above 1891 article, in the March 9, 1889 issue of the *Press and Daily Dakotaian,*

> A sensational arrest was made at Grand Valley, Buffalo County, Wednesday by Deputy United States Marshall George Wright. The arrested party is Capt. J.C. Marshall, probate judge of that county. The charge is perjury in negotiating a loan through C. M. Gregory."

So, smack dab in the middle of our grandfather's legal wrangling, a "sensational" (or perhaps scandalous and certainly dramatic) arrest was made of J.C. Marshall, the very person who had first ruled against our grandfather. Marshall, identified as probate judge of Buffalo County, was charged with perjury, which is essentially lying under oath. The online FindLaw website says that one perjures oneself by knowingly making false or misleading statements or by signing a legal document one knows to be false or misleading. Perjury is a very serious crime since it undermines the foundation of the legal system which depends on trust and credibility. Apparently, Mr. Marshall lied or otherwise made false and misleading statements while negotiating some type of loan through an individual by the name of C. M. Gregory, whose office is not given.

Whether Marshall was sentenced to jail and/or fined or perhaps even exonerated we do not know. We do know that it was not quite two years later that the Secretary (of State we presume) ruled in our grandfather's favor. Unfortunately for us, no legal description of the property in question was provided in any of these articles. Thus, our search for the exact location of this property was set in motion.

Making the Connection between Judge Marshall and Our Grandfather's First Claim

As fate would have it, we were, quite unexpectedly, permitted to view the original handwritten ledger that was used to record claim applications - retrieved for us by one of the historians from a back room at the South Dakota Historical Archives in Pierre. As sisters Donna, Sandy and myself sifted through dozens upon dozens of names and related information entered into that ledger, it was almost as if we fell into a state of suspended disbelief when we came upon the names of our grandfather and great grandfather along with several of our grandfather's in-laws. But there they were, undeniably. We were so thoroughly dumbstruck to see those names and recording dates that we neglected to note whether the signatures we viewed were those of our grandfather and great-grandfather or filled in by some person appointed to perform the task.

Although many of the entries are quite blurred due to age and thus difficult to read, we were able to discern that Vaclav's father Stephen had filed for a Homestead claim in El Dorado Township, Buffalo County on March 10, 1883. On that exact same date per another ledger entry Vaclav filed for a "Pre." (Pre-emption) claim on what we eventually determined to be the contested parcel disallowed by J.C. Marshall as discussed above. Vaclav's "Pre." claim was adjacent to the Homestead claim made by his father Stephen. For some unknown reason, Vaclav again filed a "Pre." claim for the exact same parcel of land some six months later, on September 29, 1883. This second unexplained entry came a few days before he and Barbara were married in Iowa, so perhaps Vaclav made that second entry to insure his claim.

In any case, and very thankfully, the ledger also provided legal descriptions, allowing us to trace exactly where these properties were located and later use this information to prove that our grandfather's original preemption claim of March 10, 1883 was for the same piece of property for which he inexplicably received a Timber Culture patent in 1892, finally giving him full title to this piece of property. This patent was awarded one year *after* the legal wrangling first begun with J.C. Marshall in 1887 was concluded. It might also be noted here that the type of claims Stephen and Vaclav filed in 1883 was no doubt due to provisions of the Preemption Act which excluded those with other land holdings from filing a Preemption claim. Vaclav had no other land holdings, but his father Stephen did. Hence Vaclav was able to file for a "Pre" claim while his father could not.

This same handwritten ledger also tells us how things played out for the pair as a result of their first venture into staking claims in Dakota Territory. We know for instance that Stephen relinquished his Buffalo County Homestead claim to a Bardin Sobek on July 28, 1888, which was a little over year after Vaclav began his legal wrangling with J.C. Marshall. This relinquishment was why Sobek's name appears for Stephen's homestead parcel on an historical plat map we collected from Pierre.

As mentioned in Chapter 2, on April 17, 1885, President Grover Cleveland issued Presidential Proclamation 268, closing the southern part of the Crow Creek Indian Reservation to settlement.

Both Vaclav and Stephen's claims of March 10, 1883 were located in the southern portion of the Crow Creek Indian Reservation. What effect this had on their claims or their movements, perhaps back to Iowa, we do not know. However, on April 30, 1888, this portion of the Reservation was re-opened to settlement, possibly correcting any legal problem the Presidential Proclamation may have created for our grandfather and his father.

We do know, as mentioned above, that four months after the reopening of the Reservation, Vaclav's father Stephen relinquished his claim to Bardin Sobek, in July of 1888. And we know that four months after that, on November 12, 1888, Vaclav staked a Timber Culture Claim near the vicinity of his Preemption Claim. It is therefore entirely possible, even likely, that both men returned to Iowa between 1885 and 1888 to wait out the uncertainties of their respective claims, returning when the "law" allowed. It also could explain why Charles was born in Iowa, a month after Cleveland's proclamation.

By 1890 both Stephen and Vaclav filed Homestead claims in Brule County on parcels across the road from each other. Years later, in 1901, both Stephen and Vaclav were awarded Homestead patents on these parcels, and it was on these properties, together with the Wencil Havlik parcel, that the town of Vega was built.

As indicated earlier, we hired a professional land patent researcher to help us sort out some of the details concerning when it was that our grandfather and his family first ventured into Dakota Territory. He located and provided us with two land patent documents. The first of the two documents told us that on November 12, 1888 our grandfather had filed for a Timber Culture patent in El Dorado Township, Buffalo County, South Dakota. (This patent was not in any way connected to the Timber Culture Patent awarded to our grandfather in 1892, the documents for which were not located or provided to us by our researcher for reasons we will provide shortly).

The second document showed that Vaclav had filed for a Homestead in Union Township, Brule County, South Dakota on May 5, 1890. Because there was no residency requirement for Timber Culture land, Vaclav's place of residence was listed on his 1888 patent application documents as Lyonville, county of Brule, even though this Timber Culture parcel was in Buffalo County, not Brule. Lyonville is a town southeast of Vega, thus placing Lyonville a little farther south of the Brule/Buffalo County line than Vega. Lyonville's post office had also been established in 1882, four years before the "Vega" post office was originally established in Buffalo County in 1886 with Trew Hayes as its first postmaster,

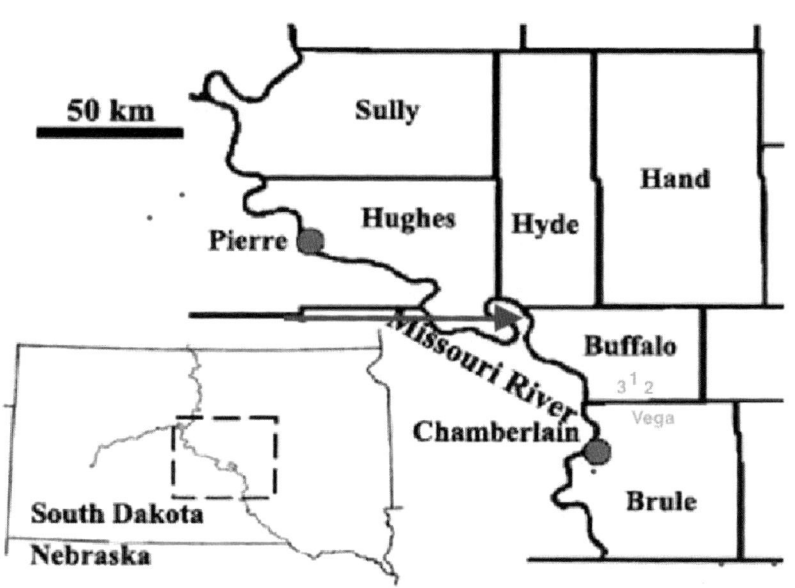

Map showing the proximity of Vaclav's 1883 "Pre." claim in Buffalo County to what would become the town of Vega in Brule County years later. The "pre." Claim is designated by the numeral 1. Numeral 2 is Stephen's first homestead claim filed in 1883 next to his son's "Pre." claim, Numeral 3 is the Timber Culture claim Vaclav filed in 1888.

and eight years before the Vega post office moved to Abraham Meyer's property in Brule County in 1890. We are left to wonder whether President Cleveland's 1885 order caused Trew Hayes to leave Buffalo County and the operation of the Post Office to be temporarily suspended with postal services relegated to Lyonville.

Sorting through all these rather confusing details caused us a significant delay in making the discovery that our grandfather had filed a "Pre." claim on March 10, 1883, placing him in Dakota Territory five years earlier than the 1888 Timber Culture application. This "Pre." claim was, of course, the very same parcel which resulted in a legal dispute with Judge J.C. Marshall that was eventually resolved in our grandfather's favor when the Secretary reversed Marshall and held that Vaclav had substantially complied with the law. Although the newspaper reported this to have occurred in December of 1891, Vaclav obtained a deed for the property for $125 from Case & Whitback Bankers on March 5, 1891. He then sold the property for $450 to Henry Schamel not quite a year later, in February of 1892. Even stranger was the fact that three months after that, in May 1892, Vaclav was awarded a Timber Culture Patent for the same piece of property. This patent we are guessing was turned immediately over to Henry Schamel, since the next record for the parcel appeared in 1909, when the Schamels turned this land over to Clement and Lillie Clark for $1.00, in a transaction described as an "indenture."

Clearly and in our grandfather's case at least, the preemption claim proved to be a much more complicated and confusing story than either the Timber Culture claim or the Homestead claim. As discussed earlier, preemption rights could be exercised by paying $1.25 per acre for the 160-acre parcel, which meant that the total cost would have been $200. However, records show that our grandfather paid Case & Whitback Bankers only $125. We are left to wonder why.

Interestingly, both the Preemption Act and the Timber Culture Act were repealed in 1891. We were unable to find the exact date the Preemption Act was repealed but the Timber Culture Act was repealed on March 3, 1891. We can fairly surmise that the Timber Culture claim that our grandfather filed on November 12, 1888 was not affected by the 1891 repeal of the Timber Culture Act since he received a patent for that parcel in 1898 but we have no idea as to why he was awarded a Timber Patent in 1892 for land that he had originally filed for under the Preemption Act.

We found no mortgages recorded for the property obtained from Case & Whitback and conjecture that our grandfather may have paid for it in cash which may have been earned while traveling back to Iowa during the winter months to earn extra money. This is supported by family lore which holds that our grandfather traveled around Iowa during the winter months, perhaps zig-zagging his way to Sioux Falls and back to make extra money by selling pots and pans. It may even have been that these travels helped our grandfather establish business relationships which would later help establish the little frontier town of Vega.

Land Titles Now Split-Estate, Not Fee Simple

Our grandfather's 1888 Timber Culture claim in Buffalo County, like his 1890 Homestead claim that was located in Brule County, were both accompanied by a "non-mineral affidavit" that required our grandfather to swear that his claim "was not made for the purpose of fraudulently obtaining title to mineral land. . ." We thought this interesting as we had always assumed that the purchase of land, or in our own personal case a home and lot, was awarded fee simple title, conferring rights to what lay beneath as well as on top of the land in question. The fee simple land title was established in early America and by the Northwest Ordinance of 1787 for new states east of the Mississippi. Somehow the mineral rights provision was later added. Perhaps it had to do with the discovery of gold in California in 1848 but we do not know that for sure.

These "split-estate" land titles may also have resulted from various pieces of Congressional legislation. Laws such as the Railroad Enabling Act (1866), the Desert Land Grant Act (1877), and the Stone and Timber Land Act (1878) essentially transferred millions of acres of land together with the resources and raw materials that lay below ground into the hands of cattle syndicates, mining and land development companies and railroads, or in other words large conglomerates.

Constitutional change, via Supreme Court decisions concerning the Commerce Clause, also contributed to the process of opening the West not just for settlement but also for those who would be awarded the economic use of raw materials that lay below the ground. For example, between 1875 and 1900 the Supreme Court not only blocked federal attempts at regulation of interstate commerce but removed many state laws that restricted interstate commerce. The limited powers of the Interstate Commerce Commission, created in 1887, were further restricted by Court decisions. Together, these decisions allowed the large and more privileged land holders to move their "booty" across state lines, while at the same time taking from ordinary homesteaders and settlers the right to profit from any minerals that may have been located on their land.

Taken together, this redefinition of the land as something other than "the people's heritage" contributed to the "populist revolt" of which our grandfather was a part.

On November 16, 1898, our grandfather was awarded a Timber Culture patent ten years after filing his application, after providing proof of citizenship (which he had received in 1894) and written testimony from himself and two witnesses. In this testimony we learn that our grandfather had dutifully planted, replanted and tended 11 acres of trees, in accordance with the 1878 downward revision of the Timber Culture Act of 1873 from 40 acres to just 10 acres that were required to be planted in trees. Unfortunately, a drought in 1894 and 1895 killed all the trees on those 11 acres.

Native Americans Help Settlers Settle

Despite the massive drought which prevented our grandfather from maintaining the required number of trees on his Timber land, a patent was awarded to him anyway, presumably because officials were learning that this "Great American Desert" might require a lot more than a few newly planted saplings to tame it. For their part, as we learn from historian Herbert Schell in an account provided to him by a certain Minnie Palm Hagen, that Native Americans were known to have offered their help to penniless settlers needing to plant the 200 seedlings required for their Timber Culture claim. Native Americans did this by pulling up enough seedlings from the area and then transplanting them on respective claims to allow settlers to satisfy requirements for their claim. We have no proof that our grandfather took advantage of such largess however.

Our Grandfather Achieves Citizenship

Included in the package of documents that we obtained for this Timber Culture parcel was a copy of the handwritten naturalization papers that were awarded to our grandfather on June 2, 1894 - five years after South Dakota became a state. An excerpt reads as follows: "The court being satisfied as well from the oath of said Vaclav Fousek as from testimony of M. Novotny and Frank Pazori, who are known to be citizens of the United States, that the said Vaclav Fousek has resided within the limits and under the jurisdiction of the United States for at least five years past, and at least one year last past within the State of Dakota, and during the whole of that time he has behaved himself as a man of good moral character, attached to the principles contained in the Constitution of the United States, and well-disposed to the good order, well-being and happiness of the same. . . ."

We know from other documents that our grandfather had applied for citizenship years before, in 1882 while living in Iowa, and that Barbara was a naturalized citizen by virtue of having been born in Iowa. Numerous facts and details of our grandfather's life indicate that our grandfather, like so many others before and after him, took his U.S. citizenship seriously, embracing its rights, privileges and responsibilities with enthusiasm and pride. Just as clearly, he retained much of his Bohemian heritage and clung to its culture by choosing to live in Bohemian communities to the end of his life.

Vega Homestead Claim Reveals Details, Lingering Questions

As detailed earlier, Vaclav had filed a "Pre." claim in 1883 which seems to have created considerable trouble for him, in part because that area had been closed to settlers in 1885 by Grover Cleveland and second because he became involved in a legal dispute that began in 1887 and was not resolved until 1891. During this time period, the area was again opened to settlers in 1888, and a few months after opening, Vaclav filed for a Timber Culture Patent in the same County and township as the "pre." claim had been filed. He was in other words following the steps laid out by Railroad propaganda that showed new settlers how they could obtain "free" or very cheap land.

Thus, we find that in May of 1890, just a few months after South Dakota achieved statehood, our grandfather filed a Homestead affidavit, this homestead being the future home of the town of Vega. Across the top of some of the pre-printed application papers were the hand-written words "Soo Indian" or "Sioux Indian" - an indication that this had been part of the Crow Creek (Dakota Sioux) Indian Reservation that was now open to settlement. On the application affidavit our grandfather states that "I am at the head of a family and have declared my intention to become a citizen of the U.S. Was living on this land and had valuable improvements."

Just how long our grandfather and his family had been living on the parcel that would then become his homestead is unclear, for reasons we have tried to lay out in this chapter. But we do know that Vaclav finally received his homestead patent on June 13, 1901. Although there were many modifications to the original Homestead Act of 1862, we understood that east of the Missouri River a patent could be awarded after five years of continuous residence (with any tax benefit expiring after seven). If this were true and since our grandfather had received his naturalization papers in 1894, we can only speculate as to why more than ten years had elapsed between application and patent.

It is possible that the Sioux Act of 1889 (passed by Congress the year South Dakota became a state) for the purpose of opening Sioux lands west of the Missouri River to settlement may have applied in our grandfather's case as well. In this case homesteaders were to pay $1.25 per acre if the homestead was settled during the first three years after opening; 75 cents per acre the next two years; 50 cents an acre the next five years. After ten years the homestead could be acquired free and clear. Since it also took Vaclav's father Stephen ten years to receive his Homestead Patent after initial formal application, it is a possibility that the Sioux Act of 1889 applied to Stephen and our grandfather and they decided together that they would wait out the full ten years in order to acquire their respective homesteads free and unencumbered.

Other than the aforementioned possibilities, including the opening and closing of the Crow Creek Reservation, the only other reason we could come up with that may have caused such a lengthy delay in obtaining a Homestead patent occurred when our grandfather spelled "Fousek" with a "c" instead of an "s" on one of the final documents, for which another document with corrected spelling was filed and duly certified by the registrar.

The same thing occurred years earlier when Vaclav's father Stephen was finalizing ownership documents for his property in Iowa, resulting in Stephen filing a separate document duly noting his version of the correct spelling of "Fousek." On the plat maps we looked at - which included Stephen's Iowa property, we found "Fousek" spelled "Foesek," "Fousek," "Foucek" and "Fouchek" - one or all of which spellings might have been used at various times or recorded differently at different times by different officials. Similarly, the name of the Wencil Havlik was shown as "W. Hawlik" on these early maps. Incidents like these are legion and indicate the kinds of problems newcomers (as well as Native American Indians) dealt with as they tried to cope with unfamiliar languages, customs and legal issues.

We also learned from our grandfather's own testimonial for "proving up" his homestead that there already was a house on the tract when he filed on it. We speculate that this house may have been put there by someone who had been there during the 1885 opening/closing of the area – or it could simply have been abandoned by someone who was unable to "prove up" the claim. The size of the original existing house was not specified, and although slightly larger than the 8' x 10' structure required by law, it is quite likely that the house was one of two 10' x 12' structures later described in the proving up documents.

One can only guess whether this original structure was exactly the kind of tar paper shack described by Edith Eudora Kohl in her book *Land of the Burnt Thigh* which describes the 1907 homesteading experiences of Edith and her sister Ida Mary west of the Missouri. But Edith's account does give us a general idea of what life might have been like for our grandfather and his young family when they first took up residence in their own tiny pre-existing structure:

> It was a typical homestead shack, about 10' x 12', containing only one room, and built of rough, foot-wide boards, with a small cellar window on either side of the room. Like the walls, the door was of wide boards. The whole house was covered on the outside with tar paper. It had obviously been put together with small concern for the fine points of carpentry and none whatever for appearance. It looked as though the first wind would pick it up and send it flying in the air.

> It was as unprepossessing within as without. In one corner a homemade bunk was fastened to the wall, with ropes crisscrossed and run through holes in the 2 x 4 inch pieces of lumber which formed the bed, to take the place of springs. In another corner a rusty, two-hole oil stove stood on a drygoods box; above it another box with a shelf in it for a cupboard. Two rickety chairs completed the furnishings.

Remarkably, inasmuch as the prairie generally provided little wood for building, forcing many settlers to build sod homes or live-in dugouts, our grandfather's "proving up" documents indicate that he had plenty of wood, and it is guessed, enough money to purchase it. Altogether improvements to the property, as of 1900, included a 14' x 17' frame house, with two 10' x 12' add-ons. In addition, there was a 20' x 40' frame barn, with two add-ons, one being 14' x 16' and the other being 15' x 36'. In addition, there was a granary measuring 14' x 18', a corn crib measuring 12' x 16' along with "several other buildings." There was also a well and a windmill, plus 200 rods of fencing. Total value, as stated in the patent documents, was $1400. These details taken together show that our grandfather and his family were very serious about building strong roots in their tiny new community.

We also learned from the "proving up" testimonies that our grandfather farmed 40 acres of this homestead land in 1891, 50 acres in 1892 and 70 acres each season between 1893 and 1900, when the final proof was filed. Operating on the assumption that up to 40 acres of sod had potentially already been broken by a previous occupant, this still meant that our grandfather had to break at least 30 more acres of sod in order to plant all 70 acres beginning in 1893. And, since we know that there was a drought in 1894 and 1895 that killed all his timber claim trees, we can only surmise that this drought did considerable damage to his 70 acres of crops as well.

These formidable challenges were of course in addition to adding all those afore-mentioned improvements, raising a family, which by 1897 consisted of eight children, and perhaps also traveling to Iowa in winters to make extra money. It is quite possible that Vaclav had been breaking sod on his timber claim as well.

Family and Friends Stick Together, Creating a Community

If you look at online plat maps you can find the homestead that Edith (Ammon) Kohl and her sister "proved up" just west of the Missouri River, not all that far from where our grandfather proved up his own homestead, east of the river. In her book *Land of the Burnt Thigh* Edith provides vivid and moving descriptions of the experiences shared with her sister when they set out to prove up their claim, and the incredible odds they had to overcome in doing so. The sisters' initial despair over the prospect of facing the wilderness alone is palpable and haunting.

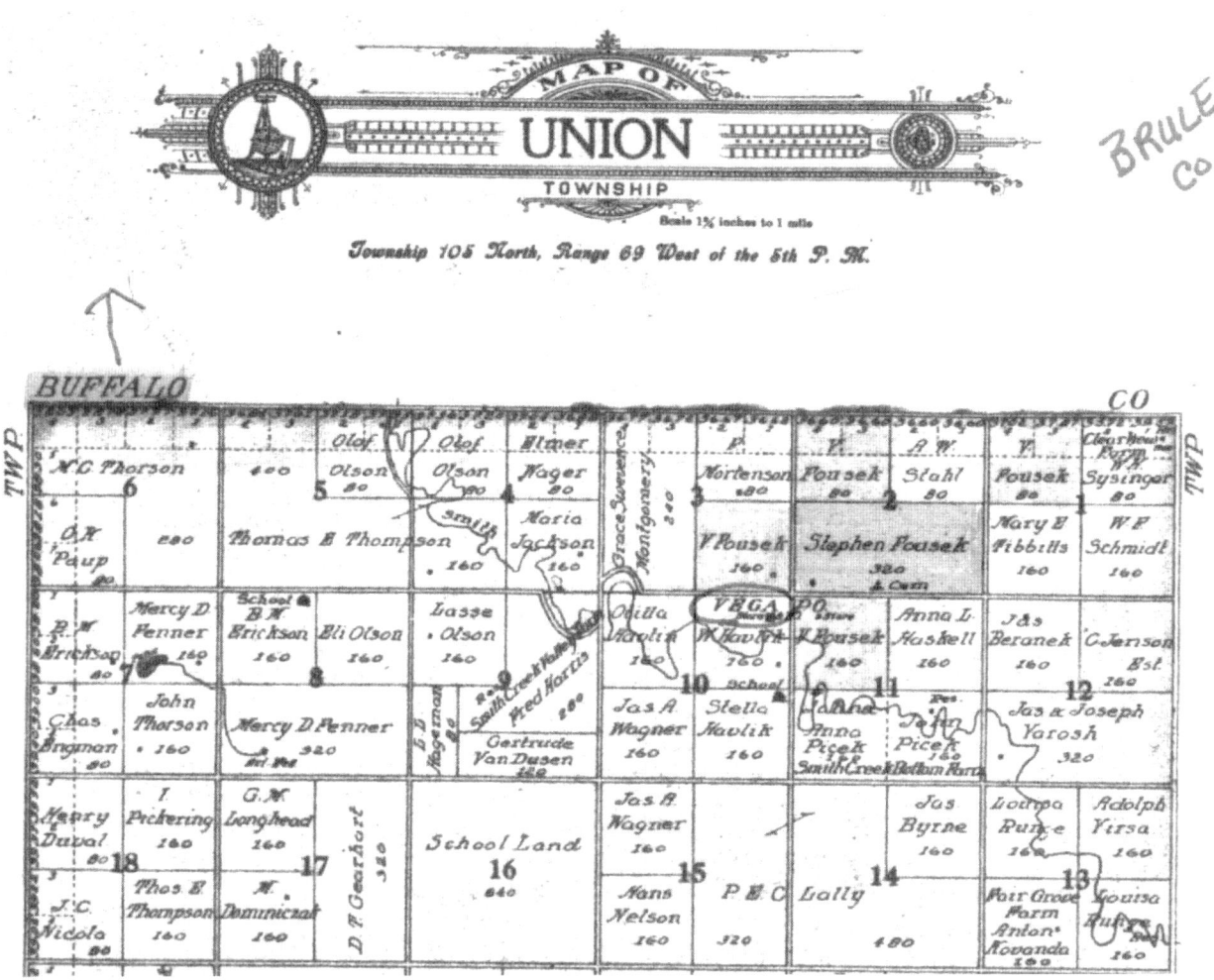

Plat maps of the northern half of Union township. Brule County circa 1911. Shows the parcels owned by our grandfather and his relatives. The town of Vega is located on the four farms of our grandfather, his father and his brother-in-law Wencil Havlik. Smth Creek runs from the southwest to the southeast through several of these parcels. The Missouri River is to the west.

Fortunately, our ancestors on both sides followed the more typical pattern of migrating in groups in the hope that they might build a new community similar to the one they left behind. So it was that both our maternal grandfather Vaclav and his wife Barbara could count on their parents, who lived on adjacent farms, as well as several of Barbara's siblings who lived nearby, for help as well as company.

Plat maps of the period show that Barbara's brother Wencil and his parents had staked out claims across the road from Vaclav Fousek and his wife Barbara's homestead at about the same time that Vaclav and Barbara were proving up theirs. One of the maps we looked at indicates that Barbara's brother Wencil Havlik had the parcel directly across from our grandfather. Meanwhile Barbara's parents had a parcel directly south of her brother Wencil, who was alternately called Waclov, Vaclav and James or "Jim". The parent's parcel was listed under Veronika Havlik, presumably to minimize confusion between her husband and son, both named Wencil, who were both sometimes called Waclov. Both of Barbara's parents, Vernie and Wencil, are buried in the Vega Cemetery, where their names appear as Veronika Havlik and Vaclav Wencil Havlik (not to be confused with our grandfather Vaclav Fousek). Wencil Jr. is also buried in the Vega Cemetery, with his name appearing as Vaclav James Havlik.

As mentioned earlier, Vaclav's father Stephen (our great-grandfather) had also staked a homestead claim on the parcel directly north of Vaclav's. In addition, Barbara's sister Josephine and her husband John Henzlik lived nearby in Buffalo County for a period of years before finally ending up in Mitchell, South Dakota. James Beranek, who was married to Barbara's sister Flora, had a parcel east of our grandfather. They had two daughters, Lillian and Violet, plus an unnamed baby girl who is buried in the Vega Cemetery, where they themselves are also buried. A parcel proved up by a Mary J. Everhart was located between the Beranek and Fousek homesteads.

Interestingly, about a dozen women had staked and/or finalized claims in Union Township during that period, most of them apparently without benefit of husbands or relatives.

A harrowing account of one such lady is provided in *Brule County History* and concerns one Maria Jackson who had a claim next to Abraham Meyers during the time that Meyers was running the Vega Post Office. It seems that in 1895 Maria had traveled by covered wagon from Sutherland, Iowa to Brule County with her husband, four children, ages 3 through 13, and fortuitously enough, two large sacks full of navy beans to keep the family from starving. They arrived on their claim June 5th, but the drought in Brule County that year forced Maria's husband Millard to go to Lake County to drill wells. When Millard died of typhoid fever in 1898, Maria had to carry on alone with her children. So, she proved up the claim next to the Meyers place and raised her children there.

Luckily, the parents in the Fousek and Havlik clans managed, during this time period at least, to escape early deaths due to disease, accidents, rattlesnake bites, or other calamities that befell early pioneers.

Barbara's brother Wencil added his wife to the group when he married Stella Bely, who had grown up in the Bijou Hills area, which was south of Vega. According to *Brule County History*, the marriage took place on November 3, 1890 just a few months after our grandfather had filed his homestead affidavit. Wencil had to borrow a coat to be married in, and the couple traveled to their home in Vega "in a wagon using a board with a comfort covering it to ride on." We are told they had a home waiting for them, but do not know whether this was a small claim shack or some other kind of abode.

Brule County History, completed in 1977, says that Stella and Wencil's home was located on the farm of our grandfather's late grandson Duane Fousek. This farm would have been homesteaded by Barbara's brother Anton somewhere around the time Wencil brought his new bride to Vega. It is highly unlikely that this parcel was indeed the location of Wencil and Stella's new home since in 1902 Anton essentially swapped this parcel with our grandfather for our grandfather's Timber Culture parcel. We do not know the reason for this swap but perhaps Anton wanted to be closer to Barbara's brother Aaron and his wife Clara. Anton died in Buffalo County in 1905 and is buried in the Vega Cemetery. His name is shown there as being Antone Havlik, while research that we have found through Ancestry.com says that his name was Thomas Anton Havlik. He was just shy of his 33rd birthday when he died.

In another section in *Brule County History,* Stella wrote down her own memories, telling us that her husband had been farming in Vega at the time of their marriage. So, we think it is most likely that Stella and Wencil moved to Wencil's home located on his homestead which adjoined the homestead of his parents. In any case, some kind of home was available for Wencil and his new bride and we are conjecturing that this structure was at some point moved to Anton's homestead when Stella and Wencil built a new home. We also find on a later plat map, circa 1911, that Wencil's wife Stella was now shown to be the owner of Wencil's mother Vernie's parcel.

Stella and Jim would go on to have eight children. Two of the eight died in infancy and another daughter named Mary who died in 1904 when she was not quite six years old. Yet another daughter named Libby died in 1894 at the age of five months fifteen days. Both Mary and Libby appear on the Vega Cemetery roles, although some of the information concerning death dates appears to be incorrect. Yet another daughter died at the age of 33, leaving her eight children in the care of their grandparents Wencil and Stella. While establishing his young family, Wencil was finding ways to support them in addition to farming. By 1901 he had a blacksmith shop, a general merchandise store, and a post office set up on his property while our grandfather Vaclav would have a store, a creamery and some kind of granary, perhaps used by the neighborhood, thus birthing the little town of Vega. Both Stella and Wencil are buried in the Vega Cemetery.

Aaron Havlik, whose actual name we have determined to be either Jaroline or Jeroline Aaron Havlik, was yet another of Barbara's brothers who lived just over the Brule County line, in Buffalo County, El Dorado Township with his wife Clara. Aaron's parcel was located near our grandfather's Timber Culture and "Pre." claims. Brule County History says that Aaron married Clara Helm in 1887 and moved into a sod house just over the Brule/Buffalo County line right after their marriage. They then proceeded to have 14 children, three of whom died in early infancy. It is quite possible that one or all three of these babies are also buried in unmarked graves in the Vega Cemetery, which did not become an official cemetery until Vaclav's father Stephen deeded over two acres on his farm to the "Vega Cemetery Association" in 1906.

CHAPTER 5

Our Grandfather the Populist

When we first learned of our grandfather's involvement in the Populist movement, we were very excited, even thrilled, but in truth we knew very little about this incredibly important moment in American history, or South Dakota's crucial role in it. In this we are not alone.

Despite the vast amount of literature that has been written about this era, surprisingly few Americans are familiar with the Populist "revolt" of the late nineteenth century. Fewer still are aware of the various labor groups and Farmers' Alliances which preceded it, ultimately culminating in the creation of the Populist or People's Party. The bulk of attention given to the Populist Party, which became the most enduring third-party movement in American history, typically focuses on the Southern Alliance, which was an agrarian group that had originated in Texas after the Civil War.

Nearly hidden from the popular narrative is the crucial role that farmers in South Dakota played in Populist thinking, this due in no small part to the tireless work of its most outspoken, nationally known leaders Henry Loucks and Alonzo Wardall. As R. Alton Lee writes in *Principle Over Party*, "South Dakota was on the cutting edge of this [Populist] development, supplying both proponents of and significant leadership for reform." Our grandfather, as it turns out, was one of those proponents.

We learned of our grandfather's participation in Populist activities almost by accident, having always assumed that our grandfather was a staunch Democrat due to tales we heard about how he helped his son Charles get elected to office on the Democratic ticket. That assumption was bolstered by the following statement in *Brule County History,* which not only mentions our grandfather but also gives one a sense of how seriously politics was taken out on the prairie: "Political lines were strong in Union Township from the start. There were a number of Civil War veterans who were generally strong Republicans, George Tipton and Henry Trump being the leaders. V. Fousek was the leader of the Democrats, and each election was a fight to the finish."

The notion that our grandfather had been a Democrat was itself somewhat surprising to us since South Dakota has for most of its history been a Republican state. In fact, both Loucks and Wardall had been Republicans before spearheading the formation of the Independent Party, which very soon after became the People's Party, or as it was also known, the Populist Party.

You might well imagine our surprise then, when we discovered that our grandfather, fourteen years younger than Henry Loucks, had been active in Populist politics. This was a circumstance made visible to us after 1894, the year that our grandfather had received his citizenship papers. Given the above statement in *Brule County History* it does appear to be true that our grandfather did eventually become active as a Democrat, but in his early years he most definitely was a Populist and not a Democrat. We know this because he ran for office in 1896 and again in 1898, on the Populist ticket.

For example, we read in the June 27, 1896 issue of the Democratic *Kimball Graphic* that "At the Populist county convention held in Pukwana Saturday, the following were elected delegates to the state convention at Huron: S. W. Duncan, J.S. Stewart, Jesse Hiatt, E. H. Ames, A. I. Troth and Vaclav Fousek" This was an historic event, and it must have been quite an experience for our grandfather to be able to participate. South Dakota being an agrarian state, we can reasonably assume that all of these delegates to this 1896 South Dakota Populist Convention were farmers. Indeed, that was the case for our grandfather.

As R. Alton Lee indicates in his *Principle Over Party,* Populist state convention delegates that year developed a platform along Populist lines without much debate. However, it seems that most of the delegates supported Populist-Democrat William Jennings Bryan of Nebraska for the presidency, while Henry Loucks and others who were opposed to what became known as fusion, fought against supporting Bryan. By way of clarification, fusion was a strategic move by the Populists to endorse and support William Jennings Bryan who had become the Democratic Presidential nominee just prior to the Populist Convention, a happenstance that will be discussed in more detail in the next chapter. Lee writes that "After three hours of debate [at the Huron Convention], the anti-fusionists lost the battle." As it happened, Bryan lost the national election, but he triumphed in South Dakota where fusionists also elected Andrew E. Lee as governor, sent a majority to the state legislature and won both seats in the United States House of Representatives.

In 1897, our grandfather ran for county commissioner, winning the endorsement of the Democratic *Kimball Graphic* on October 30, 1897 with this statement: "Vaclav Fousek, candidate for commissioner in the northern district, is a Populist, but he is all right and the GRAPHIC wants to see him get every Democratic vote in the district."

We learned that our grandfather lost the commissioner race through the following rather horrific notice in the January 29, 1898 *Kimball Graphic*: "Chamberlain, Jan.25. - the board of county commissioners, which is composed of democrats, selected John J. Virsa, democrat, to fill the vacancy caused by the death of John M. Rush, who was found at his home on the 9th with the top of his head blown off. Rush was a republican, having defeated Vaclav Fousek, populist, for the office. The populists of the county wanted Fousek appointed to the vacancy, but the county board decided to appoint Virsa, and their action meets with the practically unanimous approval of the democrats." This notice also appeared in the *Omaha Daily Bee.* Aside from the grisly details relating to poor John Rush, this article suggested to us that our grandfather had considerable support within his own county, so we briefly explored some of the factors that may have contributed to his loss.

R. Alton Lee provided some clues. It seems - perhaps not surprisingly - that the success of the newly formed Populist (or People's) Party during the 1892 election cycle led to a variety of maneuvers by both establishment and rank-and-file Republicans and Democrats at all levels of government, this to keep the newly minted, up-and-coming Populists at bay. For example, and as reported by R. Alton Lee, by 1893 South Dakota Republicans had spearheaded anti-fusion laws to prevent two or more political parties from joining forces to support a particular candidate. However, in the 1896 election an agreement was made by the national leadership of the Democratic and Populist Parties to support William Jennings Bryan as their "fusion" candidate for President of the United States.

According to Lee, this resulted in many Populists who were running for local offices to lose votes in the 1896 election. Additionally, says Lee, rank-and-file "Democrats opposed voting as Populists so ardently that they arranged a compromise name of 'free silver' for the fusion ticket." Since a "fusion" ticket only affected the presidential race, this meant that those running as Populists for local elections would not get the Democrat vote. We are left to wonder whether similar maneuverings affected the 1898 state election, since Republicans mostly swept that election, with the notable exception of the narrow re-election of Andrew Lee, Populist candidate for governor.

Whatever the case and most importantly for us is that the above articles offer proof positive that our grandfather was an active participant in one of the largest and most significant political movements in U.S. history, arguably second only to the American Revolution itself. In addition, we now know that Vaclav was a "Populist" and not a Democrat or "silverite."

Oldest son Charles, who later would also be elected to public office on the Democratic ticket, would have been seven years of age in 1892 (which was the year the Populist or People's Party was officially formed), and likely accompanied his father to more distant Populist political events even when circumstances prevented other family members from attending. All family members more than likely were part of earlier, pre-populist local Alliance chapter meetings, where a variety of social and educational activities took place.

As will be discussed in more detail in the next chapter, the formation of the Populist (or People's) Party came about because of a series of political and economic decisions and events that began right after the Civil War, nearly all of which were clearly *against* the interests of the people. By 1892, a broad coalition of groups and small political parties came together under two main issues: one being the monopolistic practices of the major railroads, the notorious cattle barons of the West, and the big corporations – along with the Eastern financial establishment and European Syndicates that made monopolies like these possible. The second, and most important issue for the Populists dealt with monetary reform, particularly the need for a government-issued "democratic" currency along the lines of the Greenback system. This was *the* critical issue because it was well understood that government-issued "democratic" money could effectively curtail the influence and power of the financial sector, and with it the monopolies.

Tragically, as we were to discover, the failure of the "Populist Revolt," particularly as it related to the money question, would seal the fate of our grandfather, his son Charles, and our paternal grandfather just two to three decades later. Moreover, and as observed by House Banking Chair Louis T. McFadden in a speech delivered to the United States Congress in 1933, the personal tragedies visited upon our ancestors were repeated many tens of thousands of times over throughout farm country, all due to the monetary system - which had been the key issue for the Populists.

The Populist Party, From Whence It Came

Originating first in South Dakota and followed by Kansas one week later, the Populist or People's Party, was formed in 1890 through a coalition comprised primarily of farmers' groups and labor organizations, together with small merchants and businessmen, rural and urban workers and intellectuals. The lineage of these groups could be traced back to the 1860s and the National Grange of the Patrons of Husbandry and the National Labor Union. Out of these two main groups grew the Granger Movement in tandem with the National Labor Reform Party, the National Greenback Party, the Greenback-Labor Party, the Knights of Labor, and the Union Labor Party among others. By the mid-1880's, in a period known as the "Great Upheaval," a number of farmers' alliances had been formed, including the Northern Alliance, the Southern Alliance, the Colored Farmers' Alliance, plus the Farmers' Mutual Benefit Association. In addition, there were the Patrons of Industry and countless smaller parties and state and local organizations.

Many of these disparate groups were formed both directly and indirectly in response to the series of drastic reductions in the money supply that began immediately after the Civil War and continued through the 1890's, thereby causing a similar decline in wages and farm prices and creating a prolonged period of agonizing deflation. The question on the minds of the populists was: should the nation's money supply be controlled by private interests or the sovereign government? This, it may be noted, is the same issue we face today.

While it is true that the National Farmers' Alliance and Industrial Union together with the Colored Farmers' Alliance with whom it had merged by 1890 formed the largest contingent of the Populist or People's Party, much of the confusion about the Populist movement stems from the fact that at one point the Southern and the Northern Alliances were two entirely different groups, with important ideological differences. It was these differences that would eventually lead to the destruction of the Party. But from a purely personal perspective, it was these differences that also helped us understand our grandfather far better than we would have otherwise been able to do.

In historical terms it appears that after an aborted attempt by a group of farmers at forming a Farmer's Alliance in 1877 in New York, the first viable National Farmers' Alliance was started in Chicago in 1880 by Milton George, a publisher and editor of a farm publication. Milton George's organization was alternately called the National Farmer's Alliance, the Northern Alliance and the Northwest Alliance, and was comprised of white and black farmers of the Midwest and High Plains, many of whom had previously been members of the Knights of Labor and/or Greenback Party. Ironically, the Northern Alliance faced strong competition in Iowa as well as Milton George's home state of Illinois from the Farmer's Mutual Benefit Association, which later became allies of the Populists.

The Southern Alliance originated in Lampasas County, Texas sometime between 1874 and 1877 under the name of the Knights of Reliance, which was soon changed to the Texas Farmers' Alliance. Once Charles Macune assumed leadership of this organization in December of 1886, it spread rapidly across the South due in large part to Macune-inspired mergers with similar organizations. Soon after assuming leadership for example, Macune completed a merger with the Louisiana Farmers' Union, which had become a secret society in 1885. The organization created out of this merger first took the name of the National Farmers' Alliance and Cooperative Union, but soon also became known as the Southern Alliance. Macune retained his leadership role until 1889, and during his tenure would introduce his organization as "a strictly white man's non-political secret business organization."

Vega Mystery, Solved

In stark contrast to the Southern Alliance, the Northern Alliance was, by 1886, not only very politically involved, but like the Knights of Labor and Greenbackers, it embraced the philosophy that anyone, regardless of color or gender, should be included in the organization if the individual was born on a farm or was involved in agrarian pursuits.

We had long puzzled over information we had come across at the online Lyman-Brule Genealogical Society which said that there are "two unknown negroes" buried in the Vega Cemetery along with an additional thirteen unmarked burials. Later, Ed Piskule, who was the great-grandson of our grandfather's youngest daughter Emma, related to us how she had told him about a black family by the name of Houston that lived north of Vaclav's homestead and that she, Emma, had helped deliver their three triplet girls who died shortly after birth. After learning this, we revisited the cemetery and found what appears to be a newer granite marker inscribed with the names of the three little girls whose last name was Houston. We found no other markers with the Houston name on them.

Our grandfather's decision to become an active participant in the Populist movement in which the Northern Alliance played a key role, coupled with the facts we learned about the Vega Cemetery, indicates to us that this was one arena in which our grandfather's philosophy was in sync with that of the Northern Alliance.

It was this surprising and seemingly inexplicable discovery that set us on our long and sometimes difficult journey to untangle not only the Vega Cemetery mystery, but other mysteries which seemed to surround our grandfather's life and times.

Growing Up in Iowa during the Anti-Monopoly/Greenback Era

Our grandfather of course could not run for office until he received his citizenship papers in 1894. We are left to conjecture whether it was the entrance onto the scene of Populism itself that inspired our grandfather's participation in politics, or had it come about due to an early awareness of the political landscape of the time? Surely, he would have acquired some of his political ideas, inspiration and insights from one or both of his parents, not to mention the farming com-

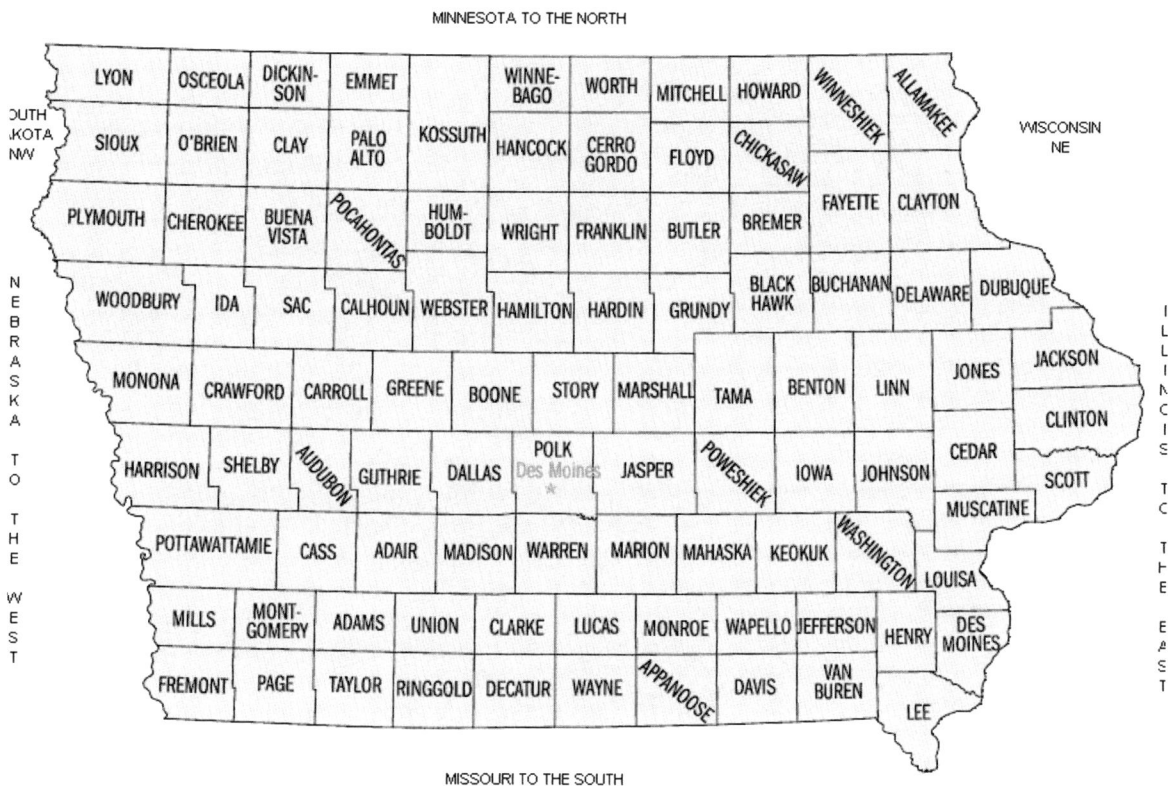

Map shows the location of Washington County in relation to Des Moines, located in Polk County in south central Iowa.

munity at large.

Having come with his parents to a farming community in Iowa in 1870, it is next to impossible to imagine that the turbulent political and economic events of the day were not frequently discussed at the family dinner table or at social gatherings, especially given the fact that our grandfather and most likely his parents were "Freethinkers," which is discussed in a later chapter. Intense and increasingly frequent discussion must have occurred after the Panic of '73, dubbed the "Crime of '73 by farmers due to the effective demonetization of silver which caused yet another sharp reduction in the money supply. This Panic not only brought widespread unemployment and civil unrest but as Henry Loucks, Alexander Del Mar and others could predict, the reduced money supply also caused a dramatic drop in wages and prices, particularly farm prices, which for the farmer are his wages. The panic also prompted the Northern Pacific Railway Company to shed its debt by establishing the notorious bonanza farms, which is covered in more detail in the next chapter.

Interestingly, the Farmer's Anti-Monopoly Party, a newly formed but short-lived political party, held its first Convention in the city of Des Moines, Iowa in 1873. We have no idea as to whether our grandfather and his family attended. But it does seem quite inevitable, given the economic and political climate of the times, that our grandfather and his family and friends heard about, and probably attended some or even most meetings and events of those earlier farm-based political organizations.

In fact, James Weaver, who had been mustered out of the Union Army with the rank of brevet Brigadier General and whose parents had staked a claim on the Iowa frontier when he was a boy, had himself become politically active as a young man, advocating for farmers and laborers. Weaver joined the Greenback Party in 1877 and was elected to the House of Representatives in the U.S. Congress in 1878 as a Greenbacker, through the support of the democrats. At various times he had been elected to Congress on the Democrat, Greenback and Farmer-Labor tickets. In 1892 Weaver was the Populist nominee for President of the United States, winning over one million popular votes and twenty-two electoral votes.

Although our grandfather was only a young boy during his early Iowa years, we cannot help but believe that very little of these political activities, not to mention financial concerns, escaped the intense interest and attention of not only our grandfather and his family, but all of Iowa farm country.

Influence of The Knights of Labor and the Greenbackers on the Populists

The Knights of Labor, which was the largest labor organization in 19th century America, established itself in 1878, which also happened to be the year of the Greenback-Labor Party's peak year of electoral success. Just a few years later the Knights of Labor would become a key ally of the Populist Party. The preamble to the Knights of Labor constitution, known as the Reading Platform, adopted much of the verbiage of the preamble to the constitution of the Industrial Brotherhood of 1873-1875, which in turn had drawn from the platform set forth by the National Labor Union in 1866. The Reading platform set the agenda for the Knights of Labor as well as the various agrarian movements of the next two decades.

Two months after the Knights issued the Reading platform of 1878, the Greenback Labor Party, which was allied with the Knights of Labor,

Political cartoon depicting monopolists dividing up the country.

issued its first platform. It echoed many of the demands of the Knights platform. As Matthew Hild writes in his book *Greenbackers, Knights of Labor and Populists,* the Reading platform offered "a system. . .which will secure to the laborer the fruits of his toil." Hild outlines the demands of the Reading Platform, many of which would find their way into future platforms of the Farmers' Alliances:

> Specific demands encompassed by this system included the establishment of cooperative institutions, productive and distributive; the reservation of public lands ("the heritage of the people") for settlers rather than railroads and speculators; the repeal of all laws not bearing equally upon labor and capital; the adoption of measures to protect the health and safety of workers engaged in mining, manufacturing, and building; the enactment of laws compelling corporations to pay employees weekly in full and in lawful money; mechanics' and laborers' lien laws; the abolishment of the contract labor system on national, state, and municipal work; the substitution of arbitration for strikes; the abolishment of the convict lease system; equal pay for equal work for both sexes; the eight-hour workday; and the establishment and issue by the federal government of a national circulating medium (currency) without the intervention of private banks, that would be a legal tender in payment of all debts, public and private.

The first local assembly of the Knights of Labor in Dakota Territory started in Fargo in 1882 and by 1890 thirty-six assemblies met throughout the new state of South Dakota. Alonzo Wardall among other Alliancemen had been a member of the Knights of Labor first. In the South, the Knights of Labor and Greenbackers entered most southern states before the Texas Farmer's Alliance and the Agricultural Wheel (whose origin was in Arkansas) got a toehold. By 1883 local assemblies of the Knights of Labor existed in every southern state. At its peak the Knights had a membership of one million nationwide. It welcomed all "producers," including farmers, small businessmen, and both skilled and unskilled laborers, without regard to gender or race. But as Matthew Hild writes:

> While both the Knights and the Greenbackers of the South worked to organize across the color line and build support among town workers and farmers, both organizations, upon the insistence of *some* whites, also organized blacks and whites into separate clubs (in the case of the Greenbackers) and segregated local assemblies (in the case of the Knights). Terence V. Powderly of Scranton, Pennsylvania who had become the Knight's Grand Master Workman in 1879 denounced, to little avail, this demonstration of prejudice writing that 'Under the laws of our Order a brother no matter what his color is can visit any Local in the Order of which he is a member so long as he is clear and in good standing.' Powderly's question: 'Can the wisest of us tell what color labor is? I doubt it.'

Remarking on the Greenbackers, Hild says that "even in the southern states where the Greenbackers fared better, they had to contend with charges of fostering "Negro domination" and with the Democrats all too successful weapon of last resort, the denial of a 'free ballot and fair count.'"

Women in the Populist Movement

As it happens, many Populist ideas dovetailed well with our grandfather's "free-thinking" ways (which were, it seems, part of his Bohemian heritage). So it only seems natural that we find that women often figured prominently in Populist politics, both in the North and in the South. Women played an especially prominent role in local sub-alliance activities, and in some parts of the Plains states they made up as much as 50 percent of the membership. Despite serving as a target of heated criticism, ridicule and abuse, many achieved national recognition. These included such personages as Mrs. Eva McDonald Valesh, Mrs. Bettie Gay, Mrs. Fannie R. Vickery, Mrs. Annie L. Diggs, Helen Gauger, Mrs. Farmer Smith, best-selling author Mrs. Sarah E. V. Emery and the very popular speaker Mary Elizabeth Lease of Kansas.

Although less well known and less studied, a number of South Dakota women played prominent roles in the early years of Populist politics. They included Sophia Hardin of Huron, who was secretary-treasurer for the South Dakota Northern Alliance. There was also Elizabeth (Alonzo) Wardall, who proved to be an "able writer and untiring worker" in the Alliance organization both statewide and nationally. Florence (Henry) Loucks was likewise active in the Alliance movement.

In late October of 1892 Mary Elizabeth Lease of Kansas toured South Dakota along with national Populist candidate for president, General James Weaver. They appeared in Aberdeen, Huron and Sioux Falls. Lease was billed as "the eloquent orator from Kansas" and usually spoke first for about an hour and a half to warm up the audience. These seemed to be all day events, with songs from local Glee clubs and parades for the opening of the evening ceremonies during which Weaver would speak for about two hours, followed by concluding remarks from Lease.

We can only wonder whether our grandfather and his family attended any of these events, but we would not be at all surprised to find that they did. Almost certainly, first-born son Charles would have accompanied his father to many if not all the more distant events. This kind of early participation on the part of our grandfather and his family in the Populist cause is made a near certainty when one considers that our grandfather was elected as a delegate to the Populist state convention in Huron a mere four years after Lease and Weaver made their tour through South Dakota.

For her part, Mary Elizabeth Lease was probably one of the better known of the Populists, male or female. While raising four children on the Kansas frontier, she earned a law degree and was admitted to the bar in 1885. In 1890 she was given a place on the Populist lecture bureau and made 160 speeches during the summer and fall of 1890 to "immense audiences." Political opponents cleverly nick-named her "Mary Yellin"- apparently not without good reason. One of Lease's speeches captured both her forceful style and the key issues of the Populists, which subsequently was echoed in the Preamble to the 1892 Omaha Platform, written by Minnesota politician, lawyer and author Ignatius L. Donnelly. The following is an excerpt, strikingly (and disturbingly) similar to present day events:

> Wall Street owns the country. It is no longer a government of the people, by the people and for the people, but a government of Wall Street, by Wall Street and for Wall Street. The great common people of this country are slaves, and monopoly is the master. The West and South are bound and prostrate before the manufacturing East. Money rules, and our Vice President is a London banker. [referring to Levi P. Morton, under Benjamin Harrison]
>
> Our laws are the output of a system which clothes rascals in robes and honesty in rags. The parties lie to us and the political speakers mislead us. We were told two years ago to go to work and raise a big crop, that was all we needed. We went to work and plowed and planted; the rains fell, the sun shone, nature smiled, and we raised the big crop that they told us to; and what came of it? Eight-cent corn, ten-cent oats, two-cent beef and no price at all for butter and eggs - that's what came of it.
>
> Then the politicians said we suffered from over-production. Over-production, when 10,000 little children, so statistics tell us, starve to death every year in the United States, and over 100,000 shopgirls in New York are forced to sell their virtue for the bread their niggardly wages deny them.
>
> Tariff is not the paramount question. *The main question is the money question. . .*
>
> The common people are robbed to enrich their masters. There are 30,000 millionaires in the United States. Go home and figure out how many paupers you must have to make one millionaire with the circulation of only $10 per capita.

There are thirty men in the United States whose aggregate wealth is over one and one-half billion dollars. There are half a million men looking for work. There are 60,000 soldiers of the Union in poor houses, but no bondholders. It would have been better if Congress had voted pensions to those 60,000 paupers who wore the blue and dyed it red with their blood in the country's defense than to have voted to make the banker's bonds non-taxable, and payable, interest and principal, in gold. [More about this in the next chapter.]

In the above speech, Lease refers to "only $10 per capita" then in circulation, which meant that when the total U.S. money supply was averaged out across the population, there was only $10 per person in circulation. This was down from a circulation of $52 per capita in 1866, which was $4 lower than the figure calculated by Thomas Jefferson as being adequate to serve the needs of the country during his own more sparsely populated era.

This dramatic reduction in the circulating medium was due to the "sound money" policies then being implemented by the politically powerful corporate business and Eastern investment banking communities and their European partners. These "sound money" policies emphasized the use of gold as the basis of US currency – instead of Constitutionally appropriate government issued paper money that was given full legal tender for all debts public and private, along with, secondarily, the bimetallic system created by statute in 1792. This mixed money system then in place is a somewhat complicated subject that will be covered in more detail in the next chapter but suffice it to say here that the 1792 statute helped prevent European influence over our money system which was why the Populists fully supported the bimetallic system and "free coinage of silver".

Let it here be said that it appears that the so-called "sound money" men were not aware of, or chose to forget, Alexander Hamilton's clear assertion that "*It is immaterial what serves the purpose of money, whether paper or gold or silver; that the effect of both upon industry is the same; and that the intrinsic wealth of a nation is to be measured, not by the abundance of the precious metals contained in it, but by the quantity of the productions of its labor and industry.*" Or perhaps "sound money" advocates did remember Hamilton's statement and chose to focus on Hamilton's predilection for "bank paper" as the founders disparagingly called it (backed by gold) through his establishment of the First National Bank of the United States in tandem with his financial system. Few in the founding generation were fooled by Hamilton's plan and readily understood, as the Populists did, that "bank paper" was in reality debt acting like a tax against the poor and that gold, as declared by William Jennings Bryan in his famous *Cross of Gold* speech, had always been "the money of kings".

Northern Alliance Timeline and Transition to Third Party Politics

Almost immediately after Milton George launched his National Farmers' Alliance aka Northern Alliance in Chicago in 1880 it spread rapidly through the northern and western states and territories. By January of 1881, delegates from twenty-five counties in Nebraska organized a state Alliance while Dakota Territory farmers in Yankton County were the first to be issued a charter to start a territorial sub-Alliance, also in 1881. In neighboring Minnesota eighty sub-alliances and a state organization had already been formed by the end of 1881.

Within eighteen months of Milton George's launch of the Northern Alliance, Kansas, Michigan, Wisconsin, Iowa and Illinois had all also organized state Alliances. According to John D. Hicks in his book *The Populist Revolt*, by the third annual meeting of the Northern Alliance, held in St. Louis on October 4, 1882, "it was claimed that two thousand alliances with a total membership of 100,000 farmers were represented." Membership went down substantially the next year due to relatively good crop prices but began to pick up again by the end of the next year as crop prices declined.

So it was that in 1884, a time during which our grandfather was just starting his family and taking the necessary steps to prove up his pre-emption claim, Henry Loucks established his own Dakota sub-Alliance almost as soon as he obtained a farm in Duel County on the eastern side of the state. Louck's singular style of leadership and his tireless work provided inspiration and ideas for others to follow as they in turn established their own sub-Alliances. The number of Dakota Territory sub-Alliances grew considerably that year, providing the conduit through which mass meetings were held in Huron and elsewhere to demand regulation of the railroads among other things. By February of 1885 the Dakota Territorial Farmers' Alliance was created as an affiliate of the Northern Alliance, and by mid-summer the number of territorial sub-Alliances in Dakota Territory tripled, with the executive committee reporting an increase from 55 sub-Alliances in February to 163 in July.

By January of 1886 Henry Loucks was unanimously elected president of the Dakota Territorial Farmers' Alliance. A few months later Alonzo Wardall established the first sub-alliance in Grant County, inspiring the formation of nine more such groups in his area within a short time. As R. Alton Lee writes in *Principle Over Party:*

> The two men most important to the Dakota Alliance were now on the scene, and as historian Robert McMath observed, in the next ten years, Loucks and Wardall 'oversaw the development of the strongest Alliance cooperative in the West, and probably the nation.' In the process, they also built a strong territorial Alliance and paved the way for a third-party movement in South Dakota.

A few months after Loucks was elected president of the territorial Alliance, the Northern Alliance, the Knights of Labor, and the Greenbackers together with other similarly aligned groups met in a national convention held in Indianapolis in the summer of 1886. This led to the formation of the Union Labor Party in February of 1887. Although not spectacularly successful, the formation of this political party signaled the desire of labor, farmers and other allied groups to join forces politically and this party, along with others, would become an ally of the Populists.

In November of 1889, South Dakota and North Dakota were admitted to the Union as separate states. The Dakota Territorial Farmers' Alliance split in two, with Henry Loucks elected president of the South Dakota Alliance and Walter Muir the president of the North Dakota Alliance. By this time Loucks was also president of the Northern Alliance, working tirelessly to strengthen the alliances of Nebraska, Minnesota and Iowa. It was through his leadership that South Dakota began showing its Independent/Populist stripes almost immediately upon achieving statehood, actively promoting the idea of a third party and then achieving it well before the Southern Alliance got on board.

According to John Hicks, author of the now classic *The Populist Revolt,* two years prior to the first Populist (or People's Party) nation-

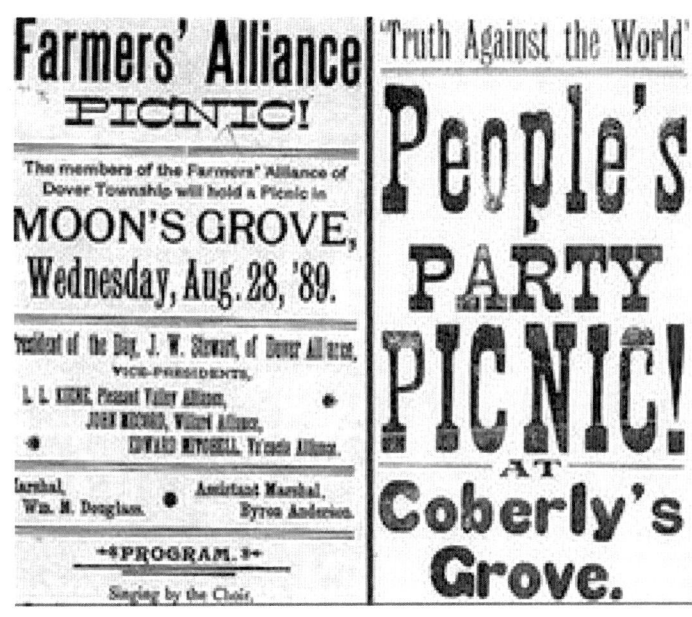

Sample promotional literature, first for the Farmer's Alliance, and later for the People's Party, advertising upcoming events.

al convention held in Omaha in 1892 "South Dakota held its first convention [in 1890] in Huron on the seventh of June, several days prior to the comparable convention held in Kansas – hence the claim, sometimes made, that the birthplace of Populism was South Dakota, not Kansas." R. Alton Lee was more emphatic and detailed, writing that at the 1890 Huron convention Loucks offered two interlocking motions. The first was to form a new independent political party, and the second stipulated that this new party adopt the Alliance platform. Both motions were accepted and as Lee writes:

> Loucks and Wardall thus abandoned the Republican Party they had supported for so many years, as did thousands of their followers. This formation of the Independent Party preceded the Kansas decision to form the Populist Party by one week. Nebraska alliances endorsed similar action, with North Dakota endorsing the move in September. In Minnesota, the editor of *The Great West* applauded the boldness of the Dakota convention, saying, "While we are growling and groaning over this side of the line, asking for crumbs from a corrupt tyranny, Dakota steps forward with her head erect and puts an Independent Party into the field."

John E. Miller, in a book called *South Dakota: A Journey Through Time,* tells us that "South Dakota was in fact one of the strongest Populist states, with farmers and their friends taking the lead in forming the Populist party. At the Huron Convention, held in June of 1890 they started the Independent Party, changing their name to Populist Party two years later."

Hicks records in *The Populist Revolt* that there were ten fully functioning state Northern Alliance organizations by 1890 and "the secretary's office reported new members coming in at a rate of 1000 a week."

The loose organizational structure of the Northern Alliance contrasted sharply with the much more centralized and secretive structure of the Southern Alliance. This was particularly so for the Dakota Territorial Alliance, which Lawrence Goodwyn describes as being made up of rural "clubs" in 1884. R. Alton Lee paints a fuller picture, remarking that with such inducements as those devised by Henry Loucks for the Dakota Territorial Alliance, the organization grew rapidly, with one source listing around sixty sub-alliances in 1884 and over eight hundred by April 1889:

> Becoming president of the Dakota Farmers' Alliance in January 1886, Henry Loucks quickly put his stamp on the organization. He later observed that the Farmer's Alliance movement seemed to take on a natural progression of functions: 'first, social; second, educational; third, financial; fourth, political.' Loucks saw each function as important in itself and envisioned all of them 'working together as a natural consequence.' Under Loucks' leadership, the Alliance rapidly became an important social, educational and financial force in the Dakotas, even as political effectiveness continued to elude farmers throughout the 1880s. Social gatherings, educational and social activities for both men and women, and strong cooperatives and businesses were the hallmarks of first the territorial Alliance and then the South Dakota Farmers' Alliance.
>
> Social gatherings were important to farm families, for whom Fourth of July celebrations were the major social events until the Alliance arrived on the scene. Local sub-Alliances held picnics, political rallies, and organizational meetings so that farm families could hear speeches, enjoy music, discuss issues with their neighbors, and engage in social conviviality. These locals usually met once or twice monthly in a schoolhouse, a member's home, or, occasionally, in their own building. The wives frequently served lunch, and the men might then retire to a barn or quiet corner to conduct a meeting, but wives and family members were encouraged to join in, and many women were quite active in Alliance affairs. During political campaigns, the territorial organization also sponsored encampments that were well-attended and in which 'the speech making was enlivened by music and other minor exercises'. . .
>
> As president of the territorial and then state Alliance, Henry Loucks also promoted the idea of circulating libraries for farmers and their families. He suggested that each sub-Alliance spend five dollars for a dozen books on 'political economy' and circulate them. The Alliance newspaper printed a list of appropriate books, each of which could be purchased for less than a dol-

lar. . . 'Education is to be the greatest factor in the revolution now pending,' Loucks asserted, 'because it is useless to hope for reform until the masses are thoroughly posted on the necessity for it."

Southern Alliance Timeline Reveals Its Achilles' Heel from its inception

Somewhere around 1875 a group calling itself the Knights of Reliance was formed in Lampasas Texas, as part of a cooperative effort to purchase supplies, round up stray animals, apprehend horse thieves and protect themselves against the emerging cattle barons. As John Hicks writes in *The Populist Revolt*, "the Alliance was also calculated to furnish effective opposition to the activities of land sharks and cattle kings, whose disregard of the rights of the small farmer was notorious." In 1878, the Knights of Reliance changed its name to the Grand State Alliance, but when an attempt was made by some members to lead the organization into the Greenback Party, the Alliance collapsed.

The remnants of the organization then limped along until 1880, when the still tiny Grand State Alliance was incorporated through the state of Texas as the Farmers' State Alliance, where it described itself as a "secret and benevolent association" thereby maintaining a non-political stance. By 1884, the Alliance began expanding handsomely, thanks to the work of a thirty-six-year-old Mississippian by the name of S. O. Daws who had been hired by the Texas Alliance as "Traveling Lecturer" and chief organizer the year before.

Hicks writes that "by December 1885, the claim was made that the Alliance had about fifty thousand members scattered among not less that twelve hundred locals". Although Hicks' numbers for 1886 vary somewhat from Lawrence Goodwyn's, it is clear that Daws' effectiveness was impressive, not to mention politically oriented. As Goodwyn reports in *The Populist Moment*, by the summer of 1886 "the [Southern] order counted 2000 sub-alliances and over 100,000 members." This coincidentally, and somewhat oddly, matched exactly the numbers reported by Hicks for the Northern Alliance four years earlier, in October of 1882.

In August of 1886, under the leadership of its newly re-elected president Andrew Dunlap, the Texas Alliance met in Cleburne, Texas where it drew up what are known as the Cleburne Demands, thereby reflecting the willingness of the majority to forego anonymity in order to assert a more political stance. Furthermore, in a move to publicly join forces with labor, several of the Cleburne Demands related to labor issues that had been brought to the fore by an 1886 strike, known as the Great Southwest Strike, which was organized by the Knights of Labor against railroads in the Southwest. In *The Populist Moment*, Lawrence Goodwyn provides insight into the substance of the Cleburne Demands particularly as they related to farmers and their sometimes-self-defeating allegiance to the Democratic Party of the South:

> The five land planks addressed agrarian grievances that stemmed from the activities, state and national, of Scottish and English cattle syndicates and domestic railroad land syndicates. By 1886 both groups had seriously diminished the remaining public domain available for settlers. . . The lone agricultural demand not relating to land policy was one designed to end capitalist activity that had never found favor with American farmers – "the dealing in futures of all agricultural exchanges."

> [But] The most explosive portion of the committee report concerned the finance question. . . In short, the plank advanced the doctrines of the Greenback Party.

By August 8, 1886 the Cleburne Demands, composed of a total of seventeen planks, made front page news across Texas. The news triggered responses that quickly turned hostile within the media and proved deeply troubling to more conservative farmers. As Goodwyn writes:

> Alliance conservatives were profoundly disturbed by the Cleburne Demands. Their attitude marked the surfacing of deeply held cultural presumptions that stood as forbidding barriers to

the long-term goals of the People's Party. While Alliance conservatives shared the radicals' concern over the plight of the farmers, they felt, or at least hoped, that they would not have to break with their received political heritage to express that concern effectively. But the eleventh demand of the Cleburne document, the greenback plank, was unacceptable to the Democratic Party, and that fact created an agonizing dilemma for conservative farmers.

[Moreover, some of these farmers believed] that the stance of 'nonpartisanship' was simple evidence that their commitment to reform was a step lower on their personal scale of political priorities than an emotional dedication to white supremacy and its institutional expression in the south, the Democratic Party. . .

After midnight on the evening of the final vote on the Cleburne Demands, a group of conservative 'nonpartisans' led by [Texas Alliance President] Dunlap met and drafted a statement of dissociation. Supporters of the demands thereupon drafted a counter-statement, providing details of the tactical maneuvering and upbraiding of the minority for publicly revealing divisions within the order. The conservatives then formed a rival 'Grand State Farmers' Alliance' of an avowedly nonpartisan character, . . .The destructive Lampasas experience of 1879-80 seemed to be repeating itself.

By December of 1886, Andrew Dunlap resigned as president of the Texas Alliance. Charles Macune, then chairman of the state executive committee, became acting president and immediately secured a meeting with the two opposing factions, who agreed to attend a special convention to be held in Waco in January of 1887. Although the Texas Alliance had, up until that time, been considered part of the National Farmers' Alliance aka Northern Alliance, Macune's plan as unfolded at the January convention was to form a separate national order that would have its main strength in the south, to wit, a Southern Alliance. As Hicks writes:

Macune's expressed objections to joining forces with the Northern Alliance were three-fold. First, the Northern Alliance was a loose, non-secret organization, having at the time no system of fees or dues and being still dependent on the good graces and charity of its founder, Milton George. Second, colored persons were eligible to membership – a condition of affairs unthinkable in the South. Third, by a ruling that any person raised on a farm was to be considered a farmer, the way was left open for members to be recruited from the nonagricultural classes. What Macune had in mind was a strongly centralized order composed of farmers only, bound together by ties of secrecy and unified in purpose and procedure.

On December 11, 1886, at about the same time as Macune began drawing up plans for his new Southern Alliance, two parallel organizations were being established for black farmers. One was called the Colored Farmers' Alliance and Cooperative Union, founded in Texas in 1886, and the other was the National Colored Alliance, this one having been established apparently with Milton George's help or upon his suggestion about four years earlier.

Columbia University historian Omar Ali remarks in a footnote of an online paper entitled *Preliminary research for writing a history of the Colored Farmers Alliance in the Populist movement*: 1886-1896, that "the first Colored Farmers' Alliance was actually established four years earlier, in 1882, but it was not recorded in the official history of the organization written by Gen. R.M. Manning Humphrey in 1891. Milton George had helped establish this [unrecorded] 'National Alliance' in Prairie County, Arkansas, as documented by Roy V. Scott, 'Milton George and the Farmer's Alliance Movement,' *Mississippi Valley Historical Review*, XLV (June, 1958), p. 107."

Thus, it seems that upon the suggestion and help of Milton George a group calling itself the National Colored Alliance had been established in Prairie County, Arkansas in 1882. This organization was led by Andrew J. Carothers and apparently the history of this first group went unrecorded. Then in December of 1886, the Colored Farmers' Alliance and Cooperative Union was established in Texas. Colonel Richard Manning Humphrey, a southern white man and Baptist missionary, was chosen to serve as general superintendent. Humphrey then complied the history of this organization in 1891. The two groups merged in 1890, with some estimates of total membership set at 1.5 million. Of special note here is that the Colored Alliances were primarily made up of landless people who picked cotton for white farmers.

Meanwhile, in 1887, Charles Macune began his campaign to "grow" a Southern Alliance by arranging a merger of the Texas Alliance with the Louisiana Farmers' Union, which had become a secret organization in 1885. The new organization was called the National Farmers' Alliance and Cooperative Union which, coincidentally or otherwise, was a name very similar to the Colored Farmers' Alliance and Cooperative Union that had been formed just a few months earlier, in December of 1886.

By December 1888 and after considerable debate, Macune's National Farmers' Alliance and Cooperative Union merged with the Agricultural Wheel, which had a membership of nearly 500,000, including African Americans who were usually part of segregated "colored Wheels". This new organization was to be known as the Farmers' and Laborers' Union. At every juncture, Macune introduced his rapidly expanding Southern Alliance, as it was commonly called, as a "strictly white man's non-political secret business organization," thus effectively setting it apart from its Northern counterpart.

Macune's reign as president of the Southern Alliance came to an end in 1889, when former Confederate soldier and Congressman Leonidas L. Polk, of North Carolina was elected president. Macune was in effect forced out, due to fundamental disagreements between Alliance leadership and Macune over strategy, which soon included accusations leveled against Macune that he was conspiring to undo the originally reluctant Polk's plans to form the People's Party. When Polk was elected President of the Southern Alliance in December of 1889, the Southern Alliance merged with portions of the Northern Alliance and formally became the National Farmers' Alliance and Industrial Union. Polk was a popular and capable leader who would be re-elected to the new National Farmers' Alliance and Industrial Union (which was still often referred to as the Southern Alliance) in 1890 and 1891.

St. Louis Convention 1889

In December 1889, one year after Macune had negotiated the merger of his Southern Alliance with the Agricultural Wheel and a mere month after North and South Dakota became independent states, the Northern and Southern Alliances held their annual meetings simultaneously in St. Louis, albeit in separate halls, in an attempt to consolidate. Significant differences between the two Alliances ran more or less along sectional lines. One of these differences, which was to open a veritable chasm only a year or two later, centered on how to solve "the money question," with the Greenbacker-inspired basis for reform at the center.

In his address as outgoing president of the Southern Alliance, Macune signaled a redirection of strategy – away from the cooperatives and "exchanges" that were designed to help farmers receive better prices for their goods, and toward the root cause of the farm depression, which was an inadequate money supply, thus echoing the Cleburne Demands concerning monetary reform. On the last day of the convention a committee of Alliance leadership was formed to determine a solution to the money problem and in the waning hours of the convention the subtreasury plan was introduced by Macune. One of the arguments in support of the proposal was that it was merely an adaptation of the system under which the banking system operated, a system that enabled chartered national banks to issue national bank notes (which were to serve as a currency with limited legal tender powers) in quantities up to ninety percent of the value of government bonds purchased by the bank and deposited with the government.

The subtreasury plan as introduced by Macune called for the government to provide loans of 80% of the value of key, non-perishable crops that would be stored in government warehouses until sale of the crop could be accomplished at a reasonable price. The amount of new money that would be created by the government (in the form of loans with an interest rate cap of 2%) would be capped when the volume of circulating currency reached $50 per capita, this being $6 less than the amount calculated decades before by Thomas Jefferson as being adequate to serve the needs of the then less densely populated nation. Although Macune has been given exclusive credit for the plan, the inspiration for it, and probably the content of it, was not entirely his. It was instead an expanded version of the concept developed by Harry Skinner who was a lawyer and Populist from Leonidas Polk's home state of North Carolina, and likely was the product of the committee of Alliance leaders that had been formed to come up with a proposal to address the money problem.

While the subtreasury proposal did meet with the approval of Polk, Loucks and other Alliance leaders, it proved widely controversial. Hicks writes that the northern farmers only reluctantly agreed to support the sub-treasury plan in the early Populist platforms in exchange for the equally reluctant Southern support of government ownership of the railways. But the plan would soon meet with even more opposition in the south, most surprisingly among officials who had been elected - with Alliance backing - on the Democratic ticket during the 1890 election cycle. C. Vann Woodward writes in his *Origins of the New South*:

> Southern critics of the Alliance, as if by concerted agreement, chose the subtreasury plan as their main point of attack. Democratic politicians who had been elected on the Alliance platform in 1890 found the subtreasury intolerable a year or two later. Governors Tillman and Hogg pronounced the plan 'paternalism' and 'class legislation.' Alliance-elected Senators Gordon of Georgia and Zebulon B. Vance of North Carolina viewed the subtreasury with alarm, and so did Senators George of Mississippi, Morgan of Alabama and Reagan and Richard Coke of Texas. Disaffected Alliance members were encouraged to organize an anti-subtreasury Alliance. With the avowed object of 'overthrowing the old organization,' a few hundred delegates from Mississippi, Arkansas, Texas, Kansas and Minnesota met in St. Louis in September 1891, but their organization was stillborn.

Among the weaknesses of the subtreasury plan, which may have revealed themselves as discussion played out, was the fact that monopolies and foreign competition could still keep prices below cost of production, at least for a time. But these potentially serious weaknesses had nothing to do with "paternalism" or "class legislation" as Tillman and Hogg had charged. In the end, the sub-treasury plan was modified for the Ocala Demands of 1890 to include real estate (under certain conditions), then diluted in the 1892 Omaha Platform with the phrase "or a better system," and dropped entirely by 1896. A call for a government issued national currency given full legal tender for all debts, public and private, greenback style, that had first appeared in the Cleburne Demands, remained in every subsequent set of "demands" and platforms, though this plank became increasingly entangled with the silver issue.

In addition to the initial reluctant reaction to the subtreasury plan, northern farmers objected to two other key issues at that 1889 meeting in St. Louis. First, they refused to reject black membership, and second, they opposed working in secret. A partial compromise was reached when Southerners agreed to admit blacks into the Supreme Council, which was to be the national legislative body for the new organization and also strike out the word "white" in a joint constitution, leaving that qualification up to the individual states.

The final sticking point was the secrecy issue, for which no agreement could be reached. Secrecy for the Southern Alliance included a vague body of "unwritten law" that Northerners feared would allow the South to dominate. Because of this, many of the Northern delegates left the convention without committing themselves. Henry Loucks, with the support of Alonzo Wardall and the South Dakota Farmers' Alliance and together with the Alliances of North Dakota and Kansas felt that enough agreement had at that point been reached to warrant a merger and elected to withdraw from the Northern Alliance and consolidate with the Southern Alliance under a new name selected by the Northerners.

The organization now would be known as the National Farmers' Alliance and Industrial Union, changing the previously used "cooperative union" to "industrial union" to signal a desire to work with labor groups. In the future the National Farmers' Alliance and Industrial Union would also be referred to as the Southern Alliance. At this 1889 convention the Southern Alliance managed to secure an official endorsement from the Knights of Labor for its full platform of "demands" even though the Knights only reluctantly endorsed the sub-treasury plan. As mentioned earlier, Polk replaced Macune as Alliance president via the 1889 Alliance election cycle. Macune would remain on the Executive Council.

From Ocala 1890 to Omaha July 4, 1892: The Formation of the National People's Party.

The same year that South Dakota and Kansas farmers launched their own third parties, the newly formed National Farmers' Alliance and Industrial Union held its annual meeting in Ocala, Florida in December of 1890. As R. Alton Lee writes in his *Principle Over Party*:

> The Ocala conference called for a national political meeting early in 1892 to chart a course, but third-party advocates objected to the delay. All agreed with Charles W. Macune's proposal, however, to participate with other reform groups in an educational program for the coming year. Nearly all delegates likewise supported Alliance president Leonidas L. Polk's call to send paid lecturers into each congressional district to promote these political efforts, as well. An issue of discord surfaced when a resolution from Mississippi delegates proposed placing the Alliance on record in opposition to the Lodge Election Bill. Then pending in Congress, the proposal would re-establish federal protection for black voters. On the last day of the convention, Alonzo Wardall presented a motion to strike the resolution from the minutes; his motion was tabled, thus killing the debate on the measure temporarily.

> The promulgation of a national platform, which became known as the Ocala Demands, was the major achievement of this gathering. Drawn from recent Alliance policies, with a few additions, these resolutions would constitute the Populist doctrine for the remainder of the decade. They consisted of thirteen demands in seven categories.

Four of the categories of the Ocala Demands are most relevant to our discussion. The first of these included the subtreasury plan along with a demand for the abolition of the national banks and an increase in the amount of the circulating medium to not less than $50 per capita which again was $6 less than that calculated decades before by Thomas Jefferson as being adequate for serving the needs of a then less populated nation. The second called for "the removal of the existing heavy tariff from the necessities of life". The third category condemned the Sherman Silver Purchase Act and in lieu of that called for the free and unlimited coinage of silver. The fourth category called for passage of laws prohibiting foreign ownership of land – and asked Congress to come up with a plan to obtain all land owned by aliens and foreign syndicates as well as a plan to reclaim all lands held by railroads which was to then be held for settlers only. The fifth category begins with this statement: "Believing in the doctrine of equal rights to all and special privileges to none, we demand. . ." The most relevant demands in this fifth category were connected to the tariff issue, the first of which was "That our national legislation shall be so framed in the future as not to build up one industry at the expense of another."

One month later, in January of 1891, those portions of the Northern Alliance that had not merged with the new National Farmers' Alliance and Industrial Union held their annual convention in Omaha. Delegates endorsed the Ocala Demands and then issued their own Omaha Platform with a hugely popular Preamble written by Ignatius L. Donnelly of Minnesota that would be a key feature of the famous 1892 Omaha Platform. This group also called for the establishment of a third party in February of 1892.

Insurgents from within the new National Farmers' Alliance and Industrial Union, (Macune's old Southern Alliance along with defecting portions of the Northern Alliance) *also* met that same month (January 1891) in Washington, D. C. Members of the Knights of Labor, the Farmers' Mutual Benefit Association, the Colored Farmers' Alliance and the Citizens' Alliance attended this meeting where it was decided to hold a meeting one month later to discuss the political situation. That meeting was delayed until May of 1891 and held in Cincinnati. Alliance members were in the majority at this Cincinnati meeting, but numerous other groups were again represented, including both the Northern and Southern Farmers' Alliances, the Colored Farmers' Alliance, the Knights of Labor, the Farmers' Mutual Benefit Association, the Union Labor Party, Greenbackers, Single Taxers, Bellamy Nationalists and others. 1400 delegates were in attendance.

As R. Alton Lee writes, this May 1891 Cincinnati convention "endorsed the demands of the Southern Alliance's St. Louis platform of 1889, the 1890 Ocala Demands and the Northern Alliance's Omaha Platform of 1891." Chief concerns having to do with land, finance via government-issued full legal tender currency, and transportation would remain throughout the period. And according to Columbia University historian Omar Ali, mentioned earlier, "when some of the Southern white delegates attempted to segregate Colored Farmers' Alliance members, the convention defeated their motion by an overwhelming vote."

After some contentious debate over establishment of a third political party, the insurgents within the new National Farmers' Alliance and Industrial Union aka Macune's old Southern Alliance decided to meet a few months later, in February 1892 in St. Louis, along with their Northern Alliance counterparts and dozens of other reform groups and minor political parties. This meeting was held for the purpose of establishing the People's Party and further, to hold a national convention no later than June 1892 to nominate candidates for the presidential ticket. The February 1892 meeting did indeed take place and the People's Party was launched, with the approval of Alliance President Leonidas L. Polk and even Charles Macune, who was on the Executive Council. The Southern delegation, along with the Colored Farmers' Alliance and other smaller allied groups also were in attendance and in agreement on establishment of the People's Party.

The nominating convention was moved from June to, appropriately enough, July 4, 1892 and was to be held in Omaha. But just weeks before the convention, on June 11, 1892, Leonidas L. Polk, who had hopes - with respectable support from both the north and south - of securing the Populist presidential nomination, died suddenly of a hemorrhaging bladder. R. Alton Lee comments that "Probably no Populist could have won in 1892, but as historian Robert McMath noted, a ticket composed of major People's Party advocates like Polk and William Peffer of Kansas [as Vice-President] 'could have generated a fuller representation of Populism's true strength.'"

Henry Loucks, as vice president of the National Farmers' Alliance and Industrial Union, succeeded Polk as president. Loucks was asked by the Alliance to write a textbook on money, and he completed the first edition in 1893. A revised edition came out in 1895 and was entitled *A New Monetary System as Advocated by the National Farmers' Alliance and Industrial Union*. R. Alton Lee writes that "in spite of Louck's admonitions for a broader advocacy of money issues, the silver plank in the 1892 platform proved to be the defining issue for Populists for several years." This broader advocacy of money issues involved a deeper understanding of "the money question" which centered on the Greenbacks, as we shall see later, and was likely undermined by a media intent on simplifying the issue into a battle between silver versus gold. The online Texas State Historical Association accurately reflects the money question from the Cleburne Demands forward:

The most controversial demands [of the Farmers' Alliance/Populists] related to monetary reform. Believing that significant relief from declining crop prices required the expansion of the currency supply, alliance farmers demanded that the government immediately use silver in addition to gold as legal tender in order to ease the contracted currency supply. They argued, however, that significant relief required a more radical revamping of the existing monetary system than entailed by "free silver"- the establishment of a fiat currency system wherein the government would issue "greenbacks" based on a predetermined per capita circulation volume, rather than on an inflexible metallic standard.

The Preamble to what is known as the Omaha Platform was written by lawyer, politician, farmer and novelist Ignatius Donnelly of Minnesota. It had been part of the 1891 Northern Alliance Platform and by popular demand was repeated for this 1892 convention also held in Omaha. While garnering rave reviews from the Populists, it led to charges (which remain to this day) of Populists' having a tendency toward conspiracy, overblown rhetoric and paranoia, despite generally copious supplies of factual evidence to back up Populist complaints. Excerpts from Donnelly's Preamble are as follows, and note the third paragraph devoted to silver and the previous paragraph with the "greenback" plank confined to the phrase "The national power to create money is appropriated" which will be discussed in more detail in the next chapter:

The conditions which surround us best justify our co-operation; we meet in the midst of a nation brought to the verge of moral, political, and material ruin. Corruption dominates the ballot-box, the Legislatures, the Congress, and touches even the ermine of the bench. The people are demoralized; most of the States have been compelled to isolate the voters at the polling places to prevent universal intimidation and bribery. The newspapers are largely subsidized or muzzled, public opinion silenced, business prostrated, homes covered with mortgages, labor impoverished, and the land concentrating in the hands of capitalists. The urban workmen are denied the right to organize for self-protection, imported pauperized labor beats down their wages, a hireling standing army, unrecognized by our laws, is established to shoot them down, and they are rapidly degenerating into European conditions. The fruits of the toil of millions are boldly stolen to build up colossal fortunes for a few, unprecedented in the history of mankind; and the possessors of those, in turn, despise the republic and endanger liberty. From the same prolific womb of governmental injustice we breed the two great classes—tramps and millionaires.

The national power to create money is appropriated to enrich bondholders; a vast public debt payable in legal tender currency has been funded into gold-bearing bonds, thereby adding millions to the burdens of the people.

Silver, which has been accepted as coin since the dawn of history, has been demonetized to add to the purchasing power of gold by decreasing the value of all forms of property as well as human labor, and the supply of currency is purposely abridged to fatten usurers, bankrupt enterprise, and enslave industry. A vast conspiracy against mankind has been organized on two continents, and it is rapidly taking possession of the world. If not met and overthrown at once it forebodes terrible social convulsions, the destruction of civilization, or the establishment of an absolute despotism.

We have witnessed for more than a quarter of a century the struggles of the two great political parties for power and plunder, while grievous wrongs have been inflicted upon the suffering people. We charge that the controlling influences dominating both these parties have permitted the existing dreadful conditions to develop without serious effort to prevent or restrain them. Neither do they now promise us any substantial reform. They have agreed together to ignore, in the coming campaign, every issue but one. They propose to drown the outcries of a plundered people with the uproar of a sham battle over the tariff, so that capitalists, corporations, national banks, rings, trusts, watered stock, the demonetization of silver and the oppressions of the usurers may all be lost sight of. They propose to sacrifice our homes, lives, and children on the altar of mammon; to destroy the multitude in order to secure corruption funds from the millionaires.

Assembled on the anniversary of the birthday of the nation and filled with the spirit of the grand general and chief who established our independence, we seek to restore the government of the Republic to the hands of "the plain people," with which class it originated. We assert our purposes to be identical with the purposes of the National Constitution; to form a more perfect union and establish justice, insure domestic tranquility, provide for the common defense, promote the general welfare, and secure the blessings of liberty for ourselves and our posterity. . .

. . .Our country finds itself confronted by conditions for which there is no precedent in the history of the world; our annual agricultural productions amount to billions of dollars in value, which must, within a few weeks or months, be exchanged for billions of dollars' worth of commodities consumed in their production; the existing currency supply is wholly inadequate to make this exchange; the results are falling prices, the formation of combines and rings, and the impoverishment of the producing class. We pledge ourselves that if given power we will labor to correct these evils by wise and reasonable legislation, in accordance with the terms of our platform. . .

Union General and former 1880 Greenback-Labor Party presidential nominee James Weaver became the Populist presidential candidate, receiving more than one million popular votes and 22 electoral votes, carrying the states of Idaho, Colorado, Nevada and Kansas. Despite Weaver's loss, the Populists did elect ten Representatives, five Senators, three governors and 1500 state and county officials, this accomplished in part by fusing with the Democratic Party in certain states. R. Alton Lee writes that just days before the July 4, 1892 Omaha convention, "the Democratic national convention rejected the Populist appeal to accept its demands in their platform and instead nominated Grover Cleveland for a second term. His nomination," says Lee, "resolved the problem for many southerners, who now supported the People's Party because of Cleveland's 'unyielding opposition to currency reform.'" This of course was not true for all southern farmers, many of whom refused to vote against the Democratic Party because of long-held notions of white supremacy.

Campaign buttons for the newly formed People's Party. James Weaver is chosen as the Presidential candidate.

The July 4, 1892 Omaha Convention was attended by eight hundred Northern and Southern Alliance delegates and over one hundred Colored Alliance delegates, together with representatives of twenty-one other farm and labor organizations, including the Knights of Labor. According to John Hicks, somewhere between 1300 and 1400 accredited delegates were on hand to be counted, even though many railroads had failed to grant the usual reduced convention rates to third-party delegates. In addition, there were thousands of observers who also attended the Omaha meeting.

Somewhat counterintuitively, Henry George, whose widely read *Progress and Poverty* had inspired the formation of "Single Tax" groups who were one of many groups in support of the Populists, disagreed sharply with the Knights of Labor and the Populists over whether tariffs should be used to protect American workers. As explained in the next chapter, tariffs during this period were being used as a political football in ways that were highly injurious to both laborers and farmers. Suffice it to say here that Henry George had, toward the end of his life, become a fierce advocate for "free" trade, a doctrine that persists, incorrectly and with the same damaging effects, to this day. It was for this reason that George himself remained aloof from Alliance and allied labor efforts.

Similarly, Samuel Gompers of the newly emerging American Federation of Labor refused to have anything to do with any of the Alliances. At that time both Henry George and Samuel Gompers were concentrating their efforts in the Northeast, and it may be that the AFL was the more damaging to the Populist movement both at the time and into the future, based on the foothold it managed to establish in the political arena.

The AFL was founded in 1886, the year of the so-called "Great Upheaval," by an alliance of craft unions who felt that their concerns were not being met by the Knights of Labor. Samuel Gompers served as president of the AFL for every year except one until his death in 1924. Gompers refused to give even a mild endorsement to the Populists, writing somewhat disingenuously and erroneously in an article that appeared in July of 1892 in the *North American Review:* "Composed, as the People's Party is, mainly of employing farmers without any regard to the interests of employed farmers of the country districts or the mechanics and laborers of the industrial centers, there must of necessity be a divergence of purposes, methods and interests."

Gompers effectively and intentionally excluded female and unskilled workers as well as immigrants and people of color. The members he sought were skilled white native male workers. The early AFL even attacked the Knights of Labor for its activities among unskilled and black workers. But by staying away from what was regarded as radical political change, the AFL maintained the support of the government and the public. By 1900 the organization had over 500,000 tradespeople on its roles.

Four months after the Omaha convention and immediately following the November 1892 election, the National Farmers' Alliance and Industrial Union met in Memphis to determine the next president of the Alliance. By this time it had become clear that Macune intended to remain a loyal Democrat and not a Populist. Hicks writes that Macune had "utterly lost his reputation with reformers by his conduct during the campaign of 1892. Although as editor of the *National Economist* he seemed to support the Populists, he was actually in close touch with the Democratic campaign managers, whom he aided in the printing and distribution of documents designed to induce Alliancemen to vote the Democratic ticket – a type of activity that seemingly paid him well. For this offense Macune was forced to resign and the official character of his paper was denied."

Little surprise then that a disagreement erupted during the Memphis Alliance meeting over whether the Alliance should remain politically nonpartisan as Macune wanted or maintain its public support for the Populists as Loucks wanted. "Macune nominally withdrew his candidacy," writes R. Alton Lee, "calling for farmer alignment with the Democratic Party. . . Louck's also requested that his own name be withdrawn from the ballot, but his supporters refused to accept this decision." Once the dust had settled, Loucks was easily elected for a full term, with the Alliance maintaining its support of the Populist Party.

Ultimately, charges of double dealing and questions concerning his handling of the finances of the *National Economist*, which Macune edited, caused Macune to also resign from the executive council of the Alliance, give up the editorship of the *National Economist* and sell his interest in the paper. Shortly thereafter Macune disappeared from public view.

Race Baiting and Other Self-Serving Political Maneuvers

By the fall of 1890 a Virginia Colored Farmers' Alliance man commented on how "the great gun of white supremacy has been loaded and primed and trained upon our ranks." This marked the beginning of an era when opportunists like South Carolina's Ben "Pitchfork" Tillman, Georgia's William J. Nothen, Democrats in Florida and others began choosing race baiting as a lucrative political opportunity. Although posturing as Alliancemen, these men proved to be no

Populists when they began successfully portraying Populists as representatives of "negro domination" and "radical misrule."

These men and others like them descended from a Reconstruction-era political coalition in the South called the Redeemers, who were the southern wing of the "Bourbon Democrat" faction of the Democratic Party. Representing wealthy pro-business interests of both the North and South, the Bourbon Democrats comprised a faction of the party that men like Ben Tilman, who portrayed himself as a champion of poor white farmers, positioned themselves to overtake — while at the same time retaining the Redeemer ideology of white supremacy. In 1896, the well-known Tillman would attempt a spectacularly unsuccessful challenge to William Jennings Bryan for the Democratic presidential nomination.

The Bourbon Democrats, north and south, were "gold buggers" as the Populists called them, and strongly anti-silver - a circumstance that would take on critical significance in the coming years. Grover Cleveland for example had been a Bourbon Democrat and a "gold bugger." In 1896 the Bourbon Democrats would start the short-lived "National Democratic Party," also known as Gold Democrats, this after William Jennings Bryan had won the Democratic nomination for President on a pro-silver platform. The Gold Democrats ran John M. Palmer, who had been a former Republican Governor of Illinois and Union General to oppose William Jennings Bryan in 1896 but most Gold Democrats ended up supporting McKinley, who was the Republican candidate.

During the late 1870s and early 1880s the Redeemers, as the southern wing of the Democratic Party and including the likes of Ben Tillman, had resorted to a whole litany of brutal, extra-legal and illegal tactics (including murder) in order to destroy the interracial Greenback-Republican coalition, thus "redeeming" their party from blacks and white Republicans. The same kind of tactics were again employed in the late 1880s against the Populists, only this time they would try to stop the Populists by absorbing them, mostly through intimidation, bribery and guile.

The abhorrent activities of the Redeemers were facilitated by the 1877 compromise reached by Congress to settle the disputed election between Republican Rutherford B. Hayes and Democrat Samuel Tilden. As the Gilder Lehrman website tells us, "the compromise gave Hayes the presidency in return for the end of Reconstruction and the removal of federal military support for the remaining biracial Republican governments that had emerged in the former Confederacy." From that time forward and despite the briefly successful attempts at interracial politics in North Carolina and Virginia, occupational choices for blacks would be mostly limited to low-paying wage labor and sharecropping.

By 1892, the Southern Democrats became focused not just on preserving their electoral power but also the culture of white supremacy that supported that power. Lynching, along with other forms of intimidation and violence, began to escalate, averaging 187.5 hangings per year between 1889 and 1899. Whites were also victims. For example, in 1892, two hundred and thirty people were lynched across the entire United States, with 90% of those lynchings occurring in the South. One hundred and sixty-one of these people were black, and sixty-nine were white.

In an article titled *The Populists at St. Louis*, 1896 convention delegate Henry Demerest Lloyd argued against the idea of Populists fusing with Democrats without including necessary conditions that would ensure the safety of southern Populists. He felt that an independent stance on the part of the Populists might even be the better decision politically, because in 1892 the Populists had gained tens of thousands of voters as a result of the Southern Democrats' despicable treatment of Populist speaker Mary Elizabeth Lease and Populist presidential candidate James Weaver during their speaking tour of the South that year. Explaining that "In the South, the Democracy (Democratic party) represented the classes, the People's Party the masses," Lloyd wrote that by the 1896 convention,

The most eloquent speeches were those of whites and blacks explaining to the convention what the rule of the Democrats meant in the South. A delegate from Georgia, a coal-black Negro, told how the People's Party gave full fellowship to his race, when it had been abandoned by the Republicans and cheated and betrayed by the Democrats. . . With thrilling passion, the white Populists of the South pleaded that the convention should not leave them to the tender mercies of the Democrats, by accepting the Democratic nominee without the pledges or conditions which would save the Populists from going under the chariot wheels of southern Democracy. . . The line between the old Democracy [southern Democrats] and Populism in the South is largely a line of bloody graves. When the convention decided to endorse Bryan without asking for any pledge from the Democrats for the protection of the southern Populists one of its most distinguished members, a member of Congress, well known throughout the country turned to me and said: 'This may cost me my life. I can return home only at that risk. The feeling of the Democracy [southern Democrats] against us is one of murderous hate, I have been shot many times. Grand juries will not indite our assailants. Courts give us no protection.'

Whether or not Lloyd was correct that "tens of thousands" of votes had been gained due to the poor treatment accorded Weaver, Lease and other Northern Populist speakers by southern Democrats, it is true that only one-half of the Southern Alliance membership voted the Populist ticket in 1892, partly because it proved to be too big a leap to abandon the Democratic Party and partly due to the violence and demagoguery employed by the new breed of Southern Democrats, anchored as they were in Redeemer ideology. As a result, Southern Populist anger and frustration over unsuccessful challenges aimed at the seemingly untouchable, entrenched political/economic powers of the South would slowly, almost imperceptibly, be transferred over to the black farmer and worker for whom the movement had offered so much hope. Thus, according to C. Vann Woodward in his book *Origins of the New South, 1877 – 1913*, was ushered in the "New South" Jim Crow period.

The Story Behind Our Mother's Mysterious Invocations of "Coxey's Army"

Even in the face of almost insurmountable obstacles the Populists actively sought out alliances with a wide variety of other groups across the entire country, this because the root cause of the people's problems was the same everywhere. So, we find that among the Populist ranks one could find small merchants, "country" bankers, lawyers, economists and businessmen. Jacob Coxey was one of the better known of these people. He, and others of his ilk, understood at the most basic level Alexander Del Mar's early cautions to labor: "Strike for higher wages whenever you can, but do not blame the employer if you do not succeed. Many of them will soon become bankrupt; most of them are losing money today – though you, and even themselves believe they are exceedingly prosperous."

Jacob Coxey had established a sand quarry business called the Coxey Sand Company in 1881 in Massilon, Ohio. He was one of thousands of businessmen who faced serious financial difficulties because of the Panic of 1893. By 1894, he organized what became known as "Coxey's Army" to protest the federal government's inaction in the face of the economic crisis. Although Coxey hoped that his "Army" of marchers would ultimately number 100,000, it only grew to about five hundred by the time it reached the nation's capital. The group's main demand was for the U.S. Treasury to be compelled to issue $500 million in interest-free treasury notes with which to employ 4 million people, ala the Greenback system.

To accomplish this, Coxey and his "army" proposed two bills. One bill would be used to construct rural roads to aid farmers, using government-issued money to do so. The other bill involved the passage of a non-interest-bearing bonds bill that would allow state and local governments to issue their own non-interest-bearing bonds. These bonds then could be used to borrow legal tender notes from the federal treasury, with the money used to build urban libraries, schools, utility plants and marketplaces. Taken together these proposals would have created millions of jobs, without attendant federal debt.

Of Coxey's protest Populist supporter Francis Schulte writes in his 1895 *The Little Statesman*:

Jacob Coxey and his sone Legal Tender in a promotional poster.

"Although Coxey's plan to issue money to build good roads and thereby not only increase the volume of currency but give employment to the idle was ridiculed and scorned by Congress, and Coxey himself put in jail ostensibly for carrying a banner a size larger than a Columbian postage stamp, and fined for walking on the grass, it is not generally known that the road he travelled from Massillon, Ohio to Washington, was built by the national government and paid for out of national funds. The great national pike is an enduring monument of the idea which inspired Coxey and is in accord with that part of our platform."

Interestingly, about a month before his famous march began, Coxey and his wife welcomed a baby boy into the world, naming him Legal Tender Coxey, as the accompanying poster suggests. Sadly, the little boy died in 1901 of scarlet fever.

In addition to his march of 1894, Coxey served as a delegate to the 1896 Populist convention and ran as the Populist candidate for Ohio governor in 1895 and 1897, losing both elections. He subsequently ran for several other U.S. offices but lost each time. In 1914 he led another protest march on Washington and again the federal government refused to listen to his proposals.

Unfortunately, the deeper implications of our mother's frequent references to "Coxey's Army" were entirely lost on us. At least until now.

CHAPTER 6

The Money Question

The years following the Civil War produced a relatively small group of ultra-wealthy tycoons, also known as "robber barons," who famously wielded more political power than politicians during this period, popularly known as the Gilded Age. At the other end of the economic spectrum stood the vast and continually growing masses of people living in abject poverty, with relatively few people between these two extremes of poverty and wealth. As the Populists knew and others have acknowledged, the chief cause of this growing wealth disparity had to do with the fact that the money supply was being deliberately reduced at the behest of the "Sound Money" advocates, who began a propaganda war as soon as the Civil War ended, denouncing the Greenbacks as "dishonest, worthless rags." Moreover, the leadership of both the Democratic and the Republican Parties supported "sound money" which is why so many Populists bolted from their ranks.

Interestingly, and quite oddly if one understands the money question as the Populists themselves defined it, the currency plank that the Populists are today most known for is the "pro- silver" plank. Coincidentally or not, it is this plank that is most connected to charges of conspiracy, overblown rhetoric and paranoia often leveled against the Populists, both then and now. The words of Ignatius Donnelly, himself a lawyer, in his Preamble to the 1892 Omaha Platform provide some insight as to how this came to be:

> Silver, which has been accepted as coin since the dawn of history, has been demonetized to add to the purchasing power of gold by decreasing the value of all forms of property as well as human labor, and the supply of currency is purposely abridged to fatten usurers, bankrupt enterprise, and enslave industry. A vast conspiracy against mankind has been organized on two continents, and it is rapidly taking possession of the world. If not met and overthrown at once it forebodes terrible social convulsions, the destruction of civilization, or the establishment of an absolute despotism.

Donnelly, and other Populists, did not just make up this "vast conspiracy" nor, as has been mentioned earlier, were Donnelly and the Populists in general advocating for silver to be the sole, or most important U.S. currency. One of their most learned sources was none other than Populist contemporary Alexander Del Mar, who is regarded by many to be America's greatest monetary historian.

Del Mar, it might be mentioned, had been the first Director of the U.S. Treasury Department's Bureau of Statistics (now part of the Bureau of Economic Analysis) from 1860-1869 from which position he was forced to resign because of his convictions concerning "fiat" – or government issued money. He then purchased and operated a newspaper called the *New York City and National Intelligencer* until 1872. In 1877 he was appointed mining commissioner to the U.S. Monetary Commission, which was created by Congress after Congress had discovered the deceptions and subterfuge involved in the effective demonetization of silver that led to the Panic of 1873, also known as the Crime of '73. Although that commission recommended a return to the bimetallic system set in place by statute in 1792 (the reason for this statute will become clear as we progress through this chapter), gold remained, after 1873, the U.S. reserve currency until the 1930's.

Del Mar remained throughout his years a firm advocate for a paper currency with full legal tender functions. Known as a rigorous historian, he was well acquainted with the myriad of ways that money through the ages, in whatever form it took, was used by the few to make themselves rich through what we will call, for the sake of simplicity, the international currency exchange. Some extended excerpts from a chapter titled "The Crime of 1873" taken from Del Mar's 1899 book titled *A History of Monetary Crimes* will help illustrate how this "conspiracy" takes place even today:

> When the Civil War ended, the federal debt was about $2,800,000,000; the debts of the various states, townships and municipalities, about $1,400,000,000; of railways and canals about $2,500,000,000; and of other corporations about $300,000,000; together about $7,000,000,000.

> Between a fourth and a third of this was owed to investors in Europe, who had lent or advanced it, in *paper dollars,* which cost them on the average about half a dollar each in gold or silver coins. [During the War, Greenbacks lost value against gold due to the "exclusion clause" explained later in this chapter]. An equal proportion had been advanced by American capitalists on similar terms. The balance was advanced before the war, or else *before* the paper currency depreciated; and was therefore lent in coins or their equivalent. Leaving this portion of the debt out of view, it is probably near to the mark to say that at the close of the Civil War there were owing nearly $5,000,000,000, which [only] cost the lenders (Europeans and Americans), about half that sum in coins.

> The whole of this debt was payable, under the act of February 25, 1862, in greenbacks; the interest on a portion of it was payable in gold or silver coin.

> The first move of the lenders after the war closed was to open a newspaper war upon the paper money which they had themselves lent to the government. The greenbacks, it was contended, were "dishonest" dollars; indeed, not really dollars at all, only worthless, disreputable rags, a disgrace to civilization, disseminators of fraud and disease, etc. This question was fought in the Presidential campaign of 1868, in which, by referring to the newspapers of the day, it will be seen that the writer hereof bore no interactive part. As the election day approached every sign indicated the triumph of Governor Seymour, the champion of greenbacks, and the defeat of General Grant, the champion of coins. All of a sudden, on the eve of election, and without warning, the then trusted organ of the Democratic party, to wit, the *New York World,* edited by Manton Marble, but owned, as it was commonly believed, by August Belmont, hauled down its flag, deserted the ticket, and left nearly two million voters to the effects of treachery, panic and disorder.

> . . . The first fruit of this nefarious [post-election] transaction was the passage of a so-called "Credit Strengthening Act," dated March 18, 1869, by which the United States government pledged itself to pay the principal as well as the interest, of its paper debt, in gold or silver *coins.* In other words, without any consideration whatever, it undertook to pay for every paper dollar which it had borrowed, a gold or silver dollar, of the long-established weight and fineness; *and by this act and its subsequent action, it compelled all indebted persons and corporations to do the like.* [Italics mine]

Del Mar then introduced some of the machinations surrounding the introduction of what is known as the Crime of '73 in the same chapter as the above as well as in a previous chapter titled *The Crime of 1870.* An abbreviated excerpt from the first segment will be followed by a more extended excerpt from the previous chapter.

> Having by these means secured to themselves the payment of a whole metal dollar for each *half* of a metal dollar advanced to the government, thus clearing cent-per-cent profit at a single bound, the conspirators next attempted to double the value or purchasing power of such metal dollars, by means of destroying one-half of them, to wit, the silver ones. . .

...The old law [prior to the "Crime of '73"] made it the duty of the Director of Mint to receive deposits of either gold or silver; to coin such metal into dollars – the silver ones to contain exactly sixteen times as much metal as the gold ones – and to return the same to the depositor; and it declared all such dollars to be money of the United States and legal tenders for all purposes and to any amount. The public debt was made payable under the act of March 18, 1869 in such dollars, whether gold or silver. [The two Acts involved in the Crime of 1873] dropped the silver dollar. It did not demonetize it, but by omitting to include it in the various coins which the Mint Director was authorized to strike, it was unlawful for him to strike any more of them...

...The act [i.e., the Crime of 1873] when passed, was not read in both Houses at length, and it is notorious that this transcendent change in the monetary system of the country, affecting the most vital and widespread interests, was carried through without the knowledge or observation of the people...

Del Mar provided more detail for the Crime of 1873 in his segment titled "The Crime of 1870" showing that the European Syndicate, as Del Mar referred to them, had a vested interest in American politics especially where it pertained to their ability to profit from their "investments." Similar to what Thomas Jefferson described during the Revolutionary Era about the "brokers in paper money" wanting to multiply their profits by, in effect, demanding to be paid forty paper dollars for every silver dollar they had loaned (even though they had supplied only one dollar of goods in the first place), so too did this "Syndicate" seek to multiply their profits by influencing, through economic chicanery, the nation's currency system.

The Monetary Commission of 1876, with which I was connected, reported that the Acts of 1873, were, one of them, passed surreptitiously, and the other upon false or erroneous assurances. This has since been vehemently denied. I am going to show you not only that the Commission was right, but that these acts were the issue of European intrigue and precedent.

At the period of this legislation the ratio of value at which silver and gold were purchased and coined at the French mints was 15 ½ weights for 1; at the mints of the United States 16 to 1. In consequence of this difference (about 3 percent) those who had silver to coin sent it to Paris, rather than Philadelphia, San Francisco or New Orleans. Had the opposition to the coinage of dollars in the two metals and the preference by creditors of the government for one metal over another been of American origin, the one metal chosen would inevitably have been silver, because in fact the silver dollar was worth 3 percent more than the gold one, and because the fundholders who notoriously promoted and supported the legislation of 1873 would no more have preferred gold dollars then, than they would silver dollars now.

But in France, indeed, in Europe generally, whose mints and markets commonly followed the vast coinages of France, the gold and silver coins of like denominations were of precisely equal value. Hence to the European holder of American bonds in 1863-64 it made no difference whether he was paid in gold or silver coins, provided – and this was the point essentially important to his interest and avidity – provided that the debtor was deprived of the option of paying in coins of the other metal. The preference of gold was certainly not American, because at the American mint ratio gold dollars, when melted down, were only 97 cents. It was therefore of European origin. We shall presently see why these "cheaper" dollars were preferred to silver ones...

...At the time when the necessities of our government compelled it to issue hundreds – nay, almost thousands of millions of 6 percent and 5 percent bonds, with interest payable in "coins," the French Court of Cassation promulgated a decision in perfect accordance not only with the entire range of legal authority, but also with the Code of Napoleon, to the effect that on this subject no man could contract himself out of the law; in short, that contracts of money were equitably dischargeable in the current money of the day of payment. This decision alarmed the European holders of American bonds. "What might those shrewd, those progressive Americans do with respect to the interest on these bonds, which was payable in "coins?"

. . .There was but one way to avert this financial calamity. This was to demonetize one of the precious metals and fix the standard of the other. But which metal should be demonetized? Gold? "Oh, no, the American government would never consent to that, because it would oblige them to pay in silver dollars, which under the operations of their own laws, as influenced by our (French mint) law, are worth 3 percent more than gold ones. Therefore, let us endeavor to demonetize silver. To us it makes no difference; to the Americans it is a gain of three percent. Let us bribe them with this three percent to surrender their option of the metals. All doubt as to kind of payment then being removed, our American bonds, purchased at forty or fifty cents on the dollar, will rise to par and over. "A la mort, l'argent!" . . .

. . . From 1865 to 1870 the fundholding syndicate into whose hands it is quite evident this intrigue had now fallen, was incessant in its operations. Numerous conventions under its patronage were held in France, Belgium and Germany: its influence plainly discernible in the treacherous defection of certain party leaders during the American presidential election of 1868; in the gratuitous "Credit Strengthening" act of 1869; in the appropriation clause of Boutwell's needless Fifteen Hundred Million funding bill; and especially in that surreptitious and scandalous alteration of the British Mint Code of 1870, which furnished the immediate example, precedent and justification for the analogous alteration of our own Mint Code, namely the alteration which demonetized silver and threw the commercial world into bankruptcy. . .

Del Mar summed up the entirety of these shameful machinations by writing that "The silver dollar was dropped purely and simply to enhance the value of the gold dollar and thus to double the debt of the American people. The proof is that the very same men, I mean identical individuals, who betrayed their party in 1868 and who doubled the public indebtedness by promoting the act of March 1869, assisted again to double the debt by promoting the surreptitious mint codification act of February 23, and June 1874 though Congress was assured by its revision that no new matter had been introduced to them. The legislation of 1865-1874 was no academic experiment but a sordid crime hatched abroad and brought into this country by the treacherous people who governed the utterances of the New York World."

Cartoon titled "John Bull's Little Game" appearing in the St. Louis Dispatch on Sept. 10, 1896 depicted England's promotion of the gold standard as the reason for the indebtedness of the American farmer

Decades later, John Hicks noted in *The Populist Revolt* that President Garfield admitted in 1877 that he had not even read the law of 1873, and "took it upon the faith of a prominent Democrat and a prominent Republican" that it was acceptable. Garfield could not even recall whether he had voted on the bill. Hicks also tells the reader that President Grant was not even allowed to know the contents of the bill he had signed, and later regretted doing so. Hicks includes these relevant remarks about this period:

There was a growing conviction in financial circles that a bimetallic standard was unsatisfactory, if not, indeed, actually impossible. An international monetary conference held at Paris in 1867 strongly favored the gold standard, and in the next five or six years the silver currency of most European countries was either limited strictly or demonetized outright. Thus the "crime of 1873" in the United States was paralleled in Europe by another "crime" that actually resulted in the sale of great quantities of silver bullion, previously used for monetary purposes. With the annual world production of gold strangely at a standstill, or even declining, the gold value of silver now dropped at an alarming rate.

Once the decline in the price of silver became clearly apparent, the "crime" was out, and the silver miners of the American West, for whom coinage at the old ratio would now have been profitable, were quick to demand that silver be restored to its former status. In this demand they were joined by a host of others who saw in the action of Congress no mere accident or oversight but rather a nefarious conspiracy on behalf of the creditor class to the everlasting detriment of the debtors. The conspiracy - doubtless international in its scope – was to throw upon gold the monetary burden that previously had been born by gold and silver together. With silver demonetized, the demand for gold would increase; with the demand for gold increasing, the purchasing value of the gold dollar would rise. And with dearer dollars the debts of the common man, contracted in a period of cheaper currency, would on their collection net the lender a handsome profit. No wonder the import of the law that perpetuated this crime was concealed from the Congress that had passed it! No wonder Grant was not permitted to know the contents of the bill he signed! For, as [Ignatius] Donnelly put it, "the demonetization of silver was intended to increase the value of money at the expense of labor, and to enrich the creditor class at the expense of the debtor class."

Though Del Mar doesn't mention it in the passages provided earlier, the first propaganda success of the "Sound Money" advocates occurred with the Contraction Act of 1866 which called for a reduction of Greenbacks. This created such distress in the economy that it was repealed in 1868. Next came the Credit Strengthening Act of 1869 which effectively doubled all public indebtedness by forcing payment of debt in gold or silver coin, both of which were not in common use at that time other than for international transactions. Then the "Crime of '73" slashed an already shrinking money supply by effectively demonetizing silver (by preventing its coinage), and thus surreptitiously putting America on the gold standard. And so it went through to the 1890s.

But even worse than the "inelastic" metallic money supply, National Bank Notes issued by chartered national banks as per the National Bank Act of 1863-64 had "reverse elasticity" because they were tied to bonds. As explained by James Neal Primm in his book *A Foregone Conclusion*, which is posted in pdf form on the St. Louis Fed website, explains:

> When increased, business activity called for monetary expansion and so both the Treasury, by lowering its debt, and the banks, by seeking higher returns elsewhere, could gain by reducing bank holdings of government bonds. Since bank note issues were tied to these bonds, their circulation dropped from $350 million in 1883 to $170 million in 1891. Having increased sevenfold between 1870 and 1900, bank deposits were a much larger element in the money supply than bank notes, greenbacks, gold and silver combined, but the increase in bank deposits was not sufficient to reverse the deflationary trend.

Primm does not clearly explain that bank (or demand) deposits largely represented, as they do today, loans which must be repaid at interest. Additionally, certain restrictions in the National Bank Act prevented farmers from obtaining loans from national banks, while at the same time the notoriously less stable state banks were often encouraged – and in some states required - to loan to farmers. Just as importantly, as Stephen Zarlenga points out in his masterful tome *The Lost Science of Money* the distribution of national bank notes was clearly skewed to the northeast;

> The National Banking Association proceeded to implement a grossly unfair distribution of the [legislated] $300 million of banknote issue. For example, the city of Woonsocket, Rhode Island

was given more circulating currency than North and South Carolina combined. Rhode Island was given $77.16 per capita. Arkansas was given $0.13 per capita. The state of Connecticut was given more than the combined circulation of Michigan, Iowa, Minnesota, Kansas, Missouri, Kentucky, and Tennessee.

One can also get a sense from Primm's statement that currency contractions and mal-distribution in the national bank note supply were causing a sevenfold *increase* in bank [demand] deposits as more and more people and businesses were forced to borrow. Thus, as James Livingston states in his book *Origins of the Federal Reserve: Money, Class and Capitalism, 1890-1913* (and as Primm confirms in the above passage), "bankers and their allies understood perfectly that demand deposits were a key element in the money supply – this, in fact, was their premise in debate with "free silver" partisans who argued that the volume of money in circulation had declined after 1873."

Of course, reductions in the money (and/or credit) supply also cause falling wages and prices, as was carefully explained by Alexander Del Mar, Henry Loucks and others of the era. As less money became available fewer businessmen could afford to pay workers a decent wage and still others had to lay off workers, or even, as in the case of Jacob Coxey, go out of business. At the same time fewer people could afford even basic necessities such as food - even at the lowest prices. Falling wages and prices in turn were the root cause of the deepening cycle of debt and foreclosure, which then caused wealth aka collateral pledged by borrowers to be seized by the bank, leading to ever greater concentrations of wealth.

Capital Is Only the Fruit of Labor

In the decades following 1866, workers' wages and farm prices dropped so low that Populists were later wont to point out that "The makers of clothes are underfed; the makers of food under-clad." Workers, aka "makers of clothes," responded with the tool available to them – the strike. Although mostly unsuccessful these strikes did not go unnoticed. Among the most well-known were the Great Strike of 1877, the Railroad Strike of 1886, the Homestead Strike of 1892 and the Pullman Strike of 1894. This last strike was all the more remarkable because of the "panic of 93" which was triggered by the collapse of the Pennsylvania and Reading Railroad and the National Cordage Company.

These events, together with plummeting farm income, were punctuated by the 1893 stock market crash and the worst depression up to that time, bringing pain and hardship to all, no matter their economic status. By the end of 1893 five hundred banks and 16,000 businesses had failed; four million workers were out of work and half the nation's railroads went under. In other words, the deflationary pressure caused by lack of money, and an excess of bank credit or loans was bad for everyone, business included.

Despite this horrific economic situation, some 690,000 workers went on strike in 1894, including those that struck against Pullman. The Pullman strike developed into a nationwide railroad strike that began in the "company town" of Pullman on the south side of Chicago. It became the largest strike in U.S. history up to that time and was led by Eugene Debs, head of the American Railway Union. Then a Populist, Debs would be a serious contender for the 1896 Populist presidential nomination.

The strike did not end well when, contrary to Illinois Governor Altgeld's express and repeated requests, then President Grover Cleveland (similar to previous administrations) sent in federal troops to stop strikers from obstructing trains. What had been a peaceful protest quickly became laced with violence and death. Interestingly, the American Federation of Labor refused to come to the aid of the American Railway Union in the form of sympathetic strikes.

Meanwhile farm prices had been going through an excruciating, multi-decade decline that began in 1866, even as the value of the dollar soared (making dollars harder to earn). As alluded to earlier, falling crop prices further compounded the debt problem for farmers by seriously impacting income. The numbers tell the story: corn that had sold for 66 cents a bushel in 1866, sold for 28 cents a bushel in 1889. Wheat dropped from $2.06 a bushel in 1866 to just 70 cents a bushel in 1889.

James Neal Primm, mentioned earlier, remarked that "By 1896, wholesale prices had fallen nearly fifty percent since 1870, farm prices somewhat more. Wheat prices declined from $1.06 to 63 cents in the December Eastern markets and cotton fell from 15 to six cents a pound." Primm's next sentence accurately describes the true pain felt by farmers: *"Harvest-time prices at the farm,"* says Primm, *"averaged half or less of these amounts."* As a result, wrote Primm, "Foreclosures had turned tens of thousands of owners into tenant farmers; in western Kansas, loan companies owned ninety percent of the land in 1893." By 1900 fully ninety percent of land in *all* of Kansas would be owned by loan companies.

Many sources of the time, from the *New York Times* to Henry Loucks, understood that "capital" represents the accumulation of savings acquired through the production and manufacture of raw materials - which materials provide the basis of a nation's wealth. Clearly, the savings of farmers and workers were next to non-existent, despite massive increases in, for example, wheat production in Dakota Territory during the 1880s and 1890s. Part of what was happening was that capital was by this time being elevated above labor due to special legal arrangements then being given to capital, this despite warnings from the likes of Abraham Lincoln and his economic advisor Henry Carey and others. Indeed, years before, on December 3, 1861, at the outset of the Civil War, Abraham Lincoln included in his first annual message to Congress a warning against "the approach of returning despotism" by those making "labored arguments" to prove that popular government was the source of all political evil, this in an attempt to elevate capital on an equal footing with, if not above, labor:

> In my present position I could scarcely be justified were I to omit raising a warning voice against this approach of returning despotism.
>
> It is not needed nor fitting here that a general argument should be made in favor of popular institutions, but there is one point, with its connections, not so hackneyed as most others, to which I ask a brief attention. It is the effort to place capital on an equal footing with, if not above, labor in the *structure* of government. It is assumed that labor is available only in connection with capital; that nobody labors unless somebody else, owning capital, somehow by the use of it induces him to labor. This assumed, it is next considered whether it is best that capital shall hire laborers, and thus induce them to work by their own consent or buy them and drive them to it without their consent. Having proceeded so far, it is naturally concluded that all laborers are either hired laborers or what we call slaves. And further, it is assumed that whoever is once a hired laborer is fixed in that condition for life.
>
> Now there is no such relation between capital and labor as assumed, nor is there any such thing as a free man being fixed for life in the condition of a hired laborer. Both these assumptions are false, and all inferences from them are groundless.
>
> Labor is prior to and independent of capital. *Capital is only the fruit of labor and could never have existed if labor had not first existed.* Labor is the superior of capital and deserves much the higher consideration. Capital has its rights, which are as worthy of protection as any other rights. Nor is it denied that there is, and probably always will be, a relation between labor and capital producing mutual benefits. The error is in assuming that the whole labor of community exists within that relation. A few men own capital, and that few avoid labor themselves, and with their capital hire or buy another few to labor for them. A large majority belong to neither class – neither work for others nor have others working for them. In most of the Southern States a majority of the whole people of all colors are neither slaves nor masters, while in the

Northern a large majority are neither hirers nor hired. Men, with their families – wives, sons, and daughters – work for themselves on their farms, in their houses, and in their shops, taking the whole product to themselves, and asking no favors of capital on the one hand nor of hired laborers or slaves on the other. It is not forgotten that a considerable number of persons mingle their own labor with capital; that is, they labor with their own hands and also buy or hire others to labor for them; but this is only a mixed and not a distinct class. No principle stated is disturbed by the existence of this mixed class.

That this message to Congress was either mis-understood or deliberately disregarded is reflected in a passage in the 1895 revised edition of Henry Loucks book *The New Monetary System,* which had been written as a textbook at the request of the Farmers' Alliance. In the first chapter Loucks drew upon a small contemporary book called *Bond Holders and Bread Winners* by Kansas attorney S. S. King which was published in 1892 by the Kansas Populist Party. In the passage that follows, Loucks illustrates that despite the "wonderful increase in national wealth," the greatest accumulations of debt were occurring in those areas of the country deemed to be the wealthiest. Moreover, debt was largely born by the producers of wealth, i.e., farmers and laborers, no matter where they lived, all in apparent disregard of Lincoln's warning, resulting in all the attendant social ills of a society plagued by wealth extremes:

> When the census reports of 1890 revealed the wonderful increase in wealth of the nation of $18,000,000,000 in ten years, the result was heralded forth as the death blow to "calamity howling."
>
> Who would dare complain now of lack of prosperity with such a record of increase in wealth? An investigation of these same census reports confirms us in the position we have taken as to the unjust distribution of wealth produced. The producers of that increase of $18,000,000,000 of wealth have become poorer than they were; even what they had before 1880 has been taken from them to add to the millions of the already millionaires. . .
>
> In the accumulation of wealth, on average, one man in Massachusetts equals 812 in the West and South. Add the three states of Kansas, Kentucky and Florida, and compare with the great state of Pennsylvania, and we find fourteen times the land, in 1880 about four times the labor (population), and twice the capital (assessed value). . .On average, one man in Pennsylvania equals 112 in the West and South in the accumulation of wealth. **Do all of its citizens share in this prosperity? No; the condition of labor is much worse there.** Our plan of protection [the tariff] protects the manufacturer but gives no protection to the laborer. The manufacturers receive the benefit. . .
>
> Prof. Joseph R. Buchanan states that in a recent conversation with a special agent of the National Bureau of Labor Statistics, who had just returned from an official investigation of labor in Pennsylvania, the latter said; 'Show me a place in Russia where the people are miserable and starving and I will match it in Pennsylvania. Show me a community in Europe where the people have lost all hope and are only waiting for death to relieve them from their sufferings and I will match it in Pennsylvania.'
>
> **From these same census reports we find that there are twice as many paupers per capita in the nine favored [wealthiest] states as there are in the twenty-one [of the West and South],** one and a half times as many prisoners in the county jails; and, sadder than all else for the future of our country, there are three times as many children in the reformatory schools in the favored states as in the West and South. . . .
>
> In Massachusetts the mortgage indebtedness increased in the ten years from 1880 to 1890, 168 per cent, while the population increased 25 per cent. The mortgage indebtedness incurred in those ten years was $508,455,550. The mortgage indebtedness remaining in force, January 1st, 1890 was $323,277,688. The per capita indebtedness of Massachusetts is second only to that of Kansas . . .
>
> **It is very clear that whilst in accumulation of wealth one person in the nine North Atlantic states equals twenty in the West and South, the distribution there is very unequal. The av-**

erage indebtedness is nearly three times as great. In proportion as wealth accumulates in the hands of the few, debt, misery, poverty, and degradation overtake the many.

While unequal wealth distribution and wealth accumulation were most pronounced in the northeast, wealth *production* from raw materials was greatest in the south and west. Another commentator by the name of Francis J. Schulte laid out the mind-boggling details by drawing - like Loucks did - from the work of Kansas attorney S. S. King, but this time from an article called *Seedtime and Harvest*. In his own article entitled *Sectionalism in American Politics* appearing in his 1895 book *The Little Statesman,* Schulte summarizes King's observations that real wealth producers were able to accumulate only half as much wealth as the eastern financial community even though the raw materials wealth they produced between 1880-1890 was nothing short of staggering:

Indiana, Illinois, Iowa, Nebraska, Louisiana, Mississippi, Alabama, Georgia, North Carolina, Kansas, Kentucky, Florida, Tennessee, Virginia, West Virginia, Missouri, Arkansas, South Carolina, Delaware, Maryland and Ohio, twenty one producing States forming the great body of the Union [South and North Dakota only entered the Union in 1889 and so were not included in official data], a wonderland of diversified resources with six times as much land and twice as many people to cultivate it, were able to accumulate one-half as much wealth in the period named [1880-1890] as the nine manufacturing, bond-holding, banking, money-lending and railroad-owning States of Maine, New Hampshire, Vermont, Massachusetts, Connecticut, Rhode Island, New York, Pennsylvania and New Jersey . . .

It was largely the states named above as the producing states that Senator Ingalls wrote (Lippincott's Magazine, June 1892): 'Sparsely inhabited, with rude and unscientific methods, their resources hardly touched, the States of the Mississippi Valley last year produced more than three-quarters of the sugar, coal, corn, iron, oats, wheat, cotton, tobacco, lead, hay, lumber, wool, pork, beef, horses and mules of the entire country, together with a large fraction of its gold and silver. *Their internal commerce already greater than all the foreign commerce of the combined nations of the world.*'

This growing concentration of wealth (and capital) continued into the twentieth century, and need it be said, even into our own. In his March 17, 1908 remarks to the Senate, U. S. Senator Robert La Follette of Wisconsin pointed out that the "great industrial reorganization" that began in 1898 actually involved the "association" of industry with banking, an "association" that led a few years later to what was oftentimes referred to as the Banker's Panic of 1907. This "association" would dramatically affect the lives of our grandfather and his entire family along with the entire agricultural sector within the first three decades of the twentieth century. Excerpts from La Follette's remarks illustrate the economic situation the Populists had joined together to struggle against, and that Lincoln warned about in 1861, as follows:

1898 was the beginning of great industrial reorganization... Within a period of three years [1898-1901], 149 such reorganizations were affected with a total stock and bond capitalization of $3,784,000,000. . . This was but the first stage in the creation of fictitious wealth. The success of these organizations led quickly to a consolidation of combined industries, until a mere handful of men controlled the industrial production of the country. . .

I have compiled a list of about one hundred men with their directorships in the great corporate business enterprises of the United States. . . .they have through reorganization multiplied their wealth almost beyond their own ability to know its amount with accuracy.

[Undeniably the] great banking institutions *in the principal money centers* have become bound up with the control of industrial institutions. (Congressional Record – Senate, page 3434, 1908 March 17, Senate Bill 3023: Amendment of National Banking Laws.)

It was the "sound money" conspirators exposed by Alexander Del Mar and referred to by Abraham Lincoln as "those making labored arguments for returning despotism" that managed to achieve this kind of concentration by 1908. In his book *Origins of the Federal Reserve: Money, Class and Capitalism, 1890-1913* mentioned earlier, James Livingston draws a distinction between the newly evolving corporate capitalism that grew out of the increasingly well organized and well-funded efforts of the various "sound money" conspirators and small "c" capitalism that was a reflection of the small independent proprietorship system (which included small farmers) that most Americans of the period believed to be not only necessary but still in operation.

CAPITAL AND LABOR

This 1883 cartoon, from "Grips Comic Almanac", Toronto .Canada effectively echoes LincoOln's famous words that capital is only the fruit of labor.

As Livingston details, these sound money conspirators began organizing themselves to counter the momentum of the Populists, whose democratic money system they believed to be not only against their own economic interests, but bad for the advancement of mankind. Comprised of a carefully constructed coalition of corporate businessmen and eastern financiers together with hand-picked intellectuals, academics and members of the press, this group began to fan out across the country to expound upon the blessings of centralized control of production and distribution and the need to create and perfect the corporate instruments of such control. It was through their efforts that the Federal Reserve System was created in 1913. Through it a new, more highly organized system of corporate capitalism would emerge, one in which the savings of society as a whole were to be converted into particular productive instruments, and which was to be managed in accordance with the capabilities and requirements of the large corporations.

Arguably, and as presented by Vernon Louis Parrington in a 1930 article titled *Alexander Hamilton and the Leviathan State,* these sound money conspirators descended from the "well born" Hamiltonians, whose guiding principle was "that governmental interference with economic laws is desirable when it aids business but intolerable and unsound when it aims at business regulation or control, or when it assists agriculture or labor." Severely marginalized, and even driven to the brink of extinction, was that class referred to by William Jennings Bryan in his famous 1896 Cross of Gold speech as the "broader class of businessmen."

Tariffs, Trade and the Industrial Revolution

The "great industrial reorganization" noted by Senator La Follette in 1908 was given legs by the post-Civil War political decision to expand the industrial revolution just getting underway in the United States. The tariff, or rather the way in which the tariff was being structured, was a major tool in this endeavor. Although the tariff did not occupy the same prominence as the "money question" in Populist thinking, and was, especially in its later renditions, denounced as a distraction employed by establishment forces to take the people's minds off the "money question," the protective tariff was an area of concern. As explained by Hicks, the tariff, as it was structured, allowed the American manufacturer to fix his prices "not in accordance with the cost of production but in accordance with the amount of protection he was able to secure."

This despite the fact that the intent of the tariff in the U.S. Constitution was not just to provide revenues for the federal government but also, and perhaps more importantly, to provide one of several methods by which to protect the domestic "exchange" economy, or to use the words of author, economist and founder of *Acres USA* Charles Walters, "to regulate the value of U.S. money in terms of U.S. production" - this through the use of tariffs and other measures.

Farmers' income, representing as it did, and still does, the first stage in the nation's wealth production process and a major part of the domestic "exchange" economy, was not protected. As explained by Walters in his book *Unforgiven,* this cheating of farmers out of their just income ultimately and always results in severe damage to the national income, unless that income is expanded by debt, in which case other evils become inevitable.

The so-called protective tariff developed, as Hicks stated, by "the genial system of logrolling, which on occasion made Democrats as good protectionists as Republicans." It also was, as the Populists decried, "a hot-bed for the breeding of trusts." These trusts included the railroads and their "line" elevator system, along with steel and other conglomerates that put ordinary workers and farmers at their mercy.

The tariff system against which the Populists protested protected only the few, compounding the problem of low wages and low farm prices. This was because it had been structured as a tax on finished imported goods, with the specific aim being to encourage and expand the U.S. industrial revolution then underway. The tariff, in other words, had been deliberately designed as a way to guarantee the American market to a select group of American manufacturers. It did this by placing a tax on imported manufactured goods, thereby making imported goods more expensive (and less appealing) for the domestic American market.

In fact, at one point in the mid-1880's the protective tariff reached as high as 50 percent. As Loucks observes in his 1895 book *The New Monetary System*, the tariff was one of the three great factors in the lopsided accumulation of wealth which involved "the system of assisting special industries by prohibiting competition and enabling them to tax the balance of the nation to sustain their business."

Monopoly snake, with its tail wrapped around the White House and Congress, threatening to swallow Lady Liberty, with Puck off to the side asking Uncle Sam: "What are you going to do about it?"

Of course, neither the farmer nor the laborer benefitted from this situation since there was nothing in the tariff that protected their wages even as they were forced to purchase needed goods at whatever price set by the tariff-protected manufacturers. However, the farmer was at particular disadvantage. Not only did he have to deal with drought and similar vagaries of farming but he, more than anyone, depended on the products and services of industry for farming. So it was that the big agriculture-related trusts like the fertilizer trust, the cordage trust and the barbed wire trust upon whom the farmer depended only exacerbated the problem homesteaders and small farmers had in trying to establish a livable income for themselves and their families, and it must be said, an income sufficient enough for him to be able to purchase the array of finished goods needed for farming. Meanwhile, and in contrast to tariff-protected finished products the farmer had to buy, cash crops were almost exclusively sold, not at domestic prices, but at world prices, forcing U.S. farmers to compete with countries whose legal and economic systems enabled their farmers to produce at much lower prices.

Even worse, the erosion of farm income caused by the tariff was magnified by the fact that the farmer was also forced to compete with cheap world prices set by the international markets in larger cities like Chicago, New York and Liverpool in order to sell his cash crops, whether said crops actually ended up being exported or not. In real terms, and after adding in transportation and other costs, this often as not meant that "a bushel of wheat that brought one dollar in Chicago in 1880 cost farmers sixty-three cents to produce and forty-five cents to ship from the Great Plains to that Chicago terminal."

As Loucks would later comment: "Our farmers are compelled to compete in the world's markets, where the price is fixed by the uncontrolled law of supply and demand, with our competitors having cheaper land, the use of money or credit for less than half the rate of interest, and public transportation untaxed for private profit. [Our agricultural sector] is unprotected from foreign competition in our own markets, discriminated against by legislation at every turn, and the prey of every protected and special privileged industrial and commercial trust."

In addition, as the Populists and their predecessors such as the Grange societies and the Alliances well knew, the problems created by cheap world prices were compounded for small, independent farmers by the monopolistic practices of the railroads as well as the "line" elevator operators associated with the railroads and the high transportation costs charged by railroads (which themselves had huge debt burdens to absorb). Not only did these hastily erected debt-and-speculative driven distribution systems result in tremendous amounts of cash crops being shipped eastward at exorbitant and often erratic freight rates, they also created handsome profits for many of the owners of the largest of the railroad conglomerates and grain brokerages, causing farmers to wonder "Why should the Kansas farmer have to sell his corn for 8 or 10 cents a bushel when the New York grain broker could and did demand upwards of a dollar for it?"

In her 1918 *The Populist Uprising*, author Elizabeth Barr writes of the railroads, and government's role in their formation:

> Instead of the people building the necessary arteries of distribution the privilege was delegated by the government to private corporations and individuals who used their power to perpetrate the most flagrant injustices upon the people dependent on them for a means of marketing their produce and securing supplies. . .

> The greed of these corporations knew no bounds. In the first place, the national and state governments realizing that railroads were essential to the development of the country, especially the vast areas beyond the reach of the waterways, gave immense grants of land outright to these corporations. The companies then required the citizens of the localities through which the road was to be built to vote vast sums in bonds, in most cases more than the road would cost. Sometimes the people were given stock for this money, but if they were, the company always reorganized and cheated them out of it later. The next step was to sell "watered stock" for several times the worth of the road, and then charge the people a tariff for service, high enough to pay big dividends on this inflated valuation. But not content with these injustices

they made discriminating freight rates in such a way that they had complete control of the distribution of products and had the industries of the people at their mercy...

But the transportation companies, not content with extortion from the people, oppressed their laborers beyond endurance. According to the Kansas Bureau of Labor for the year 1886, the railroads did not pay a living wage on which a family could subsist comfortably while employment lasted, to say nothing of saving for periods of enforced idleness.

These railroad corporations were privileged characters. They avoided taxation, secured any legislation they happened to want, and made and unmade public officials. All public officials and state and national legislators, as well as newspaper men, rode around on free passes and charged their mileage up to the people.

To their credit, so long as the nation harbored huge swaths of underfed and starving populations within its borders, the Populists steadfastly refused to accept the standard excuses that low crop prices meant better affordability or that big crop surpluses caused low prices. For one thing, cheap prices did not substantively improve the ability of a low wage earner or a jobless person to purchase food, but the situation did mean that the farmer had fewer people to sell to. As Henry Loucks remarked in his 1895 textbook, America had an under-consumption problem, due to low wages, not an overproduction problem.

Cheap crop prices did of course keep farm income low, hampering farmer's ability to pay off debt, or even survive. In turn, low farm income could and did negatively impact national income as a whole. It was in fact, as Hicks and others state, low farm income that led to the national Depression of 1893 – which depression had actually started in the late 1880s for both the Great Plains and the Southern cotton-growing regions.

The politically endorsed goal of transforming America into an industrial world power was achieved within the three decades following the Civil War, moving the United States from fourth place among world industrial powers to first. This achievement came at significant cost to the overwhelming majority of the population, farmers, small businessmen and workers alike, and it represented a marked departure from the original vision of the founding generation.

Land: The Heritage of the People - or the Speculators and Foreign Syndicates?

The increasingly untenable economic and monetary situation in the years after the Civil War played a key role in the emergence of the western farm mortgage market, created by eastern capital, which included not only money raised through foreign syndicates but also the hard-earned dollars of small investors who themselves were not immune to the allure of the "western farm craze."

As explained by R. Alton Lee in *Principle Over Party,* so effectively had the western farm craze been promoted by land and railroad agents that "Creditors readily accepted mortgages on land in Dakota Territory that they had never seen and from settlers they did not know. Securities that ordinarily could not be sold found eager speculators during the boom. Such was the promise of success in the territory that land parcels in the fictitious Capitola in Spink County, for instance, were sold many times over in eastern markets before buyers discovered that the town did not exist." Creditors were enticed into this kind of investment because of the high interest rates, which typically were around six to eight percent on real estate mortgages and 30 percent on chattel mortgages. Lee remarked that the "avalanche of credit was far greater than actual need, leading to extravagant over-investing, much like what would happen a century later."

Ironically, while wages and farm prices were plummeting, land values were increasing, oftentimes by as much as 400 to 600 percent. The reason, as observed by Lee, was rampant speculation. It was, therefore, highly probable that exploding land prices were a principle motivating factor for many homesteaders including both our paternal and maternal ancestors to move to

Dakota Territory. Not only did mountains of overly optimistic promotional material serve as exceedingly effective enticement, but also farmland in Iowa and points east had simply become priced out of reach. In fact, as early as 1871 the Iowa Railroad Land Company alone was already offering 1.7 million acres in Iowa and 180,000 acres in Nebraska for $8 to $10 an acre, making the cost of a standard size farm of 160 acres somewhere around $1600, a princely sum in those days. (This situation would of course reverse itself once foreclosure rates moved skyward.)

Lee further relates that after 1893 many small eastern investors in the newly developed securitized farm mortgage market lost everything as mortgage investment companies, tentacles of which stretched all the way to London, Scotland, France and elsewhere, went into receivership. But Western farm debt kept piling up as institutional investors such as Eastern savings banks, building and loan associations and most especially life insurance companies stepped in to fill the void.

As eastern capital flowed west and south over the decades following the Civil War, farmers and their families worked longer and harder to repay their debts, sending more and more of their products, and income used to pay off debts, to the northeastern financial centers. In this way, farms in the south and west literally fed eastern urban industrialization, and most of it was accomplished through increasingly oppressive levels of debt underwritten by Eastern capital, most of which capital represented the earnings (and savings) of the *entire* nation. Capital, as measured in money and crops, was in effect being exported out of farm country to the Eastern financial centers, due, as the Populists asserted, to a lack of government-issued money, thereby forcing down both wages and farm income and causing farmers in particular to over-rely on debt instead of their proven ability and desire to complete an honest day's work through which their families could be fed and their debts could be paid.

Although assorted family-related documents indicate that our own ancestors seem to have resisted, to a large degree and for a time, the overall trend toward heavy debt, it was the pressure of this debt that prompted many farmers, against their better judgement, to shift away from small mixed farming and into monoculture (cash crop) operations. This was especially true in the cotton south. Fading into memory was the Jeffersonian/agrarian ideal of self-sufficiency in which land ownership was a better measure of economic status than income. Gradually taking its place was a largely urban society dominated by industrial corporations and supported by soil-destroying mono-crop agriculture – and accompanied by escalating debt nation-wide.

Further compounding farmers' troubles was the fact that interest rates for Western farmers skyrocketed after the financial crisis of 1887. As alluded to earlier, the 1893 crisis actually began in farm country after Eastern flow of capital (in the form of loans) slowed to a snail's pace in 1887, eventually leading to the massive nation-wide crash of 1893. Mortgage companies were forced to dramatically retrench their activities, or they went bankrupt altogether. Tight credit and tanking farm prices led to increased foreclosures and increasingly fewer people to purchase finished goods or pay railroad freight charges.

Meanwhile the purchasing power of the dollar continued its upward course, thanks to the "sound money" advocates and the contraction of the money supply. In *The Populist Revolt*, John D. Hicks explains what this "dear" dollar, combined with debt and decreasing crop prices was doing to the farmer. Consider, explained Hicks, that a farmer borrowed $1000 on his land for a typical five-year term. We all know that the farmer must pay back that $1000 plus interest at the end of the five-year term but the problem for the farmer came in when the farmer tries to repay his loan in "yesterday's dollars." Whereas the farmer's $1000 loan at the time of signing might have meant he needed to sell 1000 bushels of wheat or 10,000 pounds of cotton (plus interest) to pay off the loan, when it came time to pay the loan off five years later, he might very well need to sell 1500 bushels of wheat or 15,000 pounds of cotton solely due to the increase in the purchasing power of the dollar. That is, the "dearer" dollar was able to purchase one and half bushels of wheat when previously the same dollar could purchase only one, requiring the farmer to work that much harder to pay off his loan. Interest, Hicks points out, must likewise be expressed in terms of produce which means that proportionately more wheat or cotton must be raised to satisfy the interest payment when the loan came due. All of this left the farmer with fewer dollars to purchase needed goods and services.

Similarly, by way of rebutting the opposition who claimed that increasing the money supply would only raise prices and upset the present financial system, Henry Loucks in *The New Monetary System*, very clearly points out the flaws of their argument:

> When the opposition is forced to admit the proposition that the volume of money in circulation regulates the value of products to be exchanged, they meet us with the counter proposition that, while it is true that an increase in the volume of money would increase the price of what we have to sell, it would at the same time increase the price of what we have to buy, which, in the end would be no benefit to us but would upset our present financial system, which, they claim, is the very best in the world, in proof of which they assert (and it is true) that a dollar now will buy more of the necessities and luxuries than at any other time during the last thirty years. *They seemingly forget that there are two sides to the question; that it will require more of the products of labor to buy that dollar now. We are on the other side.*

In the following chapter of the same book, Loucks correctly observes that:

> Stability of prices can only be maintained when money and products to be exchanged increase in relative proportion. A money that appreciates in value is just as dishonest as a money that depreciates in value, and more injurious, in that it benefits the few, the creditors, and injures the many, the debtors. A money of changing value is and has been in all ages the harvest of moneychangers and speculators. It is impossible to have a stable money responding to the demands of trade as needed, based on anything uncertain in value and depending wholly on chance or accident for discovery.

In the 1920 book titled *History of the Czechs in the State of South Dakota,* Dvorak explains the effect this economic situation had on many of the early farmers in Brule County, where our grandfather had located, who got bogged down in debt, paying from 12 to 50% interest. Some borrowed on their land, others bought merchandise on credit but when crops came up short year after year, many lost everything, and the entire area became desolate as people abandoned their land. Dvorak says that the worst was in 1894 when the entire northwest, not just Brule County where our grandfather had located, suffered such drought and hot winds that crops throughout the area were poor.

Hicks points out that by 1890, census takers counted one farm mortgage for every two people in Kansas and North Dakota and one for every three in Nebraska, South Dakota and Minnesota. This does not count those who had already been turned into tenant farmers, which Lee says represented 27 percent of all farmers in the Great Plains.

When the farmer could no longer obtain money on his real estate, he usually mortgaged his chattels, with the result in many localities being that nearly everything that could carry a mortgage was required to do so. In South Dakota, many families were kept from leaving for the East only by the fact that their horses and wagons were mortgaged and could therefore by law not be taken beyond state boundaries. Although our own ancestors seemed to have escaped at least for a while, debt followed pioneers westward regardless of the price of land, and it did so with a ferocity surpassed only by farmers in the south.

Despite the fiction that because settlers like our own Dakota Boom ancestors had access to "free" land through the Homestead Act they had only themselves or bad luck to blame if they failed, the fact was that bringing a homestead into production was anything but free, never mind all the other hardships, including debt, that went along with such an endeavor. As historian Herbert Schell says in his *History of South Dakota,* it took a minimum of $1000 to bring a homestead into production at the time of the Dakota Boom, or many times the average per capita wealth.

Economic hardships, even more than physical and emotional hardships, do help explain why only forty percent of the two million people who started homesteads under the 1862 Homestead Act were successful in earning title to their land. Perhaps even more astonishing is the fact that most of the Western land made available by the 1862 Homestead Act and succeeding acts (such as the Railroad Enabling Act of 1866) went to speculators, including foreign and domestic syndicates, mining and land development companies, and railroads. Grants to railroads alone totaled 325,000 square miles, which is an area almost equal to the original thirteen states. All told, only 80 million acres out of the 500 million acres dispersed by the General Land Office between 1862 and 1904 went to homesteaders!

It is perhaps of some interest to note here that there was an interesting difference between Federal land policy in the five public domain states of the South (which included Alabama, Florida, Louisiana, Arkansas and Mississippi) after the Civil War and land policy which was in force elsewhere in the United States. This was due to the passage of the Southern Homestead Act of 1866, which was intended to help small southern landowners purchase land at low prices instead of being forced to remain in the crop lien/tenant system that had been in place in some areas even before the Civil War. This Act reserved approximately 47 million acres of Southern public domain land for small landholders, and prohibited large purchases, but by 1876 these limitations were removed and the public domain states of the South were again open to unrestricted cash purchases.

In addition, more than 25,000,000 acres in Washington State, Oregon, New Mexico, Kansas and Colorado were opened to cash purchase by executive order. In 1868 Congress established a new land district in Nebraska and authorized the President to offer this land at public sale. And so it went in an ever-lasting back-and-forth struggle between the people and the money power, as the Populists called them.

It was no coincidence then that foreign ownership of large land tracts was another area of major concern for the Populists. We find some of the Populist objections in an article titled *The Land Question* provided by Francis Schulte in the 1895 *Little Statesman.* In this article, Schulte first comments that "foreign land-owning has much impeded the development of the Western commonwealth. These great landowners positively refuse to sell. They prefer to use a system of agencies and bailiffs, with the result that serious complications have resulted. The State legislatures have done their best to deal with the question but with only indifferent success."

Then, citing data that had appeared in the Chicago *Record,* Schulte pointed out that, per the *Record,* "nearly 20,000,000 acres of American land are owned by landlords in England and Scotland, and the *Record* omits entirely the Arkansas Valley Company in Colorado, whose enclosures embrace over a million acres alone; the Prairie Cattle Company (Scotch) another million, and dozens of other syndicates which will nearly bring the total up to 30,000,000 acres. There is also a Dutch syndicate which owns 5,000,000 acres of grazing land in the Western states and a German syndicate owning 2,000,000 acres in various states. It is safe to say that not less than 40,000,000 acres of the land of this nation is owned in Europe."

This background helps explain the following plank of the Omaha Platform of 1892: *"The land, including all the natural sources of wealth, is the heritage of the people, and should not be monopolized for speculative purposes, and alien ownership of land should be prohibited. All land now held by railroads and other corporations in excess of their actual needs, and all lands now owned by aliens should be reclaimed by the government and held for actual settlers only."*

In short and as the Populists charged, the sum total of the situation including the tariff, "tight" monetary policies, unpayable debt and a myriad of special privileges given to the railroads, trusts, foreign syndicates and the banks, had the effect of ruining legions of independent producers and taking the natural resources of the state from the hands of the people and giving them over to wealthy speculators and the large trusts and combines.

South Dakota Historian Herbert Schell pointed out that because the primary benefits accrued from a government policy of free or cheap western land went to the speculator and *not* the homesteader or small farm purchaser, the result was a perversion, if not an actual violation, of the spirit of the original 1862 homestead law. We often hear about how it was the settlers who pushed the Native American Indians off their land, starving and killing them in the process. But truth be told, it was, more often than not, the clamor of these well-funded, politically powerful individuals, conglomerates, and syndicates – foreign and otherwise - that did the Native American Indians as well as ordinary settlers in, by forcing wide scale, intensive development well before anyone was ready.

Yet bad as things were economically and politically for the newly minted Populists, Populists had no intention of overthrowing the existing government. Instead, argues historian Charles Postel in his award-winning book *The Populist Vision*, Populists sought sweeping economic and political changes that, like the Jeffersonians of Revolutionary America, were specifically designed to bring about a more inclusive society.

Farm Hierarchies of the South and West, with a connection to our grandfather

In his book *Greenbackers, Knights of Labor and Populists*, Matthew Hild points out that farms in the postbellum South could be divided into several categories. At the top of the socioeconomic ladder were the planters and large landowning "farmers" whose main focus was cash crops, especially cotton. Though representing just two or three percent of southern farmers, their land holdings and their focus on a single cash crop that was (need it be said) tended by others allowed them to be "lords of acres if not slaves." After the Civil War, cheap labor became a primary concern for this top rung of so-called "farmers."

The second and third tiers of this socioeconomic ladder illustrate why land ownership was (and is) so important to farmers. The first segment of this group was comprised of small landholding farmers, who raised both cash and subsistence crops, and usually livestock and poultry, on about one to two hundred acres. These farmers were less susceptible to falling prey to escalating debt, but they were far from immune, with increasing numbers joining the ranks of tenant farming due to foreclosure.

Below this small landholder group were the tenant farmers, who were subdivided according to the amount of land rented. Those who occupied one or two hundred acres operated their farms as if they were owners. However, the need to pay rent in either cash or crops cut into their profits, making them less prosperous than small landowners. The poorer class of tenants farmed as little as twenty to fifty acres. Landlords provided these farmers with supplies, but the farmers usually paid somewhere between one half to two thirds of the crops they raised as rent. Many tenants also were forced to mortgage their share of the crop to a merchant, or even a landlord, in order to buy food and supplies, with interest rates on these loans reaching as high as 150 percent. Little surprise that by 1880 close to forty percent of all southern farmers were tenants of one form or another.

Then, at the very bottom of the agricultural ladder were the landless wage laborers who worked for the planter class. These "wage laborers" were paid about $8 to $12 a month during the mid 1880s. This could be compared to one of our paternal ancestors who, although he lived in Illinois, worked in Iowa during the summers in the 1870s as per old family letters. There he earned $1.50 a day, "after his fare money was deducted." This would have given him $30 a month, if he worked only twenty days out of the month, or five days a week.

Hild writes that "Planters identified more closely with industrialists as employers and shared their enmity and contempt for the Knights of Labor who organized both groups [of tenant farmers and landless wage laborers]." Contrary to claims of Samuel Gompers and the AFL, "the Knights of Labor not only organized many small farmers and farm laborers but also led strikes by southern black plantation workers for higher wages."

While farming in the South was concentrated around cotton as the cash crop of choice, farming in the Northern Plains was concentrated around wheat – and of course the great cattle barons further to the west focused on beef. In terms of numbers, homesteaders were the largest group of Northern Plains and Western small landholders, but whether these small landholders had homesteaded or purchased their farms, they would, by the 1890s, increasingly be made into tenants. In fact, as R. Alton Lee reports, by 1890 fully 27 percent of farms in the Great Plains were farmed by tenants on foreclosed land.

Although they usually raised "cash" crops many small Plains farmers, like the small landholders of the South, practiced a more diversified form of farming, raising livestock and poultry as well. Not so the large Northern Plains landholders who oversaw the development of the "bonanza farms" that were made possible by an extensive land grant provided by Congress in 1864 to aid in financing the Northern Pacific Railway Company. The Panic of 1873 prompted that Railway Company to shed the debt it had acquired in the process of building its "road." It did this by exchanging its land for bonds and preferred stock. This in turn was accomplished by promoting large scale agriculture and establishing showcase farms called bonanzas – with nearly all of these so-called bonanzas located within forty miles of the Red River Valley of Minnesota and the Dakota Territory. Like the large landholders of the South, these "farms" were often managed by absentee owners.

Oliver Dalyrimple's Bonanza Farm during the 1877 harvest, showing the large crew and field supervisors.

A total of 91 Bonanza farms were developed, ranging from 3,000 to 100,000 acres. They employed as few as 15 and as many as 1,000 low paid migrant laborers per farm and were managed by professional managers. Oliver Dalyrimple, who had established himself as the wheat king of Minnesota by 1874, was one such fellow who formed a "Bonanza Farm" partnership with the Northern Pacific through which he would eventually own about 100,000 acres. The accompanying photo shows the 1877 harvest at the Dalyrimple "farm," together with a sizable team of migrant workers and crew managers required to reap the harvest.

When the partnership between Oliver and the Northern Pacific was dissolved in 1896, Dalyrimple and his sons divided the "farm" into ten units. By 1917 the Dalyrimple boys determined that the *interest income on the proceeds of selling their farms* would amount to *more* than the profits obtained through farming.

Although Dalyrimple's bonanza farm was located in North Dakota, it is intriguing to note that one of the parcels eventually acquired by our grandfather in Pershing Township, Buffalo County, South Dakota was known as "the Dalyrimple land." We have been unable to establish any connection to Oliver and his sons for this rather intriguing detail. However, and because the parcel had previously been owned by our grandfather's son Charles who had for a short time lived in North Dakota, it may be that the Charles' original intent had been to raise "Dalyrimple" wheat on that parcel.

One reason the American Federation of Labor may have mistakenly assumed that the Alliances were "composed of employing farmers" was because these Bonanza farms, owing to the promotional capabilities of the Northern Pacific Railway Company, quickly became the subject of national farm periodicals and were visited by political and business leaders of both the United States and Europe, giving the impression that the farm community as a whole was, or perhaps should be, "composed of employing farmers." Oliver Dalyrimple, for example, was one of those who received a personal visit from President Hayes and an entourage of journalists, business, and political leaders in 1879.

Despite the attention the Bonanza farms received and the misperceptions that resulted, this group of "farmers" had nothing to do with northern Populist farmers. If anything, they were disliked by homesteaders and all small farmers, who it should be noted were rarely in the position to employ anyone, much less a crew of fifteen to a thousand. Homesteaders and small farmers were also forced to compete for market share with Bonanza farms for whatever cash crops they were raising.

1877 photo of an excursion train loaded with politicians, journalists, financiers and academics who were there to observe the harvest at the Dalyrimple Bonanza Farm.

Thus, and struggling under increasing debt, they often worked from sunrise to sunset seven days a week and had to rely on the free labor of their families to get them through one crop year to the next. This while the migrant workers of the Bonanza farms left the area in off-season in search of low paid seasonal work in the mines and lumber mills of Iowa and elsewhere.

The Misrepresented Money Plank

William Jennings Bryan's famous *Cross of Gold* speech of 1896 is perhaps the greatest political speech in American history. Yet most of what is remembered and most of what is written about that speech (which earned Bryan the Populist presidential endorsement) recalls only that he demanded free coinage of silver at a ratio of 16 to one with gold. Although "free silver" was a very popular issue particularly in the West, very few realize that the "pro-silver" Democrat Bryan also called for government issue of paper money, per the main and most important Populist plank. This "mis-remembering" is a product of enormous amounts of propaganda, during and since that time. As a fair study of the period shows, South Dakotan Henry Loucks, among other Populist leaders, accurately pointed out that "no other plank in our demands has been so misrepresented as the money plank."

Particularly when it came to the money question, Populist books and writings were replete with citations from such experts and authorities as the U.S. Supreme Court, State Supreme Courts, leading monetary experts including Alexander Del Mar and the U.S Monetary Commission, Blackstone's Law, Tiffany's Constitutional Law, recorded comments of U.S. Legislators, past Presidents, the U.S. Treasury, U.S. Census Reports, widely respected philosophers and economists such as John Stuart Mill, David Ricardo, David Hume, even ancient luminaries such as Pliny, and many others. In chapter five of his Populist textbook *The New Monetary System*, Henry Loucks offers a passage from *Philosophy of Price* by contemporary N. A. Dunning that sheds some light on just why it was that "no other plank in our demands has been so misrepresented as the money plank":

> The truth is, the most enormous power known to man, or that ever can be his, lies in money—in the increase and decrease of its quantity. It is the tide of human affairs upon which all things must rise or sink. It is inevitable and cannot be resisted. This power has been obtained through the carelessness of the people, who have been and are now held in ignorance for that very purpose. So early as 1577 we find the keen and piercing intellect of Bodin saying the following; 'For men have so well obscured the facts about money that the great part of the people do not see them at all. The money era do as the doctors do, who talk Latin before women, and use Greek characters, Arab words, and Latin abbreviations, fearing that if the people understood their receipts they would not have much opinion of them.'

In the 1895 book titled *The Little Statesman*, Francis Schulte schools the reader about the history of government-issued money as well as paper money specifically, including how the greenbacks were negatively affected by the "exception clause" which gave special privilege to gold thereby allowing the false claim that greenbacks had depreciated against gold. Schulte's expose' in part:

> Legal tender paper money is usually issued in times of war when gold and silver are hoarded or exported from the country, and as a consequence, such legal tender is put to the severest possible tests, those of an impelled government, disturbed industry, and impeded foreign trade. Nevertheless, history abounds with instances to prove the entire sufficiency of this kind of money.

> In 1156 the Republic of Venice established a system of paper credits which served as the principal circulating medium of that country until 1797. This money was always at par and frequently at a premium. In 1770 the Russian government issued its own notes, which sustained the government through two wars and commanded a premium over coin. In 1797 to 1823 England issued $225,000,000 full legal tender paper with which to carry on a war against Napoleon. In his *Political Economy*, John S. Mill says of these notes: "After they were made a legal tender they never depreciated at all."

> . . . . .During the colonial period of American history, several of the colonies issued and *successfully maintained* legal tender paper money. . . .

.....During the war of the last rebellion in the United States (1861-5) the government issued a volume of legal tender "greenbacks" which on July 1, 1865 was outstanding to the amount of $432,687,966.

The first $60,000,000 of this paper money . . . called demand notes, was made full legal tender for all debts public and private. This issue never fell below and often was above par as compared to gold. In a speech delivered in the U.S. Senate July 4, 1862, Hon. John Sherman said of these demand notes: "The notes are now held and hoarded. The first issue of $60,000,000 were issued with the right of being converted into 6 percent twenty-year bonds and with the privilege of being paid for duties in customs. They are now far above par and hoarded."

In Schucker's *Life of Salmon P. Chase*, p 235, the author says: "The demand notes, being receivable for customs the same as coin, kept pace with the advances of the price of coin."

All of the greenbacks except the first $60,000,000 were purposely depreciated by the "exception clause," that is, they were made legal tender for all debts, public and private, *except duties on imports and interest on the public debt*, which latter were required to be paid in coin. This exception clause created a special demand for coin, and as a consequence metallic money rose to a great premium, at one time (July 1864) being at a premium of $2.35 in greenbacks to $1 in coin. That these greenbacks were purposely depreciated stands upon the evidence of Hon. John Sherman, who in a report as chairman of the Senate Finance Committee, made on the 12th of November, 1867, said: "But it was found that with such a restriction upon the [first issue of demand] notes the bonds could not be negotiated, and it became necessary to depreciate the notes in order to make a market for bonds."

As a matter of fact, the greenbacks, discredited by legislation as they were, did not depreciate in comparison with commodities, but gold *appreciated* owing to the special demand created for it by law. The people never lost confidence in the government paper money, even in the darkest hours of the panic of 1873. . .

Free coinage of silver was another important Populist issue that has been surrounded by considerable misunderstanding and confusion. As nicely explained by Populist W. H. Harvey, who was himself an attorney, in his 1894 *Coin's Financial School* (which is replete with actual governmental statutes and official data of the United States and around the world), the 1792 Coinage Act fixed our monetary unit to consist of 371 ¼ grains of pure silver. That amount of silver constituted one dollar, and the ratio between silver and gold was 15 to 1, meaning fifteen silver dollars containing 371 ¼ grains of silver each were equal to one gold dollar. All other money was to be counted from the silver dollar; dimes, quarters and so forth were exact fractional parts of this silver dollar. Importantly, the value of the gold dollar was counted from the silver units or dollars, meaning that gold coins were regulated by that ratio. *By these means America's monetary system could be insulated from European influence via international trade which generally looked to gold as the desired method of payment.*

When in 1834, by act of Congress, the 15 to 1 ratio of silver to gold was changed to 16 to 1, the gold dollar was made smaller by reducing the amount of gold it contained from 24.7 grains down to 23.2 grains pure gold. Thus, said Harvey's main fictionalized character Mr. Coin, "up to 1873 we were on what was known as a bimetallic basis, *but what was in fact a silver basis*, with gold as a companion metal enjoying the same privileges as silver, except that silver fixed the unit, and the value of gold was regulated by it."

America's founders, said Harvey's Mr. Coin, chose silver for good reason. First it was more reliable, being scattered among all the people and favored by them, as gold was considered the money of the rich. However, the "Crime of '73" effectively put America on a defacto gold standard by discontinuing manufacture of silver coins and according gold favored status when it came to paying off debt. Harvey has "Mr. Coin" explain in more detail what happened:

On February 12, 1873, Congress passed an act purporting to be a revision of the coinage laws. This law covers 15 pages of our statutes. It repealed the unit clause in the law of 1792, and in its place substituted a law in the following language:

That the gold coins of the United States shall be a one-dollar piece which at the standard weight of twenty-five and eight-tenths grains shall be the unit of value.

It then deprived silver of its right to unrestricted free coinage and destroyed it as legal tender money in the payment of debts, except to the amount of five dollars.

At that time we were all using paper money. No one was handling silver and gold coins. It was when specie payments were about to be resumed that the country appeared to realize what had been done. No newspapers on the morning of February 13, 1873, and at no time in the vicinity of that period, had any account of the change. General Grant, who was President of the United States at that time, said afterwards, that he had no idea of it, and would not have signed the bill if he had known that it demonetized silver.

In the language of Senator Daniel of Virginia, it seems to have gone through Congress 'like the silent tread of a cat.'

An army of a half million of men invading our shores, the warships of the world bombarding our coasts, could not have made us surrender the money of the people and substitute in its place the money of the rich. A few words embraced in fifteen pages of statutes put through Congress in the rush of bills did it. The pen was mightier than the sword.

But we are not here to deal with sentiment. We are here to learn facts. Plain, blunt facts.

The law of 1873 made gold the unit of value. And that is the law today [1894]. When silver was the unit of value, gold enjoyed free coinage, and was legal tender in the payment of all debts. Now things have changed. Gold is the unit and silver does not enjoy free coinage.

Harvey then has his "Mr. Coin" lay to rest the myth, which persists to this day, that overproduction of silver as compared with gold was at that time causing silver prices to decline:

On page 21 of my Handbook you will find a table on this subject, compiled by Mulhall, the London statistician. *It gives the quantity of gold and silver in the world* both coined and uncoined at six periods — at the years 1600, 1700, 1800, 1848, 1880, and 1890. It shows that in 1600 there were 27 tons of silver to one ton of gold. In 1700, 34 tons of silver to one ton of gold. In 1800, 32 tons of silver to one ton of gold. In 1848, 31 tons of silver to one ton of gold. In 1880, 18 tons of silver to one ton of gold. In 1890, 18 tons of silver to one ton of gold.

The United States is producing more silver than it ever did or was until recently. But the balance of the world is producing much less. They are fixing the price on our silver and taking it away from us, at their price. The report of the Director of the Mint, published the other day, shows the world's production of precious metals last year was gold, $167,917,337; silver, $143,096,239. So you see the facts are just the opposite of what you had supposed. Instead of becoming more plentiful, it is less plentiful.

Anyone can get the official statistics by writing to the treasurer at Washington and asking for his official book of statistics. Also write to the Director of the Mint and ask him for his report. If you get no answer write to your Congressman. These books are furnished free and you will get them.

You can see by Mr. Coin's explanation that "the rest of the world was fixing the price of our silver and taking silver away from us at their price." From this and from John Hicks and Alexander del Mar discussed earlier, we see how it came to be that by 1896, the price ratio of silver to gold *based on world prices* was about 30 to 1. The silver mines simply could not profitably provide silver for coinage at the 30 to one ratio, but they could do so at the old legal ratio of 16 to 1, which would still of course legally make the silver dollar "dearer" than the gold dollar. The claim that the Populists wanted to "inflate" the money supply stems from this fact since unlimited, free coinage of silver at a ratio of 16 to 1 essentially meant that, with more lawful money of certain value in circulation, debts would be more payable.

Since gold and silver commodity prices, like that of wheat and cotton, were set by foreign syndicates and their political allies, adherence to the legal ratio (as defined by U.S. law) of silver to gold would also interfere with the ability of profiteers to benefit from the fluctuations in value of those commodities, again as explained by Alexander del Mar at the start of this chapter. Thus, as Schulte writes, "The People's Party are in favor of free coinage of silver at the ratio of 16 to 1 without waiting for consent of any other nation on earth. We favor this proposition because it will increase the volume of currency in circulation and contribute not only to make better prices for the products of labor, *but to break the power which the bankers now have to control the currency.*"

Moreover, and as Populists could explain in minute detail, there were numerous problems associated with the species basis for money. Schulte explains that one of these problems gave "greedy speculators" the ability to "work a corner in gold and thus extort large sums in profits which the people eventually have to pay." And since both silver and gold were commodities which of course fluctuate in value and also are used as money, profit-taking on price fluctuations of these two metals had always been a major activity in the gold/silver trade. When the commodity price of a metal rose above its "dollar" stamp, profiteers would melt the coin down and sell it as bullion, using the profits elsewhere. Thus, as Loucks points out, "A money of changing value is and has been in all ages the harvest of moneychangers and speculators."

The major reason that "no other plank in our demands has been so misrepresented as the money plank" had (and still has) to do with the fact that so few understand what money is. In chapter four of his textbook *The New Monetary System*, Henry Loucks lays out an explanation of money as clear as any Alexander Del Mar himself came up with (but which at least appeared to be modeled after Del Mar). Loucks as follows, describing money as a unit of account, not a measure of value

> Money is a *representative* of value, made necessary by the progress of civilization. It is a unit, not a measure of value. The government could not well measure value for individuals; it can provide a unit of value for facilitating exchanges of value but each individual must for himself measure the value of that which he wishes to sell as well as of that which he wishes to buy.

> For instance, one man has a horse to sell; he measures its value at $150.00. Another man wants to purchase that horse but his measure of value for this particular horse is $125.00. The eye of each measures the value. The government cannot come in and fix the measure of value for the horse. The buyer and seller must agree on a definite measure of value before any exchange can be made and this measure is designated in units of value—dollars.

> There is not and never has been any such thing as "a money of the world." Each nation creates and regulates its own money or unit of value. Our congress has reserved this right. See our constitution, Art. I, Sec. 8, under No. 30, "To coin money, regulate the value thereof and of foreign coins, etc."

> Congress having reserved to itself the sole right to coin (create, make,) money, carries with it the right and duty to issue money and to impress its sovereign power (fiat) on something capable of receiving and retaining the impression.

Schulte fleshes out how all "dollars" whether silver, gold, paper or something else get their value through government "fiat," and asks a rather rhetorical question about how a new "greenback," issued interest free by the government and unbacked by anything other than the productive capacity of the people, might work to the betterment of humanity. Schulte as follows:

We [the Populists] are charged with wanting to flood the country with fiat money. If the same amount of money per capita we had after the war, and which Thomas Jefferson concedes as proper in his letter to Mr. Epps, is "flooding the country" we plead guilty.

We plead guilty to the charge of "fiat." We will agree to eat any kind of dollar which are brought to us that is not fiat. The "fiat fools" are those who don't know that money that is not fiat is not money at all. A silver dollar is worth 100 cents and will buy as much as a gold dollar because it is fiat. Take the fiat of the law from it and it is worth only 48 cents.

Occasionally we are told that the government can't issue paper money unless it has gold and silver back of it. This is the parrot-like repetition of what the bankers say. That is what they said during the last war. But the government did issue over seventeen hundred million of it. If the government has the power to issue it to pay men to shoot other men down, why has it not the power to issue it to pay men who are idle and suffering for the necessities of life, to construct public works?

Henry Demerest Lloyd, who was a delegate to the 1896 Populist Convention, corroborates Schulte's remarks about the true purpose and best function of government-issued money by pointing out that the Populists, or People's Party as he called them, having received most of their education from the Greenbackers, believed in a currency redeemable in all the products of human labor, and not in gold alone, nor gold and silver. Clearly, as Loucks and Bodin would both have agreed, so effectively have the facts about money been obscured that the great part of the people even today do not see or understand them at all. Yet the facts are there for those who care to look, and they were presented in well researched, digestible form by Populist leaders specifically for "hayseed" farmers who would in turn diligently study these works, then discuss them until they had absorbed enough to write editorials and other opinion pieces themselves.

Henry Loucks sums up what the Farmers' Alliance and allied groups, together with the Populists, were all about in Chapter Four of his textbook. After providing a clear explanation of what money is (provided above) Loucks cites several authorities on the government's right and prerogative to issue the nation's money, beginning with Tiffany and ending with Blackstone, followed by a summary of those authorities, and then concluding with a summary of the Populist position. Here are some excerpts as written by Loucks:

Tiffany on Constitutional law, a standard authority, Chapter XII, (power of congress to coin money) Section 400, page 221, says: *"There is legally no such thing as gold or silver money, or paper money. Money is the sovereign authority impressed on that which is capable of taking and retaining the impression. That upon which the stamp is placed is called coin; the coin may be metal, parchment or paper. THE VALUE IS IN THE STAMP AND NOT IN THE METAL OR MATERIAL."*

. . . .The great jurist, Blackstone, says, (see Cooley's Blackstone, vol. I, page 276): *"The coining of money in all states is the act of the "sovereign power."*

It is clear, therefore, that congress has the right to coin, create, make, and issue money. It has always used the power, as in stamping gold, silver, nickel, copper, or on paper, as in greenbacks, treasury notes, and coin certificates, or delegated the power to corporations, as in the national banking system. Neither gold, silver, nickel, copper, or paper, is money until the fiat of government, 'sovereign power,' is stamped upon it. When that is done it assumes a legal value regardless of its commodity value. . . .

The Farmer's Alliance together with twenty-one other farm and labor organizations, demand that the government shall make and issue the money the people need, a full legal tender for all debts, public and private, and in sufficient volume to do the business of the country on a cash basis; that it shall not be farmed out to corporations at 1 percent, who are privileged to loan it at the legal rate in the state in which the bank is situated, as national banks now do. They demand that this prerogative that has been given Congress by the people shall be exercised by Congress for the best interest of the whole people. Congress having the sole power, and having prohibited states and individuals from making money, is in duty bound to supply a sufficient volume to enable the people to do the business of the country; that is, exchange the products of labor on a cash basis. All charges for the use of money to exchange the products of labor is a tax on, and paid by, labor. A limited supply enables the usurer, who owns the money, to exact such rates for its use as to rob labor of its just reward. To be free labor must be emancipated from the power of money to oppress.

All of this should make it very clear that silver was never the main issue for the Populists; a government-issued, democratically circulated dollar with stable, debt-paying power was. Whether that "dollar" was to be stamped on paper, silver, gold or some other material was largely irrelevant. That said, and while it is true that "the money question" played a key role in the 1896 Presidential election it is equally true that well-financed propaganda together with shifting political sands played major roles in the end results.

The 1896 Election

Oddly, it had been leaders of the Republican Party, the party of Lincoln and the Greenback, who immediately after the Civil War began to carry out a policy of contracting the money supply by withdrawing the Greenbacks and putting the country on a gold basis by demonetizing silver in 1873. In response, silverite factions emerged within the Republican and Democratic Parties.

Silver Republicans were most prevalent in the West where, from the 1870s on, they succeeded in getting free silver included in Republican state platforms. With the admission of six new western states including North and South Dakota in 1889-90, these silver Republicans obtained passage of the Sherman Silver Purchase Act in July of 1890, the purported purpose of which was to get more silver-backed Treasury Notes into circulation. The actual purpose was to siphon off Populist votes for the benefit of the Republicans. Similarly, from the late 1870s on, a faction of the Democratic Party, known as "Silver Democrats" began advocating a policy of bimetallism instead of the defacto gold standard put in place by the demonetization of silver in 1873.

In addition, the American Bimetallic League, formed late in 1889, provided significant help in getting a majority of United States Senators to support a free silver bill. It is worth mentioning that a new, albeit short-lived, Silver Party had been formed in 1892 which also supported bimetallism and free silver. While this Party was strongest in Nevada, none other than the renowned monetary expert Alexander Del Mar, whose writings informed the Populist stance on "fiat" money, headed up the New York State Silver Party, and later was a California delegate to the Silver Party Convention held in Memphis in 1895 where he delivered a speech entitled "The Story of the Gold Conspiracy" which was then reprinted in his *A History of Monetary Crimes*. The Silver Party, not surprisingly, was aligned primarily with the Populist Party and to a lesser extent the Silver Republican Party via its Nevada connection.

Lest it be assumed that the Silver Party was focused on the idea of only using silver as the nation's currency, we include here a segment from the Declaration of Principles that were part of the 1896 platform of the Silver Party. Those even summarily familiar with the work of Alexander del Mar can almost see his hand in shaping these words:

First--*The paramount issue at this time in the United States is indisputably the money question. It is between the gold standard, gold bonds and bank currency on the one side, and the bimetallic standard, no bonds and Government currency on the other side.*

On this issue we declare ourselves to be in favor of a distinctively American financial system. We are unalterably opposed to the single gold standard and demand the immediate restoration to the constitutional standard of gold and silver by the restoration by this Government, independent of any foreign power, of the unrestricted coinage of gold and silver as the standard money at the ratio of 16 to 1 and upon terms of exact equality as they existed prior to 1873; the silver coin to be a full legal tender, equally with gold, for all debts and use, public and pri-

vate; and we favor such legislation as will prevent for the future the demonetization of <u>any</u> kind of legal tender money by private contract.

We hold that the power to hold and regulate a paper currency is inseparable from the power to coin money, and hence that all currency intended to circulate as money should be issued and its volume controlled by the general Government only and should be legal tender.

We are unalterably opposed to the issue by the United States of interest-bearing bonds in time of peace, and we denounce as a blunder worse than a crime the present Treasury policy, incurred by a Republican House, of plunging into debt by hundreds of millions in the vain attempt to maintain the gold standard by borrowing gold; and we demand the payment of all coin obligations of the United States, *as provided by existing laws,* in either gold or silver coin, *at the option of the Government and not at the option of the creditor.*

Second--That over and above all other questions of policy, we are in favor of restoring to the people of the United States the time-honored money of the Constitution--gold and silver; not one but both--the money of Washington and Hamilton, and Jefferson and Monroe, and Jackson and Lincoln, to the end that the American people may receive honest pay for an honest product; that the American debtor may pay his just obligations in an honest standard and not in a standard that has appreciated 100 per cent above all the great staples of our country; *and to the end, further, that silver standard countries may be deprived of the unjust advantage they now enjoy in the difference in exchange between gold and silver--an advantage which tariff legislation cannot overcome.*

We therefore confidently appeal to the people of the United States *to leave in abeyance for the moment all other questions, however important and even momentous they may appear, to sunder if need be all former ties and affiliations and unite in one supreme effort to free themselves and their children from the domination of the money power--a power more destructive than any which has ever been fastened upon the civilized men of any race or in any age.* And upon the consummation of our desires and efforts, we invoke the gracious favor of divine Providence.

It is worth briefly examining here the political context for the paragraph above concerning interest-bearing bonds, especially the phrase: "We denounce as a blunder worse than a crime the present Treasury policy, incurred by a Republican House, of plunging into debt by hundreds of millions in the vain attempt to maintain the gold standard by borrowing gold. . ." The context for this statement is briefly provided as follows.

In 1892, four years before the Silver Party platform came out, Grover Cleveland was elected President of the United States for a second term, after having lost his bid for a second term in 1888 to Benjamin Harrison. He was, and remains, the only President to be elected to two non-consecutive terms. As a gold-bugger and Bourbon Democrat who was aligned with the wealthy pro-business interests of the country, Republican and Democrat alike, Cleveland proved to be tone-deaf when it came to concerns of the Populists as well as the Southern Democrats, many of whom helped get him elected. As a result, many of these Southern Democrats, including Ben Tillman, turned to the silverites, while retaining their "redeemer" ideology.

The silver issue began to dominate politics and popular debate when eastern Republicans joined the "Bourbon" Democrats under Cleveland in 1893 to repeal the Sherman Act, to keep the country on a gold standard. A nationwide battle ensued with the Silverites and Populists, many of whom were in the Congress, taking center stage.

Consensus was that legislation that was in any way unfavorable to silver must be defeated. Additionally, it was agreed by the silverites and Populists that U.S. financial policy had to remain free from dependence on the financial policies of all other nations. Finally came the call for free and unlimited coinage of silver, for which Cleveland refused his support. Essentially, the problem with unconditional repeal of the Sherman Act was that not only would said repeal stop the purchase of silver and limit the currency to gold, but it would also limit whatever silver notes the national banks found profitable to issue. Furthermore, if the gold standard were to be maintained, the administration would need to issue gold bonds thereby increasing the national debt in a time of peace.

In a chapter entitled "Greenbackers, Goldbugs, and Silverites: Currency Reform and Politics, 1860-1897" by Paolo E. Colletta, that appeared in a 1963 book titled *The Gilded Age: A Reappraisal* edited by H. Wayne Morgan, author Colletta relates how the determined Cleveland found the authority to issue gold bonds in the refunding acts of 1870-71 which imposed high interest rates on long term issues. This enabled Cleveland to arrange two sales of gold bonds in 1894, which were made through syndicates that included the likes of J. P. Morgan and Company.

When it was discovered that much of the gold paid for the bonds had been withdrawn from the treasury, the Cleveland administration resorted to securing foreign gold through a private contract with J. P. Morgan and Company together with sixty-one European Associates in 1895. "This" says Colletta "incited raucus western and southern cries against the 'cursed plutocracy' which has 'seized control of the government,' for Cleveland could have sold the bonds by popular subscription. . .By selling bonds [Cleveland] saved the gold standard but saddled the country with a debt of about $262,000,000 from which the bankers profited."

The reader might recall that these events were mentioned earlier in excerpts from the Silver Party Platform.

Meanwhile, back on February 3, 1893, a little-known Democratic Congressman, who would serve two terms in the United States House of Representatives, voted against his President's request to repeal the Sherman Act. His name was William Jennings Bryan. As R. Alton Lee writes, the Cleveland Administration punished Bryan by "completely humiliating him at the next Nebraska state Democratic meeting, a move that served to solidify Bryan's support of the silver issue." At the 1896 national convention in Chicago, Bryan was on the platform committee and wrote the silver plank, which Lee says was "a defiance of a sitting president that was unprecedented in American history." Alexander Del Mar, monetary expert and member of the short-lived Silver Party was on hand in Chicago to endorse Bryan.

Henry Demerest Lloyd explains that the Populist leadership made what would turn out to be a serious tactical error for their 1896 convention. Lacking the more seasoned and skillful leadership of the late Leonidas Polk, Charles Macune who had disappeared from public view after resigning from the Alliance, and Henry Loucks who as leader of the Alliance was spending much of his time in Washington, D.C. working on Alliance business, the less well-seasoned Populist leaders decided to hold their convention *after* the two major parties had held theirs. Their choice was anchored by the belief that they, the Populists, would have an easy task of gathering into their ranks the bolting silver and anti-monopolist Republican and Democrats, thereby increasing their votes from an estimated two million to five million and thus allowing them to take the White House.

It is worthwhile to mention here that in the weeks leading up to the 1896 Populist convention, a well-known Greenbacker by the name of Colonel S. F. Norton, whose book *Ten Men of Money Island* had sold hundreds of thousands of copies, had been a serious contender for the Populist presidential nomination. Instead, the Democrats at their earlier convention shrewdly nominated William Jennings Bryan, who ran on the "free coinage of silver" platform, in keeping with the Silver Party platform discussed earlier. By the time of the Populist Convention, silverites dominated, forcing the Populists (against the wishes of Henry Loucks and other "old-timers") to agree to a "fusion" ticket at the presidential level. This then allowed the press and other interested parties to proclaim that the "money question" was a question of gold or silver money. As it turned out Bryan was endorsed by the Populist, Silver Republican and Democratic parties, along with other minor parties of note. Some of the "gold" democrats bolted to form the short-lived Gold

Democrat Party but most ended up voting for Republican candidate William McKinley who agreed to run as a gold-bugger.

Bryan, it should be noted, had in 1892 openly supported Populist candidate for President, Colonel James Weaver, former Greenbacker of Iowa, and he worked in his home state of Nebraska to unite the Populists and Democrats for the 1894 election. As illustrated by the following excerpt from his famous Cross of Gold speech Bryan clearly understood and supported the Populist message on "constitutional" money:

> We say in our platform that we believe that the right to coin and issue money is a function of government. We believe it. We believe that it is a part of sovereignty and can no more with safety be delegated to private individuals than we could afford private individuals to make penal statutes or levy taxes. Mr. Jefferson, who was once regarded as good Democratic authority, seems to have differed in opinion from the gentleman who has addressed us on the part of the minority ["sound money" specie advocates]. Those who are opposed to the proposition tell us that the issue of paper money is a function of the bank, and that government ought to go out of the banking business. *I stand with Jefferson rather than them, and tell them, as he did that the issue of money is a function of government, and that the banks should go out of the governing business.*
>
> . . . If they ask us why we do not embody in our platform all the things we believe in, we reply that *when we have restored the money of the Constitution all other necessary reforms will be possible; but until this is done there is no other reform that can be accomplished.*

For his part, Bryan's Presidential opponent William McKinley had been a "straddle bug" on the currency question right up to the Republican convention. His advisors and financial backers finally convinced him to endorse the gold standard over his more moderate inclination to favor bimetallism, which they claimed would lead to "inflation" (by increasing the money supply) thereby bankrupting the railroads and ruining the economy.

McKinley's supporters rewarded him by filling his coffers with $3.5 million for speakers and literally tons of literature advocating the Republican position on the money and tariff questions. This allowed McKinley to conduct his famous "Front Porch Campaign" to which Republican voters were shipped in by the trainload to listen to the candidate. As R. Alton Lee writes, Republican Party leadership also warned laborers of the dangers of foreign competition and furnished the traditional rural Republican newspaper outlets all over the country with copy on the political issues. At the same time Republican employers warned their workers that their job depended on McKinley's victory; if Bryan won they need not show up for work the next day.

In comparison, Bryan's campaign had at most an estimated $500,000, a paucity which he partially made up for with his demanding whistle-stop political tour. As Lee writes, "Bryan covered over eighteen thousand miles, and millions of people turned out to hear him speak. Many stayed at the railroad tracks where he would pass late at night in hopes of catching a glimpse of the "Boy Orator of the Platte." While Bryan campaigned most extensively in the East, he did make campaign swings through South Dakota in 1896 and also in 1900, when he again ran for President. We believe there is a very high probability that our grandfather and perhaps his whole family were on hand to see the "Boy Orator" at one or more of these "whistle-stops."

Bryan's popularity notwithstanding, D. Jerome Tweton states in an article titled *Considering Why Populism failed in North Dakota* that "in 1896, fusion came to South Dakota, but the Populists dictated the terms and maintained their separate identity [apart from the silverites]." Given that our grandfather was a delegate at the 1896 Populists' state convention in South Dakota and ran as a Populist two years later for County Commissioner, it is a near certainty that he was with the Populists and not the silverites on the money question.

The Declaration of Principles adopted by the People's Party in 1896 parallels many of the principles contained in the Silver Party's own Declaration of Principles, but it is perhaps its Preamble that bears repeating here:

> The People's party, assembled in National Convention, reaffirms its allegiance to the principles declared by the founders of the Republic, and also to the fundamental principles of just government as enunciated in the platform of the party in 1892. We recognize that, through the connivance of the present and preceding Administrations, the country has reached a crisis in its national life as predicted in our declaration four years ago, and that prompt and patriotic action is the supreme duty of the hour. We realize that, while we have political independence, our financial and industrial independence is yet to be attained by restoring to our country the constitutional control and exercise of the functions necessary to a people's government, which functions have been basely surrendered by our public servants to corporate monopolies. The influence of European money changers has been more potent in shaping legislation than the voice of the American people. Executive power and patronage have been used to corrupt our Legislatures and defeat the will of the people, and plutocracy has thereby been enthroned upon the ruins of Democracy. To restore the Government intended by the fathers and for the welfare and prosperity of this and future generations, we demand the establishment of an economic and financial system which shall make us masters of our own affairs and independent of European control by the adoption of the following . . .

In keeping with the People's Party Declaration of Principles, we have an important excerpt from Alexander Del Mar's 1899 *History of Monetary Crimes*, discussed earlier in this chapter in terms of the influence of the "European money changers" as follows:

> I would advise a return to the coinage laws prior to 1873 and the retirement of bank notes, to be replaced by greenbacks.

> These reforms will not only benefit the great mass of our people, they will save the commercial classes from what will otherwise end in widespread bankruptcy and perhaps even more serious results.

> Unfortunately, the commercial classes are too greedy to accept reforms that do not promise them unfair advantages.

Some say that the 1896 election marked the beginning of the end of the Populist Party and that it was the silver issue - which failed to attract urban voters - that did them in. Whether that is wholly true we cannot say, but we are guessing that deliberate fostering of "monetary confusion" pin-pointed by Henry Loucks played an even larger role. Intermingled with deliberate "monetary confusion" was the race card played by a faction of the Southern Democrats as well as the American Federation of Labor's choice to disavow the Populist cause, despite support of the likes of Eugene Debs and his large American Railway Union constituency and various other labor groups at the 1896 Populist Convention. Although Populists did score some big wins at the state level, including and especially in South Dakota where the Populists captured the governorship, gained control of the state legislature, elected two United States representatives, plus the attorney general's office and the members of the railroad commission, it does appear that the fusion strategy in the main and especially after 1898 did not work well enough to maintain forward momentum.

It is also highly probable that fate (or perhaps the foreign syndicates) may also have intervened as explained by James Neal Primm in his book A *Forgone Conclusion*:

> Ironically, the long deflation had run its course, the nation's gold supply, though not the Treasury's, had been rising for a number of years before 1893 but with little effect on prices, but after 1897 it rose spectacularly. Advances in mining technology and gold recovery from ore and huge gold strikes in South Africa, the Klondike and Australia did what the agrarians had tried to do: end deflation and bring prosperity. These fortuitous events were hailed by

sound-money advocates as verification of their wisdom. Between 1897 and 1914, the nation's gold stock more than tripled, and wholesale prices rose on the average 2.5 percent a year. Farm prices nearly doubled during the same period, still remembered as agriculture's golden age.

Especially in view of the Federal Reserve notes that we use today as money, one might easily counter the sound money advocates by pointing out that the Populists were right: an increase in the money supply, whether it be gold, silver or, even better, greenback demand notes, brought about a rise not only in prices but wages as well. This was good for everyone so long as price stability was maintained by allowing money and products to be exchanged in equal relative proportion. Thus, as Postel argues, the ultimate failure of Populism lay not in unrealistic goals but rather in their being "outdone by academic and corporate elites who managed to convince themselves of numerous absurdities [eventually allowing them] to claim the mantle of leadership in rural modernization."

The November 12, 1896 edition of the *Dakota Chief* devoted a full page to election results.

Taking up the center of the page was a very detailed and suspiciously professional looking artist's drawing topped by the Headline *"THIS COUNTRY IS OURS! - Populist-Democratic-Silver Combine Repudiated by a Triumphant Host of Patriots Determined to Save the Nation's Honor."* Adorning the artist's rendition of McKinley and his Vice President were the words *"Sound Money"* and *"Protection, Patriotism, and Prosperity."* The lead for a side column reads: *"Goes to McKinley. Ohio Man Elected by a Tremendous Majority. Seems a Landslide. All Eastern States Support the Gold Ticket. Solid South Shattered. Republican Gains in States Heretofore Democratic."*

Somehow, the "party of Lincoln" - which had not only saved the Union and ended slavery, but which had boldly envisioned a country filled with small, independent farmers instead of plantation oligarchs, using a government-issued Greenback dollar to do so, was now fully co-opted by the "academic and corporate elites who managed to convince themselves of numerous absurdities." Yet despite the election hyperbole, the numbers for the 1896 presidential race did indicate the widespread appeal of populism throughout the non-urban areas of America.

Presidential candidate William Jennings Bryan garnered 6.5 million votes and won 22 states, while McKinley, who, after consulting with his advisors endorsed a gold standard, garnered just over 7 million votes and won 23 states. Bryan carried all the Western states except California and North Dakota, Missouri and the former Confederate States. And as R. Alton Lee comments, although Bryan failed to carry a single industrial state, "a shift of only 19,436 votes in California, Oregon, Kentucky, North Dakota, West Virginia and Indiana would have given him the election."

But because McKinley also got nearly 100 more electoral votes, having won the most populous, and "wealthiest" states – the press was able to proclaim a "landslide" victory. In short, it appears that Bryan and the Populists were simply outshouted by the McKinley noise machine otherwise known as the national press.

In his book *The Populist Moment*, Lawrence Goodwyn sums up the Populist era as follows:

> Once established in 1892, the People's Party challenged the corporate state and the creed of progress it put forward. It challenged, in sum, the world we live in today. . . As theoreticians concerned with certain forms of capitalist exploitation, they were creative and, in a number of ways, prescient. As economists, they were considerably more thoughtful and practical than their contemporary political rivals in both major parties. As organizers of a huge democratic movement, Populists learned a great deal about both the power of the received hierarchy and the demands imposed on themselves by independent political action. As third-party tacticians, they had their moments . . .And finally as participants in the democratic creed, they were, on the evidence, far more advanced than most Americans, then or since.

Despite its mistakes, strategic and otherwise, and despite the almost insurmountable roadblocks put in its way or the money and power employed in attempts to destroy it, there can be little doubt that the Populist Party came within a hair's breadth of triumphing against the single most formidable power ever to exist, which is to say, "the money power." When fairly examined, there can be no doubt that our grandfather, along with millions like him, participated in the most important, clearly articulated grassroots political movement since the American Revolution, and even in all of America's subsequent and oftentimes turbulent history.

CHAPTER 7

Brule County: Land of the Burnt Thigh

According to the Genealogy Trails website, Brule County was created by act of the legislature on January 14, 1875. Following a familiar pattern, mere months later, in May of that same year, all of the land in Brule County was withdrawn from settlement by executive order by President Grant. It was not reopened until 1879.

The county was named for the Brule (Burned Thigh) Band of Teton Sioux, the word *brule* being French for burned. As mentioned in an earlier chapter, the area that today makes up Lyman County had been part of Brule County for judicial purposes until 1893 when it was split off as a separate county. Lyman County, which is located west of the Missouri River, is the place Edith (Ammons) Kohl and her sister Ida Mary staked their homestead claims in 1907 and 1908, nearly two and a half decades after our grandfather and his family first came to Dakota Territory.

The Ammons sisters' second claim was located on the Lower Brule Indian Reservation. Edith's descriptions of spontaneous fires that without warning could and often did ravage the tiny community were as poignant as they were memorable. The same was true of her accounts of the remarkable levels of cooperation and generosity that seemed to be everywhere evident within the tiny settlement community she and her sister helped build. In contradiction to her own early misconceptions, as she herself was quick to point out, this cooperation and generosity was also exhibited by their Native American neighbors, who were among the first to bring supplies and aid to the sisters when they were completely wiped out by fire in 1909.

While annual rainfall amounts did decline the further west one traveled (a factor that no doubt increased the likelihood of fire), the area where our grandfather settled was no stranger to such fires. Nor was our grandfather and his community immune to all the other the challenges faced by the Ammons sister, including learning to co-exist with the peoples inhabiting the Crow Creek reservation. A partially illegible obituary that appeared in the March 8, 1923 issue of the *Dante News*, provides insight into some of the difficulties our grandfather and his community similarly faced on the east side of the river twenty-some years earlier than that experienced by the Ammon sisters. This obituary, which most likely had been written by first-born son Charles who was also the editor of that paper, reads in part as follows:

> They faced the ravages of drought, grasshoppers, hail and prairie fires and although starvation at times seemed inevitable, this strong-hearted pioneer stuck to his post and was wonderfully assisted by one of the most faithful, hardworking wives and mothers that the world ever knew. With that wonderful character of the wife and her desire to labor for him and his children, they were able to weather the storm of nearly ten cropless years. During these ten years of hardship, five children were born adding many mouths to feed. . .

As a means of hanging some additional details on the above obituary we relate the story of a Brule County pioneer by the name of Matt Novak as told in *Brule County History*. Matt came to the Kimball area in April 1882 from Wisconsin together with his future father-in-law Jacob Vasicek who had also staked a claim in the area. Matt had secured two immigrant railroad cars for the two of them to bring supplies and livestock for both claims. In July of that year Matt married Jacob's daughter Mary. Here is a portion of his account of what happened next:

> Next to think about was a home, so I bought logs from Joe Laroche. In the spring of 1883, we sowed the [sod] breaking, half in wheat, half in oats. Crops were promising but a streak of hail about three miles wide cleaned up everything for another year.
>
> During this period food was very scarce. One day I walked to Bijou Hills – six miles distant, to a store operated by J. R. Lowe. I asked him for credit to buy coffee, yeast and flour but he told me that he was just as hard pressed for money as I was. I went home to a hungry family feeling quite depressed, but we had to figure out what are we going to do for food. My wife pounded corn to make flour for mush and roasted barley for coffee on which we lived until the few hens we had laid enough eggs at five cents a dozen with which to buy groceries. The only income I had was the two calves raised and sold for $15 to George Franklin.
>
> In 1884, crops were good, but prices very low – wheat sold for 35 to 40 cents a bushel. In 1885 – a half crop, so after harvest, leaving my wife with two small children at home, I drove my team of horses to Yankton – over 100 miles from home where a railroad was being built to Centerville where I got a job. Wages were $3 with a team and out of those wages, I had to pay my board and horse feed. After a month I earned $21 to call my own. You cannot imagine how happy to come home with what was big money in those days.
>
> 1886 – good crops. 1887 – no crop. 1888 – good crop and good prices – wheat $1 a bushel.
>
> On January 12, 1888 – a never to be forgotten blizzard. We had a low house which was soon covered with snow. My wife attempted to get some water at a well but [got] lost in the storm. She fortunately walked until she fell right into the doorway – if she had missed the house, she would have never found her way back. We had no fuel inside the home and didn't dare to try to get it from the outside. However, we filled our cellar with straw to prevent the vegetables from freezing which was a life-saver. We burned all of it in a drum heater.
>
> 1889 – crops poor; people began to leave the country but in spite of all hardships at this time, a wide spread neighborhood met together and built the Eagle Presbyterian Church . . .
>
> 1891 – good crops – especially corn but could never be harvested; cut worms took it all and many farmers replanted three times. John Pipal Sr. planted for the last time on 21st of July and had a big corn crop. 1892 -93 – fair crop. 1894 – complete failure.
>
> It was easier for us to get along than it is now since we had paid no taxes for 8 years. The first taxes that I paid both real estate and personal was $15.
>
> 1895 – no wheat for seed next year. The county shipped in seed wheat. Only a few got their seed back.
>
> 1896 – good crop. After that conditions and prices were better.

In her *History of Pukwana and Vicinity*, Orah Glass also paints a vivid picture of life on the plains by including the story of two English brothers who came to Brule County around 1892 with dreams of becoming wealthy and then returning to their native England. Orah relates that after crops failed and animals perished in the severe winter, one of the brothers, who was a minister, was inspired to write the following lines to be sung to the tune of Beulah Land:

I've reached the land of drought and heat
Where nothing grows for man to eat
The scorching wind doth blow the heat
O'er all this land that can't be beat.
Chorus-
O, Brule Land, Sweet Brule Land

As on thy burning soil I stand
I look away across the plains
And wonder why it never rains
'Til Gabriel blows his trumpet sound
And says the rains have gone around.
We have no wheat, we have no oats
We have no corn to feed our shoats
Our chickens are too poor to eat
Our pigs go squealing down the street.
Chorus-
Our horses are of the bronco race
Starvation stares them in the face
We do not live, we only stay
We are too poor to get away.

Another story published by *Brule County History* was a 1917 autobiography of Brule County pioneer Joseph Matousek who had settled thirteen miles south of Kimball in 1882, relates the following events after 1901:

In 1901 we built a new house 28' x 22' x 16' with a 16' x 16' x 16' [add-on?], and a cistern 16' deep x 12' in diameter, all at a cost of $1200 (our own labor we did not count). In 1905 we built a barn 56' x 80' x 16' at a cost of $1100. This barn did not stand long. On June 16, 1907, at midnight, lightning struck it and it burned to the ground. All the children were asleep and mother and I ran to the barn. I loosed and drove out 9 horses, but they all returned and perished. The tenth I led out and he and I were badly burned. I, on my face, for I was bareheaded. Also 14 calves perished and 200 bushels of corn and 70 tons of hay burned. All our harnesses and most of our machinery and many tools were burned, either in the barn or near it. I collected $1250 insurance on the whole loss. The winter before we lost all our hogs, 60 head, by cholera. We figured our loss at over $7000.

Forgetting the past, with new courage and determination, trusting in GOD, we organized ourselves and pressed forward. Good neighbors and friends lent us horses for work, for we lost all our work horses. Also they gave of their time and assistance lavishly in various ways, for which we never cease to be heartily grateful for.

Lest one assume that farming in the more hospitable climate of the eastern part of the state (where our paternal great-grandparents located) came without challenge, Henry Loucks set us straight. Having purchased a relinquished homestead in Duel County in 1884, Loucks provides the following details:

Agriculture is the only great industry (except mining) that by natural or climatic conditions is forced to take chances. When the farmer plants his seed, he has no guarantee that he will have a full crop, or any crop at all. He must continue the expense of cultivation; for destruction by hail, drought, rust or frost may come on the eve of harvest, or during harvest. In my own personal experience, in one of our best agricultural counties (Duel) on the eastern border of the state, this has happened to me more than one-third of the time.

All of the above clearly shows that it was no small feat to make it through such adversities and still come out whole, but of course our grandfather and his family were part of the minority that did somehow manage. Land patent documents tell us for example that they made it through the particularly brutal drought of 1894-1895 that killed all the trees on the Timber Culture Land, and more than likely, the homestead crops as well. Per the accounts of other Brule County settlers as well as the obituary account excerpted above, our grandfather and his family also lived through insect scourges, rattlesnake infestations, hailstorms that wiped out crops within a matter of minutes, and they lived through the fire of 1899 that burned over 50,000 acres in Brule County alone – causing many farmers to lose everything, with some families saved only by going into outside caves. They also made it through the infamous "Childrens' Blizzard" of 1888, when temperatures dropped within a matter of hours to 38 degrees below zero and an avalanche of snow killed 213 people, mostly children, along with countless animals and livestock. They even made it through the depression of 1893, an event that, who knows, perhaps spurred our grandfather to become an active Populist.

Whether Barbara was able to join our grandfather in his political activities is not known, but clearly, she too led an active, challenging life, with childbearing being among the more challenging of these activities during those years. For example, we found census information that indicates Barbara may have given birth to more than the eight children accounted for in *Brule County History*. The 1900 U.S. Census shows that there were twelve children born to Barbara and our grandfather, with eight living at the time of the Census. Somewhat oddly, the 1910 U. S. Census shows that there were ten children born to Barbara with seven children living. We learned through a news article and a discussion with

Wedding photo of our grandfather and his first wife Barbara Havlik, October of 1883.

a great-grandson of our grandfather, that little Libby, as one of the eight, had died of Diphtheria in 1903. But why the number of children born was reduced from 12 in 1900 to 10 in 1910 is an unsolved mystery. In any case it seems that Barbara had carried to term at least two more babies than we originally believed. It is possible that these babies are also in unmarked graves in the Vega Cemetery.

Surprisingly, nutrition among settlers suffered mightily in the early years of establishing a farm, this due to the vagaries of weather, prairie fires, grasshoppers and other scourges. New settlers often relied on mountains of canned goods shipped from the east, along with flapjacks made with water and flour, or biscuits and gravy. Since there were no refrigerators, there was usually little in the way of fresh meat in the summer, even in the best of situations. Moreover, severe winters could and sometimes did decimate the wildlife population, making even wild game scarce. Homesteaders had to make do with meager subsistence fare for months and even years at a time in order to get established, as our grandfather's obituary above indicates. Poor nutrition was especially a problem if the family had not yet been able to afford a dairy cow and some chickens, or if blizzards, grasshoppers or similar events wiped out livestock and crops. And many settlers struggled, often under a substantial burden of debt, to first establish a cash crop that would be sold to outside markets for much-needed cash.

In addition to his family's help, a good part of our grandfather's success, as compared with so many other pioneers who were forced to give up early on, was no doubt due to his decision to settle near Smith Creek in Union Township, which *Brule County History* tells us "was fortunate about having plenty of water in shallow wells, especially along Smith Creek where good water could be had by digging only a few feet, and stock raising became an important industry as soon as the settler got means enough to buy cattle."

Based on the number and type of buildings described in our grandfather's homestead "proving up" documents, it appears that by 1900 our grandfather had established a "mixed" farming operation that included livestock and corn – both of which might be used as food. Corn of course could also be used as animal feed, and any excess could be used for seed for next year's planting or even offered for sale. If prices were too low, corn cobs could be used as fuel. Since the homestead also had a well there likely was a vegetable garden that could have been sufficiently maintained during all but the driest periods. In other words, the farm could sustain the family, if only meagerly, through lean years when crops or crop prices were poor.

We have found one or two testaments in newspapers speaking to the fact that times were hard for the Fousek clan in the early days of pioneering. Nevertheless, and unlike the unprepared and completely impoverished settlers trying to escape the slums of New York and other large urban centers, it appears that our grandfather's apprenticeship on his parents' Iowa farm, as well as his own industriousness, served him well.

The first inkling we get that debt had begun creeping into our grandfather's life is an article appearing in the February 17, 1900 edition of the Kimball Graphic which says that the Brule County Board of Commissioners granted Vaclav Fousek a "school loan" of $225 on his homestead land. Several other applicants also received "school loans" that session. What the proceeds of these loans were used for we have no idea.

A few months later, on October 9, 1900 our grandfather purchased a nearby farm that had been lost to foreclosure. According to court records our grandfather had secured this land with a mortgage at 8% interest that was paid in full on October 9, 1905. The previous owner of this farm was Lars Peterson who had been awarded a land patent for his farm in 1895. The same year as Lars Peterson received the patent award, a deed was issued recording a mortgage to him for $350. In 1897 a Sheriff's Deed is recorded, meaning Lars defaulted on "indenture of mortgage." The default is recorded as follows:

a. A $250 5-year note which also carried 10 coupons representing a bank fee of $1.75 each.

b. A $25 one-year note has two coupons representing a bank fee of $1.25 each

c. A second $25 one-year note with 4 coupons representing a bank fee of $1.25 each.

All three of Lars' notes carried an annual interest rate of 10% in addition to the coupon fees, which totaled $25, or the amount of one of his loans. Lars lost the parcel to the Iowa Land Company and it was to the Iowa Land Company that our grandfather paid $500 for the deed to the property, obtaining from them a mortgage carrying an interest rate of 8%.

The source of money for these loans was, generally speaking, raised by principals of the Iowa Land Company who would borrow money from their mother country, which was most often England, at something like four or five per cent interest. The principals of the Iowa Land Company (and others like it) made their profit by tacking on an extra 3 or 4% on the loans they provided to farmers throughout the country, but especially those in the west and south. This situation underlay much of the monetary criticisms that inspired the Populist movement.

It is worthwhile to mention here that the Iowa Land Company had been one of many foreign syndicates coming under fire sixteen years earlier, in 1884, as evidenced by bills that were then being introduced in Congress. These bills were designed to restrict or prevent acquisition of public lands by "leviathan squatters" who together had, as of 1884, already bought up nearly 21 million acres of public land thereby driving up land prices. Despite the brouhaha, nothing was done to slow the acquisition of vast quantities of land by foreigners nor were steps taken to aid settlers who alleged that they had moved on good faith to the frontier only to find themselves "in a desperate struggle against corporate greed and combined foreign capital." Thus, the essence of these legislative attempts at reform would soon show up in the platforms of the Farmers' Alliance and the Populists.

Reflecting the harsh economic and farming conditions of the period during which our grandfather was active in Populist politics, the population of Brule County had decreased from a high of 6,737 in 1890 (up from 238 in 1880) to 5,401 by 1900. Lars Peterson's misfortune became a good opportunity for our grandfather, especially since the population of Brule County would steadily increase over the next two and a half decades, reaching its zenith of 8,110 in 1925. Yet, however tempting it might be to chalk Peterson's loss up to incompetence or bad luck, the steady, unrelenting rise in farm tenancy rates, up in Brule County from 17% in 1890 to 35% by 1920, provided yet another clear indication that the underlying "money question" of the Populists remained, in 1920, unsolved.

In 1901, both our grandfather Vaclav, and his father Stephen received patents for their Brule County homestead claims. In 1902 our grandfather essentially swapped his Timber Culture parcel in El Dorado Township, Buffalo County for his brother-in-law Anton Havlik's parcel which was located just west of his father Stephen's land, just north of the Wencil Havliks, and kitty-corner to his own homestead. Later, in 1904 Stephen purchased the parcel adjacent to his homestead from a Jens Larsen for $1600. Having just sold his farmland in Iowa, which he most likely had been renting out, Stephen may have used a portion of the proceeds from that property to purchase the Larsen farm. Larsen moved to a neighboring farm, about a mile away.

It had become very clear by this time that the entire Fousek/Havlik clan had no intention of giving up their homesteads and had in fact set about building even deeper ties to their growing community.

CHAPTER 8

Vega, The Little Town That Was

Somewhere between 1890 and 1901 the little town of Vega began to take shape. Unlike many towns, Vega was not situated along a river or railroad, where dependable outbound transportation for marketable farm surplus might attract the establishment of nearby farms. Nor was it, as railroad towns were, carefully platted out in advance by railroad officials or their agents at specific intervals along railroad routes, to maximize economic efficiency. Railroads that platted these towns sold town lots as the means by which to attract residents who would help manage the train depot and provide other needed services. Growth of the railroad town would encourage nearby settlement of farmers who would, it was hoped, come to depend on railroad transportation services, the profits from which would help the railroad meet its own debt repayment obligations.

By contrast, Vega grew haphazardly into a thriving community, not on Railroad "town lots" but right there on the farms of our grandfather and his brother-in-law Wencil, and our great-grandfather Stephen – and, after 1902, on the former homestead of our grandfather's brother-in-law Anton which farm our grandfather had purchased (or really swapped since the recorded purchase price was the same on both) in exchange for his Timber Culture parcel.

Vega's anchor was the Post Office, and its main purpose clearly was not to move crops and other raw materials to distant markets but rather to provide services and supplies to the local farm community. Vega was, according to *Brule County History,* the trade center for the area, while Kimball, due to its railroad facilities, was the market center out of which marketable farm surplus could be shipped.

Kimball was one of two nearby railroad towns, being about seventeen miles southeast of Vega. The other was Pukwana, being about eleven miles southwest of Vega. Both Kimball and Pukwana were established in the early 1880s along what was then the Chicago, Milwaukee and St. Paul Railroad line. Pukwana would later figure in Charles' life when he purchased the *Pukwana Press Reporter* which is still in operation today. Kimball was, no doubt, chosen as the market center for Vega area farmers because it was several miles to the east of Pukwana, thereby offering a savings on transportation costs for area farmers.

Regardless of how they were established, small frontier towns of all shapes and designs were immensely important to the farming community because they provided a source for things like machinery that farmers themselves couldn't make or food items they themselves couldn't raise. Towns also served as social centers and gathering places for otherwise isolated farmers. Vega for instance not only had at least two general merchandise stores but it also hosted weekly baseball or horseshoe games that often drew the younger set from area farms. Because of this social component, frontier towns also served as a sort of primitive but quite effective "communications hub" through which neighbors could share information about farming and housekeeping, as well as learn about and provide aide to struggling families or orphaned children.

The seasonal nature of agriculture and continually shifting crop prices encouraged members of communities such as Vega to find ways to work together in order to keep their local "exchange" economies viable and better equipped to serve the needs of the entire community throughout the year. This exchange culture seems to have been, at least in part, a carry-over from the Grange societies that sprang up all over Iowa in the early 1870s and which had, by 1873, created a networking system effective enough to provide critical assistance to thousands of farmers in fifteen counties in Northwestern Iowa that had been left destitute by a grasshopper scourge that occurred in the summer of 1873.

The Grange societies also established farm cooperatives to assist farmers in the buying and selling of their livestock and produce. Farm elevator cooperatives not only broke the power of the line elevators stationed along railroad lines, but they helped pave the way for more local control over grain storage and distribution. These ideas then spilled over into Dakota territory under the Dakota Alliance leadership of Henry Loucks and Alonzo Wardall, who by the late 1880s had increasingly begun to turn to politics in search of opportunities to influence the laws and policies of the Territory and soon after the new state of South Dakota. The state and national success of the Alliance cooperatives and other types of assistance programs established by Loucks and Wardall helped many farmers gain more of an economic foothold on their land.

A Local Exchange Economy

By the late 1890s local communities were forming their own co-ops. Communities such as Vega that were formed by family and friends moving en masse to Dakota Territory of course had a decided advantage over communities such as the Bonanza farms composed entirely of itinerant strangers, in large part because close knit communities were far more amenable, and motivated, to establishing cooperative arrangements of all kinds. One example might be a group of farmers pooling their resources to purchase a relatively expensive piece of equipment, such as a flour mill, which co-op members then used on a time-share basis.

Another way the local "exchange" economy was enhanced in Vega was through the decision of the town's leading businessmen to continue to farm while expanding their businesses, this usually being accomplished by hiring neighboring farmers or recruiting family members for whatever odd jobs might need filling. As opposed to income being sent to eastern financial centers in payment of debt, this practice helped recirculate available cash money throughout the local economy, multiplying its value and offering tremendous benefits to the community.

It worked something like this. Let's say that our grandfather paid his brother-in-law Anton three dollars to shuck some corn for him (as family records indicate he did in fact do). Then let's imagine that Anton in turn used those three dollars to purchase some layer hens from his neighbor, who in turn used the money to purchase goods or services from one of Vega's business establishments. The business establishment then used those three dollars to pay an employee. When kept in the local community that three dollars did the work of twelve dollars and could do even more than that if more transactions occurred before the money exited the community in payment of debt, taxes, railroad transportation fees or the purchase of goods from outside markets.

Everyone in these frontier communities knew that when farmers' incomes declined, town businesses suffered too. The exchange economy of the entire community contracted simply because there was less cash money coming into the community by way of crop sales to outside markets, and so various mechanisms, including borrowing and buying on credit as well as use of various cooperative arrangements were set in place to deal with such events. In contrast, the big bonanza farms, composed as they were of highly transitory migrant workers and reliant upon large scale cropping systems, never developed a strong local exchange economy or the sense of community or interconnectedness that most if not all small rural agricultural towns had. Of course, it goes without saying that farmers who practiced mixed cropping systems were less dependent on outside markets for their survival since they were able to raise and use more of their own food and fiber.

One very typical, very important way the local economy was supported was through a kind of exchange economy credit system, where town merchants would extend credit to farmers in order that they might purchase needed supplies, thus helping to tide a farmer over till the next crop came in. Of course, part of the cost of doing business this way meant that merchants were forced to absorb losses whenever a farmer could not meet his obligations to the merchant due to crop loss, bankruptcy or other calamity.

It goes without saying that these kinds of arrangements did not help merchants like our grandfather pay *their* creditors, who did demand cash, plus interest. And, of course, the merchant, like the farmer, had expenses to account for, including paying for the merchandise with which to stock their businesses, as well as all associated financing, warehousing, advertising, holding and improvement costs. This is why poor Matt Nowak, mentioned in the previous chapter, walked six miles to the nearest store in 1883 in the hopes of securing credit with which to buy some food for his hungry family, only to be turned away by the merchant who was just as strapped for cash as he was. Luckily, our grandfather and the town of Vega not only had the residual if not direct benefits of programs established by Populists such as Loucks and Wardall in the late 1880s, but they also had extended family and the greater Vega community to rely upon for sustenance in hard times.

Another common practice among frontier merchants, including our grandfather, was to accept fur pelts, grain, eggs or other farm produce as payment in lieu of cash – or, in a word, "barter" which was a form of exchange Native Americans heavily favored. Treatises we have read on the subject suggest to us that this barter business seems to have eventually led our grandfather into a career as a grain merchant.

As explained by these treatises we are guessing that our grandfather's earliest activities began as a cooperative arrangement with his relatives and involved collecting the surplus produce of the neighborhood, perhaps storing it in the granary mentioned in the proving up documents, and then forwarding the whole on for sale, thus providing a savings for everyone on transportation and storage costs. The second granary mentioned in will documents may have been built in response to more area farmers requesting this service as Vega expanded. At this point, our grandfather may have been called upon to credit a farmer for his produce at a fixed price, or he might even have provided the farmer an advance if the grain was to be handled on a commission basis.

In the first case of providing credit, our grandfather may have issued a receipt showing the grade and amount of grain the farmer was to contribute. Since receipts like these were "fungible," that is to say, the same as money, it meant the farmer could then use this receipt at any establishment that recognized such receipts in order to purchase the goods he needed. In other words, the farmer could make purchases at the store owned by our grandfather, or the store owned by his brother-in-law Wencil Havlik or any other local business that recognized the signature of our grandfather, using these receipts. Once the grain was sold our grandfather could use the proceeds from the sale of the grain to pay his own obligations. This was essentially a barter system, but it did require our grandfather to, in effect, finance the farmer out of his own pocket, as did the practice of providing an advance to the farmer if our grandfather was selling the grain on a commission basis.

In the grand scheme of things, and for the rural farm economy that desperately wanted to "make a go of it," the use of barter and pooling of resources for specific tasks, the use of local merchant credit, and most especially the extensive reliance upon loans or mortgages from outside sources were inevitable, necessary responses to the "money-shortage question" so clearly articulated in the Populist era. An illustration that would soon parallel our own grandfather's situation comes by way of future South Dakota Governor Peter Norbeck. As the father of South Dakota's ill-fated Rural Credit System and a leader of the progressive wing of the Republican party, Norbeck knew as well as any the difficulties involved in acquiring adequate funds needed to operate – never mind improve – a business.

Having achieved state-wide prominence because of his successful artesian well-drilling business, Norbeck's account books show that in 1908, he was carrying over $150,000 in notes and accounts receivable, that is to say, debts owed to and by him. This debt was against an annual income that by 1917-1919 was averaging about $90,000. Suffice it to say that Norbeck's debts may have been even higher in 1917 than in 1908, but fortuitously enough for him, Norbeck and similar businessmen always had access to ample credit. It should be noted that balance sheets like Norbeck's were not unusual. Indeed, they seemed to be typical for merchants as well, as figures provided by Lewis E. Atherton in his seminal book *The Frontier Merchant of Mid-America* indicate.

The Crop Lien System of the South and the Impact of Debt

Luckily for businessmen like Norbeck, Western merchants like our grandfather and Western farmers as a whole, both the economy and the banking system in the North had not been paralyzed by the Civil War in the same way as in the South, where the brutal "share" or "cropping" system soon took hold between merchants and tenant farmers. Massive devastation resulting from war and a rather disjointed money system lacking in cohesion and uniformity (starkly contrasting with the Greenback North), created an extreme shortage of easily recognizable cash money in the postbellum South. Lack of money then led to a scarcity of credit, and both together very quickly led to a situation in which some three-fourths to nine-tenths of the farmers of the cotton South became ensnared to a greater or lesser degree by the crop-lien system. The co-op system developed by Charles Macune experienced a much more limited success than that developed by Loucks and Wardall in part due to the heavier pressure of debt.

Importantly, the crop-lien system that developed in the South stood in stark contrast to the merchant credit system of the North. For example, the crop liens of the cotton South allowed merchants to dictate such things as which crops the farmer was to raise and what merchandise the farmer could buy and what he was to pay for that merchandise. A crop-lien farmer was also typically forbidden to deal with other merchants except on an all-cash basis, and similar contractual relationships were also forged.

As Hicks recounts, the effect of the crop liens was to establish a condition of peonage throughout the cotton South. It also contributed heavily to the one-crop evil that did more than its full share to insure to the farmer a permanent condition of indebtedness. For their part, Southern merchants were forced to obtain funds from eastern banks at ruinous rates, commonly 1 ½ % a month. Thus Hicks says, contextualizing the assertion of another writer: "The road to wealth in the South, was doubtless merchandising, but for many it was also the road to bankruptcy."

Essentially the greater availability of credit and eastern capital (as well as Greenbacks) allowed the local economies of the rural North to develop along much different lines than in the rural South. This despite the fact that merchants and businessmen, both North and South, were well accustomed to extending credit to customers at their own risk as well as depending on loans as a means by which to build or just to operate their businesses.

In the case of our grandfather, evidence points to his having taken out some relatively small mortgages in order to be able to extend credit to local farmers and operate his merchandising businesses. He most likely, like other merchants of the era, also relied on "advances" provided by his merchandise suppliers although we have found no concrete evidence of this. Land and mortgage documents we have obtained do indicate the distinct possibility that our grandfather was mortgaging some of his land in order to build his businesses and also, most probably, to allow farmers to buy on credit. This is especially true prior to 1909.

As already mentioned in the last chapter, our grandfather took out a "school loan" from the County Board of Commissioners in the amount of $225 in February of 1900. Two years later, in 1902, Vaclav essentially swapped his Timber Culture parcel for the parcel of one of his brothers-in-law that lay across the road from Stephen's, our grandfather's and Wencil's parcels, thus making Vega into a square. Based on some non-specific details provided in *Brule County History*, we believe that it is quite probable that George Caufman, who was the father of two of Vaclav's future daughters-in-law, may have at some point during this period rented out the empty building that stood on this parcel to use as a store.

Documents do tell us that in 1902 and again in 1903, Barbara and our grandfather took out mortgages on this swapped parcel. The first loan was from their brother-in-law John Henzlik for $550 and the second was from M.L. Davison for $400. The Henzlik loan was paid in full by 1906 and the Davison loan was paid in full in 1908. This was during the time that several businesses were being established on the farms of Wencil and our grandfather, and possibly Stephen as well. It is very likely that Wencil was similarly making use of loans, either from his parents or on his land, to establish his businesses.

In 1909, Barbara and our grandfather took out two loans from Stephen (our great-grandfather) totaling $2750, both of which were paid off by January of 1915. Since our grandfather purchased another quarter section of land in 1909 for $2750 we are guessing that the loan was used to purchase this new parcel. It is also perhaps an indication that any excess cash from our grandfather's business ventures was being utilized and thus not available to purchase land.

In short, and unlike the crop lien economy of the South and unlike the short-lived "Bonanza farms" of the North, most rural communities that developed in the North after the 1890s were better positioned to devise what might be thought of as quasi domestic exchange economies. They did this by making liberal use of a variety of cooperative arrangements that, despite a chronic and often severe shortage of government-issued money, allowed the local economy to function as smoothly as possible for as many as possible even in the off-season and during lean years. Without question, this is what allowed Vega to persist through all manner of economic downturns that would come its way over the next couple of decades.

Vega Becomes a Town

We know from *Brule County History* and other texts that in 1890 Abraham Meyers had taken over from Trew Hayes as postmaster of Vega, moving the Vega post office from Buffalo County to his Brule County property and then combining the post office with a store and upstairs dance hall. In 1900 Meyers sold "Vega" (meaning both the building and his property) to Tom E. Thompson who made a home out of the building, thus allowing Meyers to move to Chamberlain where he ran a store until his death. The post office was moved to the farm of our grandfather's brother-in-law, Wencil Havlik.

Interestingly, *Brule County History* also says that the "Vaclav Fouseks lived in a one room building, probably 24 feet by 24 feet, and lived in that until they built the store. In fact, they lived upstairs and used the other building for a kitchen added to the store." Because proving up documents tell us that there were numerous buildings on the homestead by 1900, this rather confusing, partially inaccurate statement suggests to us that our grandfather may have been operating some sort of store prior to 1900, and in tandem with Abraham Meyer's operation, which was about a mile west of our grandfather's homestead. In addition, we have entries taken from what appears to be a "Day Book" of the kind used by merchants of the day.

Although this Day Book contains family information recorded at a later date by our grandfather's son James, and thus may have been the Day Book used by either our grandfather or perhaps James for the store, we find on page 100 some interesting, if sparse, entries belonging to our grandfather. At the top of the page we find: "V. Fousek Dr. to year 1899." We are guessing that "Dr" meant "Daily Record." Under this are the following few entries: March 1 of 1898 our grandfather paid his father Stephen the $30 he owed him. He also paid Anton Havlik $4 for cutting grain. On March 19, he paid Anton Havlik $30 for one mare and he paid Anton $3 for husking corn. Unless we can locate the earlier entries for this Day Book, these details and most especially

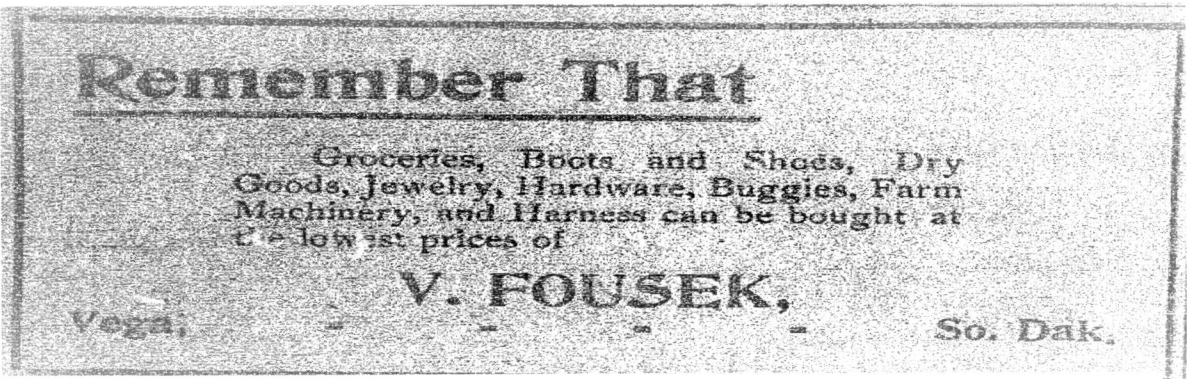

This ad appeared in the December 1903 Kimball Index.

the existence of this "dr." will remain merely an intriguing possibility that our grandfather was operating a small store prior to 1900.

Weaving together details provided by *Brule County History* and *Of Rails and Trails* we can say that the Vega School and the Kovanda School were the first schools in Union Township. The Vega school was originally held in the abandoned claim shack of Thomas Nelson, whose parcel was located on Smith Creek on land that had once been part of the Crow Creek Reservation. Miss Elvalena Rossman was the first teacher and it was also her first school. Children from the families of V. Fousek, Olaf Olson, Tom E. Thompson, Lasse Olson, and others attended this school. The school board consisted of Mrs. Rindy, D.C. Miller and our grandfather "V. Fousek."

Presumably Miss Rossman would have taught at the Vega School through all or most of the 1890s, perhaps till 1901. By 1902-1903 Emma Brooks was teaching at the Vega School, receiving a salary of $28. It seems Miss Brooks had her hands full because the school had a seating capacity of 21, but 24 students were enrolled that year. Seven of the eight Fousek children were among her students: James, age 11, Milo, age 9, Libbie, age 8, Otto, age 6, Tillie age 12, Emma, age 4, and Rosie, age 13. Charles, we believe, had just started college in Iowa. Later teachers at the Vega School included Clara Anderson, Ellen Brady, Marie Fousek, Emma Vesely and at least two of the Gearhart sisters, Flossie and Goldie. Per *Brule County History* the highest annual salary earned by teachers of Union Township was $85.50 attained in 1926. Salaries then dropped to a low of $67.50 in 1943.

By combining information from *Brule County History, Of Rails and Trails,* phonebooks and newspaper articles we have come up with the following picture of Vega's growth from its rudimentary beginnings just outlined into a thriving town in its own right. Its businesses included an award-winning creamery, at least two general merchandise stores, a blacksmith shop, a farm machinery repair shop, a post office, dance hall/meeting hall, possibly a cafe of some sort, farm machinery sales at both the Havlik and Fousek farms, buggy sales, and wood sales. In addition, regular dances, baseball games, horseshoes and wrestling matches added to Vega's social scene.

Quite likely there was a flour mill and a cane press as well, with an evaporative tank to dry the cane juice. This is per an account in *Brule County History* which said that since most farmers grew sugar cane – or more likely sorghum which grew better in drier climates - every community had a cane press where farmers could have their cane pressed and processed on shares. Whatever was not evaporated into sugar could be stored in barrels as molasses. Similarly, every town had a flour mill where farmers had their grain ground on shares, and the miller sold his share to do business. We are surmising that Vega had both a flour mill and a cane press/evaporator which operated on shares.

Somewhere around 1898 and 1900 the V. Fousek Creamery, as it was referred to in *Brule County History,* was started. Our first real clue as to its initial formation comes via an entry in the December 11, 1897 Kimball Graphic that says: "V. Fousek attended the creamery meeting at Strouds school house in Buffalo county Saturday."

The expense attached to setting up a creamery was substantial and so we are guessing that the "V. Fousek Creamery" must have been a joint venture with at least some of the Havlik clan and perhaps Vaclav's own parents as well. The June 9, 1898 edition of the *Dakota Chief* gives us an idea of the expense involved in starting up a creamery when it tells us that an unnamed creamery

Photo of the V. Fousek Creamery, also known as the Smith Creek Creamery and the Vega Brule County Creamery. It was located on the northwestern edge of our grandfather's homestead.

required $1000 in cash and $1,435 in notes (with one half due in six months and one half due in one year) to get said creamery up and running. Since the Kimball Creamery along with the Pukwana Creamery and several other creameries in the vicinity were already in operation in 1898, we are conjecturing that these particular notes may well have been for the V. Fousek Creamery.

An indication that the "V. Fousek Creamery" was a joint business venture and not a co-op is provided by a 1904 article in the Kimball Index which says that the stockholders of the Smith Creek Creamery Company held their annual meeting the previous Saturday and elected John Henzlik (husband of Barbara's sister Josephine), Fred Harris and James Beranek (husband of Barbara's sister Flora) for the Board of Directors. Our grandfather was appointed Manager and Wencil Havlik Jr. was Treasurer. The Board decided to contract for hauling butter "provided not more than ten cents a hundred is charged for hauling." In addition, a Martin J. Norton of St. Paul Park Minnesota was selected "to take charge of the Smith Creek Creamery as butter-maker." Mr. Norton it seems, came "well recommended, with many years of experience as butter-maker."

A promotional brochure we came across put out by the *General Passenger Department of the Chicago, Milwaukee and St. Paul Railway* and printed, per our conjecture, around 1901 stated that the five creameries located in Brule County were among the best in the state. The "wonderful natural grasses" were given as the reason that the butter from these creameries was able to command "the very highest prices in New York and Boston markets, even commanding a higher price than the famous Elgin creamery butter." This document also said that "The Vega Brule County Creamery was granted the silver medal at the Paris Exposition for the best butter." Aside from being a remarkable honor, the multiple references to 1902 bringing even better prospects for farmers that are contained in this brochure tells us that the Vega Creamery was in operation by 1901 and probably for a year or more earlier.

According to *Brule County History* the "V. Fousek Creamery" was located across the road east of the Havlik store and just west of the windmill on the Fousek farm. Everyone hauled milk to the creamery. They would test the milk and then give the patrons back the skimmed milk. Later managers would include Jensen, Pipal and Riggs. After ten or so years of operation, business began to fade as farmers began bringing their milk to the Kimball Creamery instead, in which our grandfather held one share of stock as per will documents. The V. Fousek Creamery building was sold to Elmer Wager, who had land just north of the Elvin Peters place. Wager later sold the building to the Clarence Thorsen farm.

Even when our grandfather was manager of the V. Fousek Creamery in 1904, it must have had a fair number of employees, as evidenced by a February 18, 1904 announcement in the *Kimball Index* alerting readers that "creamery pay day is this week." This is an indication also that the creamery was operated as a business and not a cooperative as the cane sugar and perhaps even the flour operations likely were.

Our grandfather's General Merchandise Store with repainted marquis to reflect transfer of ownership to James in 1917.

We also get a glimpse into the type of jobs our grandfather (and likely his brother-in-law Wencil Havlik and other businesses) provided through news articles. For example, in the same edition of the *Kimball Index* that announced Creamery payday we find that a John Thornson was invoicing V. Fousek's stock of merchandise. In another edition of the *Kimball Index* that same year we find that V. Kovanda hauled some fruit from Pukwana for V. Fousek and later that year an Elvin Peters is hauling fruit for our grandfather. That same year the Gann Valley newspaper reported that "V. Fousek pays the highest price for eggs," which he then presumably sold at his store. Another article says that our grandfather "has been getting a lot of hides lately and it is because he paid the highest prices." A 1913 article in the *Dakota Chief* said that Libbie Vesely was clerking at the store, while her sister taught at the Vega School.

All of this indicates that Vega even then was providing employment and income opportunities to the community

Bargains On Machinery

Desiring to close out some machinery I will sell it at reduced prices. This is your chance to buy certain Farm Machinery at less then Factory Price.

Here Are Some Bargains.

Queen City Strap Moldboard 16" Sulky Plow, Just the plow for gumbo soil Regular price $45. Special price to close out $34. Rock Island 16" Sulky Plow Regular price $45. Special price $34 John Deere 14" Gang Plow Regular price $70. Special price $55. John Deere Double disc Plow for gumbo soil Regular price $60 Special price $45. Van Brunt 7 foot Drill Regular price $85. Special price $70. John Deere Swinging Hay Stacker Regular price $65. Special price $45. Janseville Disc Harrow with drill attachment Regular price $60. Special price $50.

I also have a large supply of Breaking Plows, Corn Cultivators, Corn Planters Listers and Listed Corn Cultivators at attractive prices.

V. Fousek   Vega   S.D

This ad appeared in the Green Valley Chief Newspaper, March 23, 1915.

In 1901, Barbara's brother Wencil (or Jim or Vaclov) opened a general merchandise store and about a year after that our grandfather built a general merchandise store, perhaps replacing the smaller one we suspect he had been operating prior to 1900. When Wencil opened his store, he also became Postmaster for Vega. His annual salary for the position was $48.68, increasing annually until 1911 when our grandfather became Postmaster for an annual salary of $130. After Wencil died in a car accident in 1930, Stella rented the store to George Caufman, whose daughters Marie and Katherine married our grandfather's sons (our half-uncles) Otto and James in a double wedding in 1916. The store burned down sometime after 1930, on the night that George had thrown his daughter Marie a birthday party, after which time, according to *Brule County History*, George rented the Stephen Fousek house to use as a store.

Wencil also ran a blacksmith shop. Apparently, he continued farming as well, which indicates to us that family members assisted him in many of these activities. Wencil's store had a large second floor that was used for various types of events and as a dance hall. Dances were held about once a month. Wencil's wife Stella later recalls in *Brule County History* that "people for miles around came by horse and buggy to dance all night and drive home by early morning light." Other accounts say that some of these dances lasted all night with farmers going home in the early morning to do chores and then coming back to resume dancing.

An account provided by Earl F. Hall in *Brule County History* says that "Although we lived in Buffalo County, during my teen years I spent many Saturday nights and Sundays at Vega, which was a great place for Saturday night dances and Sunday baseball games. One Sunday one of the attractions was a wrestling match in which Al Ackerman agreed to throw John DeLoria and John Badger both twice in an hour and ten minutes which he did quite easily." In addition to the events just mentioned, Earl recalled the Wencil Havlik store and dance hall, the V. Fousek store and Post Office, and a couple dozen individuals who frequented Vega. Wencil played the violin and furnished entertainment for many of the dances held above his general merchandise store. Willis Henegar contributed by playing a big harp. The "Bunny Hug" was a new dance at the time, and "some even tried it." Beer was passed around in buckets from which individuals would use a common dipper with which to take a sip. Family lore indicates that beer and "Apple Jack" wine were often homemade, and it is quite possible that the beer sold at these dances was homemade.

There was a 25-cent admission charge for men at these dances, but women and children were free. As Stella tells it "an all-you-can-eat lunch could be had for 25 cents" but we do not know whether this was just offered after dances or on a more regular basis in some type of area serving as a cafe. The winter menu was oyster stew and summer was sandwiches and cake, plus coffee. *Of Rail and Trails* says that this same menu was offered after dances, except that in summer ice cream took the place of oyster stew. One does wonder where the oysters came from.

At some point Wencil added two pool tables in a small addition at the back of his store and began selling beer. Apparently selling beer was not an acceptable activity for a Postmaster and the job was passed to our grandfather in 1911. Wencil also became a dealer for McCormick machinery, while our grandfather was a dealer for John Deere Buggies, John Deere plows and other John Deere farm equipment, Deering Harvesting Machinery and J. I. Case Threshing Machines. According to an ad in the 1910 Gann Valley phone book, our grandfather also handled "a large line of repairs" for farm machinery. This phone book listed the phone number for "Vega" and for our grandfather as 817.

Enlarging Vega

As early as 1903 our grandfather was advertising that he had "Groceries, Boots and Shoes, Dry Goods, Jewelry, Hardware, Buggies, Farm Machinery, and Harnesses for sale at the lowest prices." By 1904, he was offering tailor made suits, and he and his father were "moving buildings to town, thus enlarging Vega" in the winter months. Stephen would have been in his early 70s at this time.

Since homes and claims shacks were often moved hither and yon during this period, it was

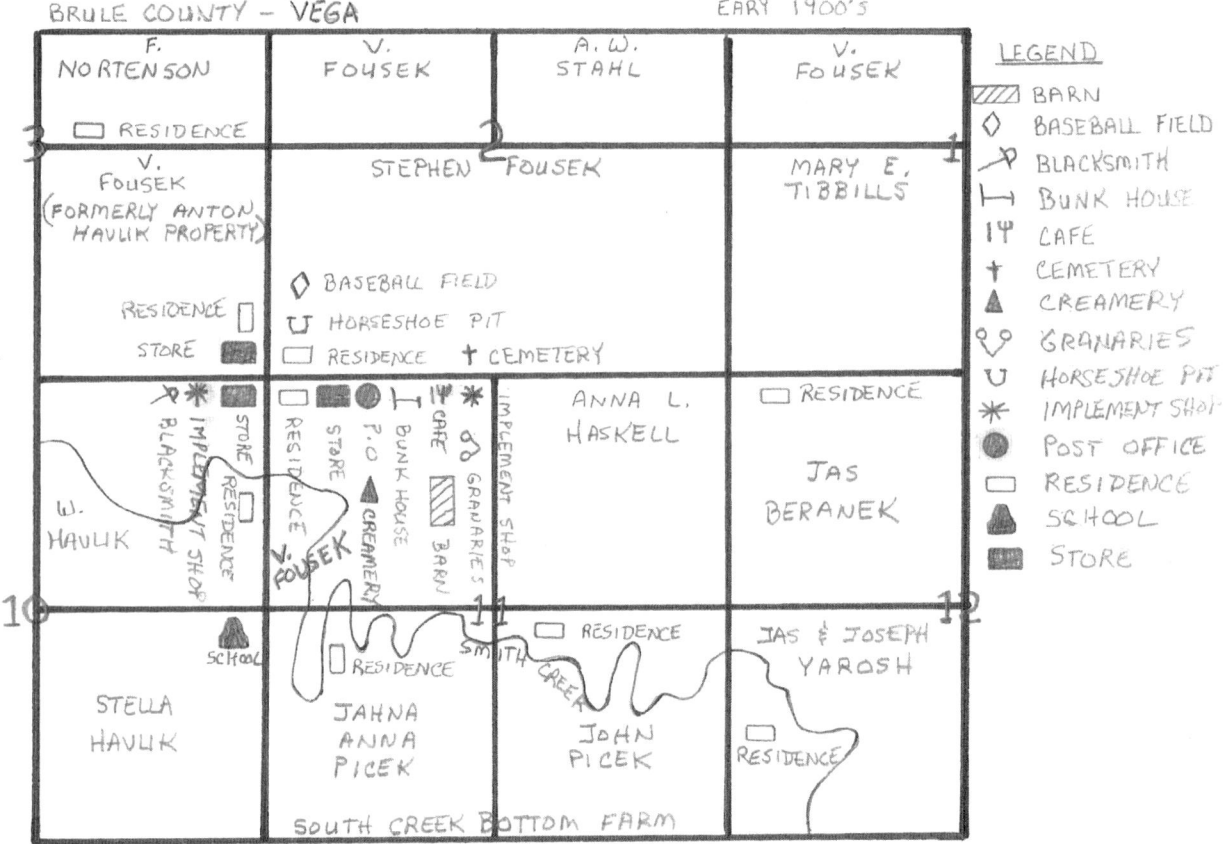

116

very interesting to us that, as news articles indicated, our grandfather and great-grandfather were moving abandoned homes and claim shacks to Vega. What the buildings were used for is a mystery, but we can guess they included bunkhouses, rooming houses, or "hotels" of some sort for workers and/or visitors, and perhaps some of the buildings might have housed businesses such as a carpenter shop, shoe cobbler or barber shop with very restricted hours of operation that could thus be run by nearby farmers, or perhaps serve as office space for a visiting dentist or doctor. The home that Anton had lived in before moving to Buffalo County, after swapping his parcel for our grandfather's Timber Culture parcel, may have been used for some sort of business, one of which may have been a store operated by George Caufman until Otto purchased the parcel from his father (our grandfather) in 1916.

We also find that our grandfather had the only phone in Vega, per the 1910 Gann Valley phone book. As mentioned earlier, our grandfather's phone number and that of Vega was 817. His brother-in-law Aaron, who lived in Buffalo County, was the only other family member who had a phone. Our grandfather also ran an ad in this same 1910 phone book. As our map shows, the Vega community also included more individuals than those mentioned in our narrative. Per our map, the following were among them: F. Nortenson, A. W. Stahl, Mary E. Tibills. Anna L. Haskel, Jas & Joseph Yarosh, John Picek and Jahna Anna Picek.

Our grandfather also apparently continued to farm and, per news articles, deal in cattle, hogs and horses while in Vega. There is a notice in a 1904 issue of the Kimball Index indicating that our grandfather had rented Section 16 of school lands for the term of three years. Based on his other activities we have surmised that this "school land" may have been used for hay and grazing land for his horses and cattle. In 1913, the Gann Valley newspaper reported that "V. Fousek commenced plowing with his engine this week and is turning old Mother Earth over in the right kind of style." So, it seems that our grandfather was still farming in 1913. And in keeping with his Populist and "Freethinking" ways we have concluded that the engine in question was a combustion engine on a tractor fueled by hemp oil, flax oil or maybe gasoline.

CHAPTER 9

Our Grandfather the Freethinker

Religion was an important part of pioneer life, and even today one can see tiny churches from days gone by dotting the Dakota landscape. Some of these churches have incredibly intricate and beautifully ornate carvings and detail work on the interiors while others are quite small and very basic structures. However, there were no indications of a church in Vega, not even a tiny church, not even after our grandfather and his father enlarged Vega by bringing in buildings from the surrounding territory. But as we were to discover, religion did play an important role in our ancestors' lives though not in the way we had first assumed. The key to our conundrum concerning the way our grandfather approached religion lay in the Freethinkers or Freethought Movement that erupted after the failed revolution of 1848 in Bohemia and which seems to have made its way to the Dakotas around the beginning of the twentieth century.

The roots of the Freethought Movement can be traced back to a time when Bohemia was one of the leading and most enlightened countries on the European continent, long before any other Western European nation knew much of anything about enlightenment. The people of Bohemia were centuries ahead of all of Europe in their cultural development, educational system, and economic, political, and religious freedoms. Bohemia was also during that time known as the breadbasket of Europe due to its farms and produce. As we understand it, animosities developed towards the freedoms and beliefs enjoyed by the Bohemian people. These beliefs and freedoms threatened certain power structures particularly within the Roman Catholic Church and the Hapsburg Empire, setting up a struggle that would last several centuries.

The struggle took shape in the 15th century when Jan Hus, religious reformer and martyr, was burned at the stake for being a heretic. In a failed attempt to destroy all of Hus's followers, known as Hussites, no less than three Crusades were embarked upon by the Catholic Church. All ended with the Thirty Years War (1618-1648) which devastated Bohemia and her people, transforming Bohemia into a nation enslaved by a neighbor state. The Thirty Years War resulted in the takeover of Bohemia by the Hapsburg Empire, and it ushered in a period known as doba temna or Dark Age, when for 150 years the Catholic Church sought to stamp out all vestiges of Bohemian identity, including its language. By the mid-19th century the people of Bohemia became nominally Catholic as the Austrians imposed Catholicism as the state religion.

Ultimately, the failed revolution of 1848 reflected the schism that had developed within the Bohemian community between those who remained with the Catholic faith and those who seized upon the opportunity afforded in America to make an open break with both the Catholic and Protestant church without fear of consequences. Nearly all who broke from the Church refused to affiliate with any church and referred to themselves as "liberals," "rationalists" or, most often, as "freethinkers."

According to the book *Prairie Churches of Bon Homme County Dakota Territory,* author Maxine Schuurmans Kinsley says that "freethinkers was a name given to those in the Tabor, Tyndall and Scotland areas who preferred not to submit to clerical and theological dogma. As such these people were welcomed into Czech fraternal lodges, non-denominational in nature, which for many created a social avenue separate from the church." The author goes on to say that Scotland, Tabor and Tyndall formed ZCBJ lodges in 1883, 1885 and 1900 respectively. Tyndall apparently also formed a CSPS Lodge at some point. According to Kinsley, ZBJC translates to "Western Czech Brotherhood Association." The author also states that the Tyndall and Tabor Lodges continue to exist on paper and still meet annually at least, as of the date of publication of her book, which was 2004. All the lodges at one time provided halls for plays, dances and gymnastics as well as opportunities for summer school in the Czech (Bohemian) language.

Our first inkling that "Freethinkers" had anything to do with our grandfather came when we found what was to us at the time obscure references found in Brule County History indicating that the ZCBJ, a Bohemian Lodge, held dances at the Wencil Havlik store. One of these Brule County History references included a photo showing about three dozen people who had attended a ZCBJ meeting in Vega. Another reference was found in the August 1904 issue of the Gann Valley newspaper, which said that "Mr. and Mrs. W. Havlik, Mr. and Mrs. J. Henzlik and Mr. and Mrs. V. Fousek drove to Bendon Sunday to attend the C.S.P.S. fiftieth Jubilee."

Another reference is provided by Stella Havlik in Brule County History, when she says that

Certificate of Marriage
Oddávací List

THIS IS TO CERTIFY — DOSVĚDČUJE SE TÍMTO

that in pursuance of the Marriage-License, No. *733969* issued by the County Clerk of the County of Cook, in the state of Illinois
že na základě povolení k sňatku, vydaného okresním klerkem okresu Cook, ve státu Illinois

_____ Mr. *Vaclav Fousek* _____ and _____ *Miss Stephanie Veselak-Brovec* _____

were united by me in
uzavřeli přede mnou svůj

MATRIMONY
SŇATEK MANŽELSKÝ

at Chicago, Illinois, on the *9th* day of *July* in the year One Thousand
Nine Hundred and *fifteen 1915*

in the presence of undersigned witnesses
v přítomnosti spolupodepsaných svědků

Witnesses
Svědci
Albert J. Anthony
John Pazour
Fr. Smolka

[signature]
Minister of the Congreg. of Boh. Freethinkers
Řečník Svobodné Obce.

Marriage Certificate for our grandmother and grandfather, issued by a minister of the Congregation of Freethinkers.

she joined the Z.C.B.J. Lodge at Vega in 1907. Yet another is provided by Dvorak's 1920 History of the Czechs in the State of South Dakota, where Dvorak says that "Brule County has two lodges: one is 'Jerome Prazsky' (Jerome of Prague), No. 152, C.S.P.S., which holds meetings in the school at Bendon; the other lodge is in Vega and is named Z.C.B.J. Lodge, 'Dakotska Osveta (Dakota Enlightenment) No. 184." Our last inkling that our grandfather, along with all or most of Vega, was a Freethinker is the 1926 deed we found that showed that the Vega Cemetery was deeded over by the "Vega Cemetery Association" created in 1906 to Camp Dakota Osveta (Dakota Enlightenment) No. 184 of Z.C.B.J.

Of note here is that Bendon, to which the Fousek/Havlik clan traveled in order to attend the fiftieth Jubilee of the CSPS, also had a Catholic Church. Yet we found not one mention of the Havlik's and Fouseks traveling to Bendon to attend church. The Bendon Catholic Church building was later moved to Kimball, where visitors can arrange an appointment to see its exquisitely beautiful interior carvings and also visit the headquarters of the Brule County Historical Association in the church basement.

Because marriages among Freethinkers were for generations performed by Justices of the Peace, we can now understand why the double wedding of Otto and Marie and Katherine and James was held, per Brule County History, in Otto's home rather than a church. We also can now understand why there was no certificate of marriage issued by St. Procopius Church of Chicago for the marriage of our Catholic grandmother and our Freethinker grandfather. Instead, we have included here a copy of the Certificate of Marriage for our grandparents, which was issued "pursuant to Marriage License No. 733969." The couple "were united in matrimony" by a minister of the Congregation of Bohemian Freethinkers in Chicago, Illinois on July 9, 1916. One of the witnesses was a Fr. Smolka, who may possibly have been from St. Procopius Catholic Church, where our grandmother had married her first husband.

Indeed, we were surprised to learn that the early Bohemian arrivals in the Pilsen neighborhood where our grandmother lived not only built their own Church (St. Procopius), but that not all Pilsen area Bohemians were churchgoers. As the online "History of Pilsen" page of Window to the World (WTTW) website relates:

> Many more were Bohemian Freethinkers, agnostics who valued reason and logic over tradition and church doctrine. In 1870, they formed a secular institution, The Congregation of Bohemian Freethinkers of Chicago, or *Svobodna obec Chicagu*. It served many of the same social functions as a church, conducting weddings and secular baptisms and becoming a social nexus for Pilsen's Freethinker community, eventually creating an extensive network of schools, athletic clubs (or sokols), benevolent societies, organized discussion groups, and forums for political debate. When a Pilsen church refused to hold a mass for one of their members, they established their own cemetery on Chicago's North Side.

> Downtown banks at the time refused to loan money to blue-collar workers, so the Freethinkers formed their own credit unions and savings and loan associations, providing the means for much of Pilsen's earliest and grandest development projects.

The following slightly edited excerpt from the online *Encyclopedia of the Great Plains* edited by David J. Wishart explains some of the key characteristics of freethinker "lodges" and the gradual re-assimilation into more traditional religious organizations. It also explains that not only was the ZCBJ Lodge an offshoot and rival of the CSPS but gives reasons as to why the community of Vega would choose to establish the ZCBJ Lodge:

> At least half of all Czech immigrants up to 1914 were "freethinkers" who chose not to affiliate with any organized religion and who established fraternal and benevolent associations to advance many of the same goals as those promoted by churches: fellowship, community solidarity, and civic service. Outstanding among these associations were the Sokol, dating from 1862 in Bohemia and 1864 in the United States, and the various benevolent associations, including the CSPS and its trans-Mississippi offshoots and rivals, the ZCBJ founded in Omaha in 1897, and the SPJST founded in Texas in 1898 and affectionately referred to as the "Special People Jesus Sent to Texas." The founding of the ZCBJ by trans-Mississippi members of the CSPS reflected their desire to admit women to membership on the same terms as men and to obtain lower insurance premiums for western lodge members, who tended to be younger and have longer life expectancies than eastern industrial workers.

Nearly half of all Czech immigrants were practicing Catholics, who established Czech speaking parishes in almost all urban and rural areas with sizable Czech populations. Protestants numbered no more than 5 percent of the Czech American population and organized independent congregations only in Texas. In the other Great Plains states, fledgling Czech Protestant congregations developed with the support of mainline Protestant denominations, notably the Presbyterians. After several decades of acculturation, tens of thousands of Czech freethinkers and their descendants joined liberal Protestant denominations or returned to their ancestral Catholic faith.

In keeping with the value freethinkers placed on cultural development, education and civic involvement, we found a 1903 article appearing in The Iowa Citizen which said that our grandfather's first-born son (and our half-uncle) Charles had joined a "number of Bohemian students at the university for the purpose of organizing a Bohemian Literary Society." This initiative, said the newspaper, "was a new one for the students in this university and indeed there are but three other similar organizations in the United States." Charles was appointed secretary of the new organization.

After Charles graduated from the College of Liberal Arts, he entered the College of Law, where he and some fellow students came up with a plan to run for public office. In 1909, Charles was subsequently elected for the first of two terms as Brule County Auditor. During his second term he became editor and owner of the Pukwana Press, which is still in operation today. In 1914 the Democratic Party asked him to run for State Auditor but he, along with nearly all Democratic candidates on the ticket that year, lost as Republicans swept the state. We assume that our grandfather, as leader of the Brule County Democrats, was doing his best in each campaign to see Charles elected. Newspaper articles indicate that Charles remained involved in cultural activities all his life.

According to Brule County History, James attended college in Sioux Falls after which he was employed in a lumberyard before returning to Vega. Since there was a business college in Sioux Falls at the time, we are speculating that James may have attended this business school in 1914. We say this for two reasons. One is that a May 1913 news article that we found said that James had returned home after attending high school in Chamberlain. Then we found another article that shows that in December 1915 James had obtained articles of incorporation for the "James Mercantile Agency at Sioux Falls."

For various reasons, including apparently personal choice, none of our grandfather's other children attended college, thus breaking with the freethinkers' emphasis on formal education. These children were Tillie, Otto, Milo, Emma and Rosie, along with our mother Elsie and her brothers Clarence and "Buddy."

CHAPTER 10

Our Catholic Grandmother Comes to Vega

As event-filled as our grandfather's life had been up to this point, 1916 brought yet an even greater whirlwind of events. On March 14, 1916 our grandfather's youngest child Emma married Edward Piskule. Emma would at some point, perhaps after our grandfather's death, be tasked with caring for her older sister Rosie, who had been rendered incapable of living on her own as a result of her ordeal with Diphtheria that had killed her little sister Libbie in 1903.

On July 19, our grandfather traveled to Chicago to marry our widowed grandmother, who like our grandfather was a native of Bohemia. Immediately after their marriage our grandfather brought our grandmother and her three children to live with him in Vega. Around this time our grandfather seems to have moved away from farming, as he listed his occupation as that of "merchant" on the marriage certificate. However, he was still the Vega Postmaster. Per family lore, our grandmother Stephanie frequently pinch hit as Postmaster during the remainder of 1916 and part of 1917. In September of 1917 James officially took over as Postmaster, to be followed in 1921 by Otto's first wife Marie.

In September of 1916, Stephanie and Vaclav sold Vaclav's son Milo, age 22, the parcel that had been sold to Vaclav by his father Stephen the year before. In a deal that matched Milo's exactly, they also deeded over, or sold, to Vaclav's son Otto, age 20, the parcel north of the Wencil Havlik property that our grandfather had purchased from Anton Havlik in exchange for our grandfather's Timber Culture land. To cap off the year that our grandmother came to Vega, Vaclav's son James Fousek and Katherine Caufman together with Otto Fousek and Marie Caufman were married in a double wedding on December 14.

Charles had married his college sweetheart Irene C. Yvorsky in 1908 and Tillie had married Rudolph Piskule in 1909 so all the Fousek children, with the exception of Rosie, were pretty much grown and establishing lives for themselves by the time our grandmother arrived in Vega. Tillie in fact had four children by 1915, a year before our grandparents were married, and Charles had three. Thus, our grandmother acquired seven grandchildren when she married out grandfather.

In April of 1917 James and Katherine welcomed their first and only child George into the world. And on May 6 our mother Elsie was born to Vaclav and Stephanie. Our mother Elsie was followed in 1918 by our uncle Clarence (who was Ken's father), and in 1919 by our uncle Stephen (Buddy). On July 27, 1917 Stephanie and Vaclav deeded one acre of the homestead and the Vega store to James, aged 25. In 1919, Otto and Marie welcomed their first child, Edith Lorraine, into the world, providing yet another grandchild for our grandfather and another step-grandchild for our grandmother.

On April 2, 1917 Democratic President Woodrow Wilson, who had been re-elected five months earlier on a "no war" slogan, asked Congress to declare war on Germany. Congress, by strong bipartisan majorities, obligingly issued a Declaration of War two days later. Despite this seeming strong approval, public opposition to the war was strong and the government went to considerable lengths to suppress that opposition. For example, and not unlike our second U.S. President John Adams or certain present-day policies, Wilson pushed the Espionage Act of 1917 and the Sedition Act of 1918 through Congress to suppress pro-German, anti-British and anti-war statements. He also had antiwar groups targeted by the Justice Department, resulting in the arrest of many of their leaders for incitement to violence, espionage or sedition.

Our grandmother Stephanie, at about eighteen years old. Printed detail at the bottom of phot indicates that our grandmother was living in Chicago at the time of the photo.

Through Executive Order, President Wilson established the first western propaganda office called, disarmingly enough, the United States Committee on Public Information. Headed by investigative journalist George Creel, this Committee was also known as the Creel Commission. Its main activities involved the circulation of patriotic, anti-German material and the censorship of material judged to be seditious. Creel staffed the committee with psychologists, fellow journalists, artists and advertising designers. The magazine illustrator Howard Chandler Christy drew "Liberty" as an attractive young woman dressed in a see-through gown cheering on the troops. This committee developed many of the techniques now associated with modern advertising. It also laid the groundwork for the public relations industry and served as the model for future government efforts to shape public opinion.

Despite all this, Americans did not immediately rush out to buy Liberty Bonds and their eventual sale often included a bit of arm-twisting to meet quotas. Nor did Americans rush to enlist in the army and so Congress voted in the draft. Somewhat surprisingly, some 10,000 Native Americans volunteered for service, and that number excluded those who had not yet obtained citizenship.

We have no idea what our grandfather thought about America's entry into what was to become one of the deadliest conflicts in world history, and what the media, thanks to the Creel Commission, was calling "The War for Peace" and "The War to End All Wars." Perhaps our grandfather had already become concerned about the fate of his native Bohemia as war clouds began to gather over Europe in 1913-14, and the Czechs and Slovaks, in a struggle to establish a common republic, joined the Allies against their old enemies the German and Austrio-Hungarian Empires.

We do know that our grandfather signed the draft cards of both his son Charles and his son Milo. We also know that six of Vega's finest marched off to war, Milo among them. Joining the army were Tom Cummins, Stanley Burian, Vladimir Kroupa, Joseph Piskule and Milo Fousek. Henry Thompson joined the navy. Tom Cummins, age 27, and Stanley Burian, age 23, did not survive, having died in camp of disease. Both are buried in the Vega Cemetery.

During the first two decades of the 20th century our grandfather managed to accumulate a considerable amount of land and property, some of which he sold to his sons Otto, Milo and James in 1916 and 1917, and some of which he at some point rented to his son-in-law Ed Piskule and a number of others. And in addition to helping build the little town of Vega during these two decades, he was busy improving his own homestead.

Our grandfather's barn, around 1917, looking pretty much the way it looks today.

Will documents show that this homestead had, at the time of his death, an additional 10 acres under cultivation, bringing the total to 80 acres. A new larger home measuring 38' x22' x16' had been built, and it is, we assume, to this home that our grandfather brought our grandmother in 1916. A new, larger barn measuring 28' x 72' x 20' had also been built. (Half of this barn was at some point rebuilt but the entire barn still stands today on the old homestead.) In addition, there was a second granary added, plus a hog house, and a hen house. The work was most assuredly hard, but it appeared to be paying off. Economic conditions, which had vastly improved since the days of the Populist Revolt in spite of the Panic of 1907 and the serious recession of 1914, also helped considerably.

Farm prices overall had increased over the intervening years, and so had land prices. Using figures taken from the *Kimball Graphic* for May 8, 1891 and December 1919, we can see that in 1891 wheat sold for between 55 and 65 cents a bushel, flax for $1 a bushel, butter for fifteen cents a pound and eggs for 20 cents a dozen. In 1919 wheat sold for $2.35 to $2.70 a bushel, flax for $4.50 a bushel, butter for 50 cents a pound and eggs for 35 cents a dozen. Notably this was the first time wheat had gone above $2 a bushel since 1866, at the end of the Civil War.

Land values reflected the increase in commodity prices and farm income, with good plow land in some areas going for over $100 an acre in 1919. Indeed, in 1920 Irwin D. Aldrich as Commissioner of Immigration was busy touting the attractiveness of land west of the Missouri River, which he said would never be cheaper than the going price of $15 to $40 an acre due to its income potential.

Crop and land price increases like these seem to indicate that our grandfather was a man of amazing foresight when he purchased a parcel in 1909 for $2750, or a little over $17 an acre. This land had been awarded to Civil War veteran Mikkel Kalsted for his service in the war, at a time when land could be had for a small filing fee under the Homestead Act. When Kalsted died his heirs sold the parcel to a William Wager for $670. Wager then sold the parcel to our grandfather for the then princely sum of $2750, a princely sum at least in view of the fact that our grandfather had only 9 years earlier purchased the Lars Peterson land for just $500. Will documents indicate that there were no fences or buildings on this land, and that there were 50 acres under cultivation. By August of 1924 it had an appraised value of $3200.

As previously mentioned, and somewhat curiously to us, the 1916 marriage license between our grandmother and grandfather says that our grandfather's occupation was that of merchant. We had always assumed that this meant he was a store merchant. But since he and our grandmother Stephanie had deeded over the store to James in early 1917, and James may have been managing the store for some time prior, we are left to wonder what kind of merchandise our grandfather was dealing in. It is possible that the farm machinery business was still under his control, although we do not know this for sure.

We do know that as late as 1919 our grandfather was still dealing in livestock, as indicated by a June 12, 1919 entry in the Gann Valley Chief which said "V. Fousek returned home Sunday morning from Sioux City where he had accompanied a car load of hogs that he shipped the past week." Another entry dated July 31, 1919 in the same newspaper said: "Ed Piskule returned home Thursday from a trip west of the river where he and V. Fousek had been buying cattle. Mr. Fousek will return the first of the week with the cattle they bought."

Since will documents show that our grandfather was renting two parcels he owned in Buffalo County to his son-in-law Ed Piskule as "hay land" (with these two parcels being "commonly known" as the Piskule land), it is possible that he and his son-in-law had some sort of business venture dealing with cattle. Similar ventures may have been set up with other farmers in the Vega area, since will documents also show rental income from other individuals, as well as a "Corn share" arrangement with Hans Nelson. But these activities would not qualify our grandfather as "merchant." Instead, we believe that because he added a second granary (nebulous though that term may be), our grandfather may have become a grain merchant, perhaps utilizing or even serving as a forwarding or commission agent.

In order to understand this aspect of our grandfather's life we managed to find an academic essay dealing with the historical development of the grain merchant. This following excerpt seems to fit well not only with the way Vega developed but also seems to indicate how our grandfather's grain business may have evolved over the years:

> As population grew large enough to support a town, a local general merchant *[in this case our grandfather]* began to provide the service of collecting the produce of the neighborhood and forwarding it for sale. The merchant *[our grandfather]* would credit the farmer for the produce at a fixed price, or the merchant [our grandfather] would credit the farmer an advance if the grain was to be handled on a commission basis. The farmer could then purchase goods that he could not produce for himself against this credit.

> The merchant *[our grandfather]* provided storage until a sufficient quantity of grain had been assembled. The merchant *[our grandfather]* then sold the assembled grain (providing transportation) or engaged the services of a commission merchant in larger city to find a buyer. The merchant *[our grandfather]* used the proceeds from the sale of the produce to pay his own obligations because the goods in merchant's store had most likely been purchased on credit of six months to one year. . . .

> *[It perhaps goes without saying that]* The general-merchant-cum-middleman must be trusted by the farmer in order to maintain the barter in produce that financed the retail trade. Middlemen earned the trust of their clients — who were also their neighbors *[and in our grandfather's case, his very own relatives]* — in part through developing reputation in the rural community. In order to develop personal reputation, middlemen needed to interact with clients and potential clients repeatedly in a variety of circumstances, both economic and social. . .

> *[Gradually]* The barter business of the general merchant gave way to the more specialized business of forwarding and commission merchants *[perhaps our grandfather?]* Forwarding and commission merchants handled grain for both farmers and merchants. Forwarding and com-

mission merchants were agents of the seller; that is they were to try to sell at the highest price, and they arranged transportation and provided storage and insurance along the way. They charged a fee (2 1/2 percent was customary) and did not take title to the produce.

Forwarding and commission merchants "adopted the policy of extending cash advances to country merchants [our grandfather?] with whom they had consistently dealt." . . . In essence, then, the trade in grain was conducted on the basis of inland bills of exchange, a slight adaptation to the dominant method trading since the merchants of Venice were in ascendance.

. . . .After the systematic grading of grain was adopted, warehouse receipts could be used for more than just security on credit. Because the receipts specified a quantity of a commodity with characteristics known to all, the receipts themselves became a commodity. Warehouse receipts became tradable. Trading in warehouse receipts evolved into futures trading through the use of so-called "to arrive" contracts. Excerpted from: *Middlemen in the Market for Grain: changes and comparisons* by Mary Eschelbach Hansen, The American University (Essays in Economic and Business History, (2000)). Bracketed text added.

Another online book, published in 1921 under the title of *Marketing: Its Problems and Methods* by Carson Samuel Duncan added the following salient details:

[The merchant-middleman] by himself or through his agents reaches out to touch the producer; he draws from many sources into the reservoir of his storehouse. . In so doing he is a collector, grader, standardizer, storer, packer. In this process he is also a risk taker. He buys and sells upon his superior knowledge of demand and supply. It is often necessary for him to finance the transaction before it takes place.

A commission merchant, if true to type, never owns the commodities which he handles, but receives a certain percentage of the sale price for his services. This middleman was more prevalent formerly than at present. . . The commission merchant needs the equipment required for handling the commodities with which he deals, this may be a warehouse, cold-storage room, coal bins, grain elevators and so forth. He must also establish the necessary connection both with producers or local dealers, and jobbers or retailers. He must be capable of inspecting, grading, judging what he buys.

The real service of a forwarder is to collect from various producers small lots until he accumulates a carload, thus saving in transportation rates. He gets a fee for his services.

A "factor" is almost an anomalous type [of farm commodities merchant], but is most nearly a commission merchant. He never holds title to the goods; he receives them only on consignment; he stores them; he finances the producers. He sells, like the broker, under orders.

Will documents indicate that our grandfather had received fairly sizable commission checks from entities such as the "Albers Commission Company," leading us to believe that he may have indeed served as either (or both) a forwarding and a commission agent, or some variation thereof at least by the time he arrived in Dante, and perhaps before.

Will documents also show that our grandfather was buying grain from area farmers on a regular basis, raising the question as to whether he might also have been providing cash advances to some or all of these farmers. Did he mill some of this into flour, sell it as feed, or store it temporarily in his elevator while awaiting a buyer (or higher prices)? And might he also have financed the purchase of at least some of this grain, using the grain in his elevator as collateral? Perhaps this is why he went to the trouble and expense of licensing his Dante elevator. Will documents also indicate that our grandfather had sold "graded" wheat to large milling companies in Minneapolis and Omaha, so perhaps he had begun to trade his warehouse receipts as well?

CHAPTER 11

The Move to Dante

Originally known as Mayo, Dante was a railroad town that was built in the middle of Indian country, surrounded by Native American allotments both occupied and unoccupied. The land on which the town was located had originally been allotted by the federal government to a William (Santohu) One Wing in 1887, and in 1907 One Wing's heirs sold the land to Hardin T. Mayo.

The idea of a town had come about because of a group of area farmers, including Mayo, who decided to petition the Chicago, Milwaukee & St. Paul Railroad to build a spur line between the towns of Avon and Wagner to make it easier for these farmers to get their grain to market. Since family lore indicates that our grandfather helped start two towns and because he traveled frequently and fairly extensively to conduct business, we are speculating that he may have joined the petition with these more local farmers to get this spur built.

It is certainly very likely that by 1907 our grandfather was acquainted with at least some of these farmers, particularly since Dante was, like Vega, a Czech community. It is also possible that various family obligations, including shepherding a lawsuit involving the alleged rape of his daughter Tillie in 1908 through to the State Supreme Court, may have delayed our grandfather from making the move to Dante at this early date.

In any case there must have been enough prospective railroad business to warrant the cost of building such a spur because the railroad agreed to build it, and in 1907 the town was platted as "Mayo." In 1908 the Mayo Townsite Company of Mayo was incorporated, giving it the right to sell town lots and transact all needed business.

The train depot was completed in 1908 by Joseph Kuca, who had been one of the original petitioners seeking the addition of a spur line to what eventually became Dante. As soon as the town site had been confirmed, Kuca, who was a carpenter as well as a farmer, set about building the train depot, a store, his elevator and stockyards. According to Leona Kotab's book on Dante, passenger service was not yet available, only freight and mail. Among the items shipped to the Omaha Cold Storage in Omaha, Nebraska, the Harding Creamery in Harding, and points east including Sioux City, Iowa were cans of cream, a variety of produce and crates of chickens. Cattle, hay and hogs also were shipped. And of course, grain. In 1908, the Kuca elevator became the first grain elevator that was open for business in the town of Mayo, soon to be known as Dante. By August 1912 the town of Dante was officially incorporated.

Various clues provided in will documents lead us to believe that the livestock venture that our grandfather and his son-in-law Ed Piskule had been engaged in in 1919 was not a one-time arrangement but rather on-going. However, it hardly makes sense for our grandfather to make the move to Dante in 1920 for the sole purpose of shipping livestock, hay or even grain that was grown in Vega out of the Dante terminal. But if, as we posited earlier, our grandfather had established himself as a credible, reliable, knowledgeable grain merchant while in Vega, then the move to Dante in late 1920 makes sense.

By the time our grandfather arrived, Dante had three grain elevators lined up along the tracks that intersected with Main Street. Per information gleaned from the Board of Railroad Commissioners for the State of South Dakota, sometime between June 30 of 1921 and June 30 of 1922 our grandfather purchased the largest of the three grain elevators. It had a capacity of 28,000 bushels of grain, compared with its next largest competitor owned by Owen Harty with a capacity of 20,000 bushels. Because of its size we believe this elevator was purchased from the previous owners described as "Melmer and Melmer" one of whom may also have sold our grandfather the four town lots on which his Dante home was located.

The elevator went under the name of "V. Fousek Elevator Company: Dealer in Flour, Feed, Grain, and Coal" and was one of two Dante Elevators that was bonded. The other bonded elevator was owned by Western Terminal Elevator Company, and it had a capacity of 15,000 bushels. Bonded warehouses, or elevators, were allowed to store grain and charge a fee for doing so, issuing receipts to farmers for grain stored. As we understand it, license holders needed to meet a set of minimum financial standards to hold the license. The license also meant that storage facilities and financial records would be periodically inspected without notice to determine whether or not enough grain was available to meet the amounts indicated by outstanding receipts. The license fee allowed the state to maintain a warehouse contingent fund in the event the dealer or elevator was forced to go out of business.

There were other possible, albeit not wholly satisfying, reasons that our grandfather may have selected Dante as the place from which to run his new business. One was that sometime around June of 1920 his oldest son Charles had been named cashier of Security State Bank of Dante, a very prestigious position for the time period. In fact, South Dakota State Historian Doane Robinson provides a list of banks and bank officers on pages 474-75 in his *History of South Dakota* published in 1904. This list always named the President and Cashier. If there was a Vice-President he was listed also. In other words, the position of cashier had a very different connotation in those days than it does now.

Dante also had more "modern" amenities compared to Vega. In addition to the bank, these amenities included a movie hall, a bowling alley, a lumber yard, a hotel, cement sidewalks and electricity, not to mention a wider range of businesses – and even a jail, used mostly for inebriated individuals who had gotten out of hand. The town's population at the time was 300 people, excluding area farmers who depended on Dante's services. Dante also had a Catholic Church, thus perhaps making Dante more attractive to our grandmother. Though Dante has today dwindled to a population of only 73, the Church is still in operation.

In any case, on December 3, 1920, about five months after Charles was named cashier, our grandfather purchased "Lots 1-2-3-4 in Block 4 of the original town of Mayo, now Dante, in the county of Charles Mix State of South Dakota" from Joseph A. and Rosie Melmer. The purchase price was $4500, which seems to have been paid for in cash as no evidence of mortgage against it exists until 1931. The same is true of the elevator, which we suspect was purchased in early 1921 due to the date of the residential lot (and home) purchase.

There was no mention of a house in the deed, but Leona Kotab says in her book on Dante that the house on lots 1-2 & the north half of 3 was built in 1915 by Joseph Melmer and was occupied by "Jim" Fousek in 1920. Because there was no mention of a house on the deed and because Dante residents frequently moved their homes back and forth between town and the farm, we are guessing that this house may have been paid for separately.

While doing research at the Lake Andes Courthouse, we were told that the original house was taken down when a Mr. Kostel purchased it from our grandmother in 1933, so he could put in a gas station. We have only a small fragment of a photo that may possibly include part of the front porch of the original house, together with some fairly large pieces of furniture left by our grandmother. But just the fact that the house took up two and a half lots seems to be a good indication that it must have been fairly large. We are guessing it to be about the size of the "merchant's house" at the present-day Living History Farms just outside Des Moines, Iowa.

However, even a large house (relatively speaking) would have been quite full because living

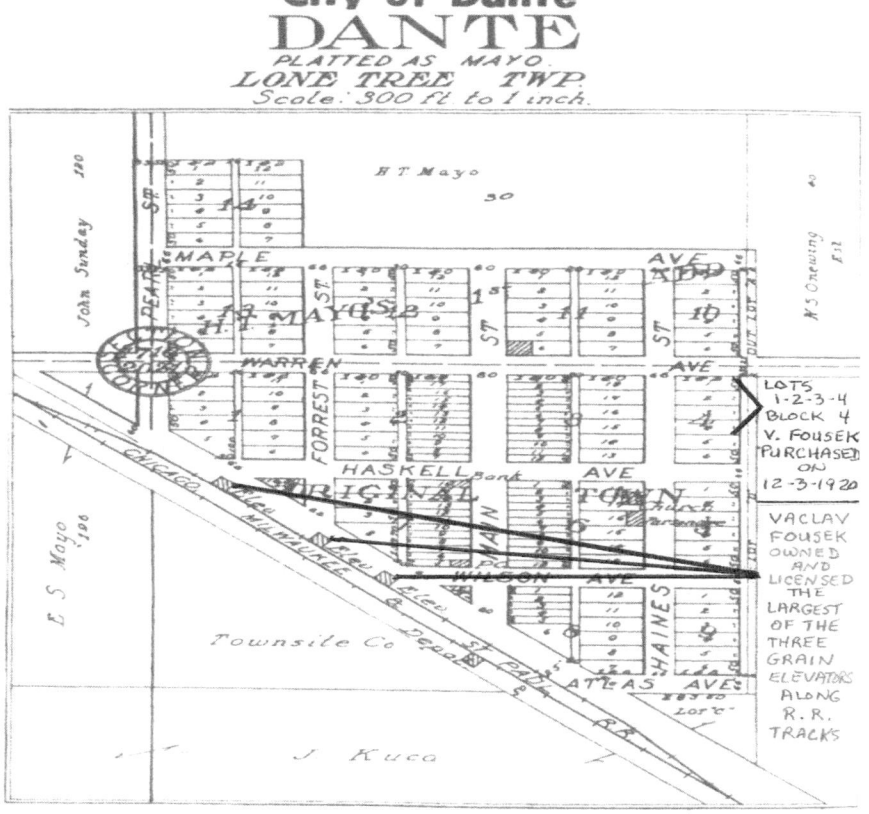

with our grandparents were the three children from our grandmother's first marriage, perhaps our grandfather's daughter Rosie who was not able to live independently, and the three children Vaclav and Stephanie had together, these being our mother Elsie and her two brothers Clarence and "Buddy." All the other adult Fousek children, with the exception of Charles and his family and perhaps Rosie, remained in Vega.

Somewhat surprisingly, our grandfather together with his son Charles, and his brother-in-law John Henzlik became majority shareholders in Security State Bank in May of 1922, a mere year and a half after moving to Dante. Whether these three had owned any bank stock before May 19 is unclear but it is quite likely that, as Henry Loucks remarked in his 1916 book on the creation of the Federal Reserve, they, like most stockholders in state banks, were more interested in developing other business relations than in banking.

This said, the details surrounding this particular stock acquisition are especially curious because on May 19, 1922 James A. Wagner, who as President of Security State Bank had built a new two-story brick building for the bank in 1920, suddenly decided to transfer his 175 shares of stock to our grandfather, his son Charles and his brother-in-law John Henzlik. It was an unusual transaction to say the least since Wagner *paid* the three recipients $1 each to take over his stock. Documents indicate that these shares were valued at $100 each in 1924. The obvious question becomes: Why would Mr. Wagner *pay* to have someone take his stock shares, when 1924 figures indicate these shares had a book value of $17,500?

Hindsight makes it clear that 1920 was perhaps the worst possible time for our grandfather (and his son, our half-uncle, Charles) to make the move to Dante to establish themselves in new businesses. This may seem like an odd statement, given that this was the beginning of the "Roaring Twenties" - which was after all a period during which America's total wealth is said to have more than doubled.

Unfortunately, and just as in the Populist Era, much of this wealth was built on debt. Through much of the Roaring 20s Urban America managed to continue expanding its income through debt and so Urban America largely escaped the pain and consequences of inevitable economic collapse until the crash of '29. For farm country it was an entirely different story.

Just as in the years leading up to the big crash of 1893, a bone-numbing farm depression was about to take hold, paralyzing the entire agricultural sector within a span of eighteen horrific months. Though farmers for a time made up for reduced farm prices by increasing production, this depression would, in reality, continue on for an entire generation, to be joined by labor after the crash. The root cause stemmed from "the money question" so clearly articulated by the Populists, but unlike the aftermath of the Crash of '93 in which gold coin became more available thus raising prices and wages sufficiently enough to create the so-called Golden Age of Agriculture, in this case farmers may have been purposefully maneuvered into accepting the necessity of expanding income through debt in the years following the Panic of 1907, also known as the 1907 Banker's Panic.

The Panic of 1907 and the Creation of the Fed

In 1916, Henry Loucks described what happened as a result of that 1907 panic, including what happened to him personally, saying in part:

> The panic of 1907 came like a clap of thunder out of a clear sky. The people were wholly unprepared. Even the bankers of the nation, outside a small group in New York City, seemed to have had no hint of it. . . In violation of the national bank laws, the New York banks refused to honor the drafts of the interior banks, and they in turn were forced to violate the banking laws and refuse to honor checks of their depositors, and without an hour's warning there was no money in the interior to pay for our grain, and other farm products. The reason given was that the eastern correspondents had wired the local banks that they could not honor drafts, because the New York banks had ceased to honor their drafts. Everything locked up in New York.

> Never was the power of the New York banks to paralyze commerce and industry the nation over so quickly and so thoroughly demonstrated as on that fateful October morning in 1907. I speak from personal experience as to the effect on the farmers of the nation. I had an unusually large crop of barley, and a large surplus to sell. I was selling four large loads a day, receiving from 90 to 95 cents per bushel. Sent in two loads in the morning, and was advised over the phone that they could not buy.

> Why? No money. Banks closed all over the nation, and local banks advised to pay out no money. Later in the day I was advised that if I would agree to take a check on the bank with the understanding that I would not draw out the money, just check against it, that they could pay me 45 cents per bushel. The price was cut more than in two. Most of us had to make the sacrifice to meet our obligations and avoid foreclosures of mortgages. Those who could afford to, held back, but it did no good, because prices did not recover for that year's crop.

> The trust-protected industries suffered temporary embarrassment only. There was no reduction of prices, because no forced sales.

> What did the government do to help agriculture in this great crisis? Nothing. The sympathy of the President and the Secretary of the Treasury was wholly with the pirates of Wall Street who had planned the coup and were making their millions and billions of dollars out of it.

As evidence for his statements, Loucks includes a portion of Senator Robert La Follette's address to the Senate, which describes the chain of events as they occurred. Excerpts as follows:

> The floor of the stock exchange was chosen for the closing act. October 24th the time. The men who had created the money stringency, who had absorbed the surplus capital of the country with promotions and reorganization schemes, who had deliberately forced a panic and frightened many innocent depositors to aid them [the money power] by hoarding, who

had held up the country banks by lawlessly refusing to return their deposits, never lost sight of one of the chief objects to be attained.

The cause of currency revision was not neglected for one moment. It was printed day by day in their press; it passed from mouth to mouth. The phenomenal interests were impressing the public in a way never to be forgotten. High interest rates must be paid for emergency money through the telegraphic dispatches of October 24th in every counting house, factory and shop in America. The banks refused credit to old customers; all business to new customers. Call loans for money were at last denied at any price. This put operators caught short or long on the rack. It spelled ruin. . .

How perfect the stage setting. How real it all seemed. But back of the scenes Morgan and Stillman were in conference. They had made their representations at Washington. They knew when the next installment of aid would reach New York. They knew just how much it would be. They awaited its arrival and deposit. Thereupon they pooled an equal amount. But they held it. They waited. Interest rates soared. Wall Street was driven to a frenzy. Two o'clock came and interest ran to 150 percent. The smashing of the market became terrific. Still they waited. . . .Then at precisely 2:45 the curtain went up with Morgan and Standard Oil in the center of the stage with money, real money, twenty-five millions of money – giving it away at 10 percent.

So it happened that the 1907 Panic started on Wall Street and eventually spread across the country forcing many state and local banks and businesses into bankruptcy. Fortunately, America was pulled from the brink of total disaster because, as would happen in the Great Depression and similar to the Vega "exchange" economy, cash substitutes (including checks and small-denomination IOUs written by banks) began to circulate, although not without sacrifice by ordinary wage earners and farmers, as Loucks indicated in the passage above. The total value of this "illegal emergency cash" was somewhere around twenty times greater than the infamous bailout organized by J.P. Morgan, but it saved the country from total meltdown and by 1909 the economy was growing again. Meanwhile, Morgan and company were hailed as heroes.

The aftermath of the 1907 Panic made it very clear that the "money question" was still on the minds of many. Farmers again rallied around the old Populist charge that too few eastern banks had too much influence over credit and the money supply. But following the same pattern set by J.P. Morgan and John D. Rockefeller ten years earlier when they organized what became the Indiana Monetary Commission, the big eastern banks lost no time in getting out in front of the issue. By 1911 $5 million in contributions had been collected from the big New York banks, the purpose of which was to establish an "educational" fund to be used to finance hand-selected university professors who would endorse the concept of creating a private central bank.

Soon after the Panic, in 1908, the Aldrich-Vreeland Act was passed by Congress, establishing the National Monetary Commission, also known as the Aldrich Monetary Commission. More study groups were formed, followed by a twenty-volume report. Republican Congressman of Minnesota Charles A. Lindberg Sr. (1907-1917), who is said to be the only man in Congress to have read all twenty volumes of the Aldrich Monetary Commission report, charged that the "king bankers" used the Panic of 1907 to put in motion a scheme whereby they could gain control of the nation's financial system through what was to eventually become the Federal Reserve System. The scheme precipitating the Panic, said Lindberg, involved "manufacturing" stocks and bonds by pyramiding and re-pyramiding them on mere speculation, causing their value to become "watered down" and thus leading to an inevitable and quite predictable crash. Democratic Senator from Wisconsin Robert La Follette. made similar charges in his March 17, 1908 remarks to the Senate, using the *Wall Street Journal* and other authorities as his sources. He added that:

The men who had created the money stringency, who had absorbed the surplus capital of the country with promotions and reorganization schemes, who had deliberately forced a panic and frightened many innocent depositors to aid them by hoarding, who had held up the country banks by lawlessly refusing to return their deposits, never lost sight of one of the chief objects to be attained. The cause of currency revision was not neglected for one moment... How beautifully it all worked out. They had the whole country terrorized. They had the money of the deposits of the banks of every State in the Union to the amount of five hundred million, nearly all of which was in the vaults of the big group banks. This served two purposes—it made the country banks join in the cry for currency revision and it supplied the big operators with money to squeeze out investors and speculators at the very bottom of the decline, taking in the stock at an enormous profit.

Almost as a harbinger of things to come, La Follette also described the problem as being traceable to the fact that . . .

legitimate commercial banking [was] being eaten up by financial banking. The greatest banks of the financial center of the country have ceased to be agents of commerce and have become primarily agencies of promotion and speculation. By merging the largest banks, trust companies, and insurance companies, masses of capital have been brought under one management, to be employed not as the servant of commerce, but as its master; not to supply legitimate business and to facilitate exchange, but to subordinate the commercial demands of the country upon the banks to call loans in to Wall Street and to finance industrial organizations, always speculative, and often unlawful in character. . .

With this enormous concentration of business it is possible to create, artificially, periods of prosperity and periods of panic. Prices can be lowered or advanced at the will of the "System." When the farmer must move his crops a scarcity of money may be created and prices lowered. When the crop passes into the control of the speculator the artificial stringency may be relieved and prices advanced, and the illegitimate profit raked off the agricultural industry may be pocketed in Wall street. If an effort is made to compel any one of these great "Interests" to obey the law, it is easy for them to enter into a conspiracy to destroy whoever may be responsible for the undertaking.

It seems that farmers, more than any other group, were aware of Loucks', Lindberg's and La Follette's objections to the 1908 amendments to the National Banking Laws (which amendments included a plan to allow commercial banks to emit "emergency" currency based on bonds or other securities during times of extreme stress). Evidence lay in the fact that farmers already were petitioning their state legislatures for more reliable sources of cheap credit. Small, rural state banks proliferated, and South Dakota became one of several agricultural states that adopted some type of state-sponsored rural credit plan between 1910 and 1925 for just such purposes.

In 1912, Progressive Democratic President Woodrow Wilson was elected on his "New Freedom" platform, which included a promise to revise the currency system. Two opposing groups vied to get their version of banking and monetary reform passed (with Wilson's Treasury Secretary also weighing in). One group was led by Senator Nelson Aldrich, of the Aldrich Monetary Commission, whose plan called for a system controlled by the large privately-owned banks, with the bulk of the nation's currency to be issued by private banks, in the form of loans. The other group, led by the still popular and then Secretary of State William Jennings Bryan, essentially sought a government-owned central bank that could print the nation's money as Congress required ala Greenback style (as well as handle the book-keeping needs and payment systems required to operate the federal government).

Democratic Senator Robert Owen from Oklahoma, himself a banker and the first chairman of the newly created Senate Banking and Currency Committee, countered the Aldrich Plan by saying that "it provided for the private control of what should be a great public utility banking system." With Bryan's support, Owen became the Senate sponsor of the Federal Reserve Act. Also known as the Glass-Owen Act, the Federal Reserve Act was signed into law on December 23, 1913. Despite the well-known Populist complaint against eastern banks being given too much power, President Wilson immediately appointed Paul Warburg and other prominent Eastern bankers to direct the new system.

Prior to the formation of the Federal Reserve System, the nation's governing financial authority had been the National Bank Act of 1864. This Act did not allow national banks to lend their credit as would happen under the Federal Reserve System, and it imposed a heavy penalty tax on state banks not joining the new system. By tying National Bank Notes to government bonds the government eliminated the 10,000 or so different "shinplasters" (or debt/money) being issued by countless banks that had proliferated in the years leading up to the Civil War. At the same time that Act restricted the power of all banks to create money as debt.

While the elimination of shinplasters did establish a more uniform currency in the form of National Bank Notes (which only served as currency in limited ways) it left the heart of the "money question" unresolved. Thus, after the Civil War the country endured one money panic after another, in order, it would appear, to get a central bank that could more or less be seen as an updated version of Alexander Hamilton's First Bank of the United States. The financial establishment, acting in concert with Republicans and Democrats alike, and often in concert with what monetary expert Alexander Del Mar called the European Financial Syndicate, accomplished these panics in a number of ways that were well known to the Populists, including creating a money shortage through recall of the Greenbacks in 1866, as well as the effective demonetization of silver in 1873, and the shipping of gold out of the country at a time when gold was promoted as the only "sound" money.

The new Federal Reserve System began operations in 1915 and played a major role in financing the American and Allied war effort, during which time the United States went from being a debtor country to a net creditor by war's end. As a result, New York's Wall Street surpassed the City of London (London's one-mile square financial center) as the center of the world capital market. This was a dubious achievement at best for ordinary Americans because, as in London, said "capital" was not really a fount of capital but rather a fount of credit built on the earnings of ordinary Americans. In other words, the new Federal Reserve System was not designed to add anything whatsoever to America's capital structure or to the formation of capital which might be used to improve commerce and industry. As the central bank of issue, it was instead organized to lend its credit, primarily to the commercial sectors.

After America's entrance into World War I, the Treasury Department mounted a series of war bond or "liberty loan" drives to raise additional funds needed to prosecute the War. In fact, the law that Congress passed to introduce these bonds still stands as the legislation that allows the issue of all U.S. Treasury securities. Essentially this new system allowed the government to raise money by borrowing from the public, in two ways.

First, it could sell interest-bearing bonds to the general public, who paid for said bonds with their own cash money. Second, it could sell interest-bearing bonds to the Federal Reserve System, which would pay for these bonds by creating a deposit account, "ex nihilo" (or "out of nothing") for the government. The government could then draw from this account to pay its expenses. At the same time, the Fed could use the value of the bonds as "reserves" by which the banking system could expand the money supply via "bankmoney" or debt.

The whole procedure essentially gives cover to the banking system by creating the illusion that the government prints the nation's money. This is of course a much more roundabout way of providing the nation's money than if the government simply issued Greenbacks (especially the true legal tender demand notes), which Greenbacks it must be recalled did not come with interest attached.

During this period, the American public was urged, often with a bit of arm twisting, to "borrow and buy" $1000 Liberty bonds by financing their purchase at local banks, or in lieu of that to purchase War Savings Stamps in smaller denominations. In his popular book *War Is a Racket*, published in 1935, Major General Smedley Butler, the most decorated soldier in U.S. history up to that time, described how soldiers paid for their bonds (while the "more privileged few" made profits of up to 1800%):

> Thus, having stuffed patriotism down [soldiers'] throats, it was decided to make them help pay for the war, too. So, we gave them the large salary of $30 a month. All they had to do for this munificent sum was to leave their dear ones behind, give up their jobs, lie in swampy trenches, eat canned willy (when they could get it) and kill and kill and kill. . . and be killed.

> But wait! Half of that wage (just a little more than a riveter in a shipyard or a laborer in a munitions factory safe at home made in a day) was promptly taken from him to support his dependents, so that they would not become a charge upon his community. Then we made him pay what amounted to accident insurance – something the employer pays for in an enlightened state – and that cost him $6 a month. He had less than $9 a month left.

> Then, the most crowning insolence of all – he was virtually blackjacked into paying for his own ammunition, clothing, and food by being made to buy Liberty Bonds. Most soldiers got no money at all on pay days. We made them buy Liberty Bonds at $100 and then we bought them back – when they came back from the war and couldn't find work – at $84 and $86. And the soldiers bought about $2,000,000,000 worth of these bonds!

The Federal Reserve Banks, then as now, coordinated and managed bond sales, and the bonds could be purchased by the public at any bank that was a member of the Federal Reserve System. The Fed also supported bond sales by lending to member banks at low interest rates when the loan proceeds were used to buy bonds. Reserves at banks that sold these bonds were thus increased, helping the bank maintain a healthy balance sheet and keep making new loans.

The phenomenon concerning the use of bonds to fund government did not go unnoticed, as is indicated by this statement by Thomas Edison which appeared in the December 4, 1921 issue of the *New York Times*, echoing the Populist demand for Greenbacks some three decades earlier:

> If our nation can issue a dollar bond, it can issue a dollar bill. The element that makes the bond good makes the bill good also. . . If the Government issues bonds, the brokers will sell them. The bonds will be negotiable; they will be considered as gilt-edged paper. Why? Because the government is behind them, but who is behind the Government? The people. Therefore, it is the people who constitute the basis of Government credit. Why then cannot the people have the benefit of their own gilt-edged credit by receiving non-interest-bearing currency . . .

Differences of view over the Federal Reserve's mandate began to surface almost immediately, and like Bryan and eventually Wilson himself, Senator Owen eventually began to express remorse over the part he had played in getting the bill passed. In 1938 testimony before Congress, he remarked that:

> I wrote into the bill which was introduced by me in the Senate on June 26, 1913, a provision that the powers of the System should be employed to promote a stable price level, which meant a dollar of stable purchasing, debt-paying power. It was stricken out.

> The powerful money interests got control of the Federal Reserve Board through Mr. Paul Warburg, Mr. Albert Strauss, and Mr. Adolph C. Miller and they were able to have that secret meeting of May 18, 1920, and bring about a contraction of credit so violent it threw five million people out of employment. In 1920 that Reserve Board deliberately caused the Panic of 1921.

The Panic of 1921

The labor market recovered quickly from the Panic of 1921 mentioned above by Senator Owen but the same could not be said for the farm sector, which by that time was not only awash in debt but whose crop prices began dropping precipitously due to the contraction of credit caused by the sudden and dramatic rise in interest rates.

Farmers had taken on added debt because, from the War's outset in Europe and throughout America's participation in the "Great War" Herbert Hoover, who was named Food Administrator in 1917, continually urged American farmers to increase production to feed Europe. At the same time, farmers were encouraged to accomplish this feat by borrowing to buy more land and farm equipment. Banks and other credit facilities expanded nationally as well as in individual states, all while the Fed itself pursued a policy of cheap money and easy credit - everywhere that is but in rural America.

As an example, Henry Loucks provided a statement made by the Comptroller of Currency before the Kentucky Bankers Association, before the Rural Credits Congressional Committee and in the Comptroller's official report for 1915: "[Usury rates] prevailed principally in the agricultural regions where rates should be normal. Yet, in every part of the country today businessmen get money at very low rates, except when it comes to the farmer. Now [war time] is the time to help the poor farmer. Nearly all of these extortionate rates are rates charged to the farmer." Loucks then remarked that the interest rates given by the Comptroller ran all the way from 12 percent to 2,400 percent!

Loucks also asserted that the policies and laws put in place in the years following the 1907 Panic. . .

> laid the foundation for a complete change of the financial system. The change is from money to credit, as I have clearly explained. At present [1916] the system is that of lawful money, currency and credit. The lawful money is being rapidly destroyed, or stored in the vaults of the men who control. The currency is being rapidly contracted, and permanently withdrawn from circulation. Then all that will be left is the credit of the national banks, and a limited amount of Federal Reserve bank notes for counter use.

In other words, in response to the Panic of 1907 and for the most part beginning in 1915, the Federal Reserve authorities put in place policies and mechanisms that were specifically meant to stimulate the creation of credit, with most assistance being directed at the commercial classes. As a consequence, in 1916 Owen spearheaded the passage of the Federal Farm Loan Act due to his becoming dissatisfied with the way the Federal Reserve was operating. As Owen and others saw it, the Federal Farm Loan Act was necessary as a means of improving the machinery needed for granting loans to farmers in much the same way that the Federal Reserve Act was being used to improve the machinery for granting loans to the commercial classes.

The Federal Farm Loan Act met with immediate criticism, including from South Dakota's Governor Peter Norbeck, who wanted his own state-sponsored rural credit plan installed. Norbeck, who represented the progressive wing of the Republican Party, had been part of the Republican Sweep of 1914 when our grandfather's son Charles ran for state auditor on the Democratic ticket.

Norbeck's Rural Credit Program, which Norbeck had developed while still Lieutenant Governor, ran from 1917 through 1923 and was supported by representatives of the cooperative grain elevator movement and other farm groups, and, it appears, even Henry Loucks himself. However, Loucks warned, unsuccessfully, that there was a serious defect in the bill:

> The committee [that examined and approved the bill] assumes that there is now and will be in the future an abundant supply of money for investments in farm mortgages. They overlook the fact that we are rapidly developing a complete change in our whole financial system as advocated by the National Banker's Association and provided for in Federal Reserve law and other laws passed during the past five or six years [prior to 1916]. The change is based on the

theory that we do not need money for the transaction of business, just credit and a check-book.

Due, as Loucks detailed, to an increasing shortage of "lawful money," demand for South Dakota's Rural Credit loans was unexpectedly heavy right from the start, and by 1921 the state had already loaned $37 million of the $46 million total it would eventually lend out during its six-year existence. In addition, South Dakota's banks had $22 million in mortgages on their books and insurance companies had $55 million in mortgages, all by 1921. This did not count farm mortgages and other types of farm-related programs obtained through the War Finance Corporation or the Federal Farm Loan program. Suffice it to say that by 1920-21 South Dakota, like the rest of the farm belt, was awash in debt.

In 1921, our grandfather's sons Otto and Milo, in apparent moves to consolidate previous debt, took out loans from the Rural Credit Board. Our grandfather also had Rural Credit loans on two of his farms, one of which was the Homestead. The second loan had been assumed as part of a purchase agreement between himself and his daughter Emma and her husband Ed Piskule for their parcel, on August 18, 1920. A similar arrangement had also been made between his son Charles and himself.

By the latter part of 1924 about 1/3 of Rural Credit loans (4,308 out of a total of 12,116) were in default as to interest or principal. 465 of these were either in foreclosure or already foreclosed upon, but the state made little or no effort to sell the accumulated real estate because there was already, by 1924, very little demand for farmland. Moreover, foreclosure was proving to be an expensive procedure that the state would rather avoid if it could. Despite this, the state eventually ended up with millions of acres of farmland at radically deflated prices, the costs of which were born by farmers and taxpayers, who were often as not one and the same. By 1927, the legislature barred further lending, and the process of liquidation began. The whole process was not complete until 1960.

While the underlying cause, as Loucks repeatedly warned, was lack of sufficient amounts of "lawful money," the immediate cause of problems in the Rural Credit Program stemmed directly from the deep agricultural distress caused by actions taken by the Fed. Beginning in mid-1920 the Federal Reserve abruptly and without warning began to raise rediscount rates (or the rates banks charge each other for loans) with the express goal, it said, of countering inflation, especially in the farm sector. This had the effect of raising interest rates – and restricting credit, which was serving as a kind of "substitute money." By 1921, mere months after the Fed's decision, South Dakota's Rural Credits Board felt obliged to "pursue a liberal policy towards borrowers" by granting "forbearance in cases where worthy borrowers were unable to pay in full or in part," this because too many farmers were already running into problems making interest payments.

In point of fact, a farm catastrophe of epic proportions was set in motion specifically because of the decision made by the Fed in May of 1920 to "counter inflation." In this endeavor and unbeknownst to anyone but themselves and a handful of Congressmen, the Fed began to abruptly and very dramatically reverse its former policy of low interest rates and easy credit (i.e., "cheap" money). This move led to sudden and severe shortages in the credit, or "substitute money," supply. As Nobel prize-winning economist Milton Friedman would later remark, the economic catastrophe of 1921, like those of 1929-33 and 1937-38, was "directly attributable to acts of commission and omission by the Reserve authorities." This was a bad system Friedman concluded, because it gives a few men so much power without any effective check by the body politic.

Two tools were used by the Fed to, ostensibly at least, curb inflation. Both tools led to the sudden and severe reduction of credit – which for many people, especially farmers, was serving the purpose of money. Both tools together began to send shock waves through the farm sector within eight short months' time.

First, the rediscount rates (or the rate which banks charged to borrow from each other) were raised during these eight months from 2% to 5%, to 7%, to 8%, to 9% until for some farm banks the rates were much higher. Second, the twelve Reserve Banks began selling those Liberty bonds which had been purchased from the government "ex nihilo" and which heretofore had been held as "reserves" for member banks. This action not only lowered bank "reserves" available to larger

Security State Bank of Dante, built in 1920, as it appeared in 2017.

member banks, but the sudden influx of these bonds into the market resulted in depressing the prices of all Liberty bonds, so all those wishing or needing to sell their bonds were forced to accept an average of 20% less than they paid for them. So it was that people across the United States who needed the money to live were being forced to cash in

their bonds for eighty cents on the dollar. Even worse, falling bond prices decreased reserves in small rural community banks, putting added pressure on the balance sheets of these banks. Farm banks began to fail as early as 1920.

By 1921 a nationwide panic occurred, throwing, as Owen said, 5 million people out of work. Far worse, both in terms of the affected population as well as duration, would be visited on farm income and land valuations - and the farm community as a whole.

As one example, the market price of wheat, which was one of South Dakota's leading crops, fell from well over $2 a bushel in 1917, 1918 and 1919 to around 90 cents a bushel (on average) by the end of 1921. Other farm prices declined precipitously as well, with lower farm prices soon being reflected in declining land values. The entire farm belt population watched its income get sliced by half or more in less than eighteen months, even as it was forced to pay premium prices for farm tools, transport costs and supplies, as well as normal living expenses. Even worse, these conditions remained throughout the 1920's, forcing some 450,000 farmers off their farms nationwide and resulting in countless failed rural businesses, and countless suicides. Farmers would by 1925 begin to make up some of the shortfall in income by increasing crop production, while rural businesses often sent one or more family members to larger cities for jobs there. This helped - but as foreclosure stats reveal, was not enough.

Leona Kotab's *History of Dante* indicates that the 1922 market price of wheat in Dante was $1.20 per bushel, corn was 40 cents a bushel and so on. Will documents for our grandfather indicate that in October of 1923 the International Milling Company of Minneapolis paid the V. Fousek Grain Elevator Company $1.10 per bushel for one batch of wheat and 77 cents per bushel for another batch of wheat for an average of 93.5 cents a bushel. This represented quite a dramatic decline from the 1919 wheat prices of $2.35 to $2.70 a bushel reported by the *Kimball Graphic*. No wonder that Leona Kotab reported that through all of 1922 there were many court cases in Dante that involved money, these cases being the result of people not paying for their purchases or services rendered them.

Wave after wave of bank failures followed the collapse of farm prices for the simple reason that such sharp and sudden declines in income rendered many farmers and rural businessmen unprepared and unable to repay their loans. In Iowa, 167 banks closed in 1920 and another 505 in 1921. Bank failures remained high in Iowa for several more painful years as more and more depositors lost all or most of their savings with each new failure. In the less populated state of Kansas, 220 banks failed between 1920 and 1929, and even though Kansas had instituted a deposit insurance fund, the sharp increase in bank failures beginning in 1920 quickly swamped the resources of the fund. Depositors of most Kansas banks that failed after 1920 found little protection under this program.

South Dakota, according to state historian Doane Robinson, had the highest rate of bank failures for any state in the Union. And despite the state's having created its own Depositors Guaranty Fund in 1915, many of the state's own citizens lost most or all of their savings during much of the so-called Roaring 20s. Tens of thousands more lost their farms, their businesses and their livelihood through foreclosure and bankruptcy.

Overall, across the nation, an average of 600 banks *per year* failed between 1921 and 1929, most of them small, rural banks; *half* of all small banks in agricultural regions failed during that time period. Investors and businessmen were erroneously led to believe that these small banks were weak and badly managed and so, they believed, the demise of these banks only served to strengthen the banking system overall. But as Milton Friedman, Robert Owen, and many academics and scholars since that time have understood, these failures were due almost wholly to the deflationary policies enacted by the Fed in mid-1920. The whole fiasco had nothing to do with mismanagement on the part of the small banks, who were for the most part as much victims of the Fed's disastrous decision as any other farmer or rural businessmen.

CHAPTER 12

Security State Bank of Dante

In his 1916 book on the Federal Reserve System, Henry Loucks pointed out that the Federal Reserve Act laid the groundwork for defining "current funds" to mean Federal Reserve bank notes, which were not "lawful money." Included as "lawful money" at the time of Loucks' writing were the national bank notes issued under the National Bank Act of 1864 (which were at the time of Loucks' writing being retired) along with coin certificates, gold coin, and a proportionately tiny number of Greenbacks still in circulation.

In contrast to the previous period from 1897 to 1914 when gold coin was in relative abundance, Loucks also observed that "gold coin has [as of 1916] practically disappeared from circulation the world over, but in no other nation are we decoining it as we are here." Why, asks Loucks, should it be stipulated that a loan be in current funds, which may or may not be "lawful money," and further stipulated that *payment* should be made in gold or lawful money? This stipulation alone meant that there would very soon be a serious shortage of lawful money in circulation. Loucks carried this line of logic to its conclusion:

> Most of our farm mortgages are now payable in gold coin of the present standard of weight and fineness. The same is true of the greater part of present obligations, estimated at all the way from $100,000,000,000 up. Suppose the creditors demand payment as stipulated in the contract, where will borrowers get the gold coin? It is a dangerous trap to set for the farmer who borrows "current funds" and obligates himself to pay in gold or lawful money.

Seen in this light, South Dakota's Rural Credits system provided one of the few alternatives then available to rural America. Clearly, wrote Loucks, the plan of the Federal Reserve System was to retire all currency, except a small amount of Federal Reserve notes for counter use. As proof, Loucks reported that in just five months, since February 1, 1915 they [the Federal Reserve Board and its Governors] had contracted the volume of currency by $42,201,550 – or about one-fifth of what it had been. The reason, Loucks concluded logically enough, was that they want to loan their credit instead of money, which meant that the schoolteacher, wage earner and everyone in between would no longer be paid in money but by a check against a credit.

All of this had far-reaching implications for state banks, which in postbellum America had played an important role in the banking system, this due to the fact that they were able to organize with a smaller capital, in smaller communities. But under the Federal Reserve system, the national banks, with whom the state banks were in competition, were able to do business without money deposits. Instead, as Loucks explained, the national bank was able to "loan the credit of the parent bank, for which it would be required to pay neither tag [Transaction Account Guarantee] nor interest." In other words, there would be "no limit to the amount of credit the national banks could loan and no gold reserves needed to back it up." In stark contrast to this arrangement, the state banks were wholly dependent on the deposits of their customers for their ability to issue loans, which were the main source of their profits.

Subsequent changes to the Federal Reserve Act similarly threatened the future of small banks. The first change, adopted June 7, 1915 dealt with the minimum amount of paid-up, unimpaired capital stock a bank was to have in order to apply for admission into the Federal Reserve System. Thus, for cities or towns such as Dante that had less than 3,000 inhabitants a bank was required to have a minimum of $25,000 in unimpaired, paid-up capital for admission to the system. This, said Loucks, "at once ruled out more than 6,000 state banks with less than $25,000 capital and a very large majority of the balance because of the rapidly graduated increase of capital required." Loucks summarized by saying, almost prophetically, that he did not see how the small independent state banks could compete for very long because...

> First, they must depend upon customers' money deposits with which to do business, and as shown, we have practically ceased to coin or issue money, and what we have is being rapidly retired, or demonetized. So there will be less and less of money in circulation to deposit in state banks. Second, the state bank cannot loan its credit; it must limit its loans to a certain percentage of its money deposits, and with a powerful opponent in control of our legislative machinery, they will insist, as they are now doing, that the state banks must keep larger reserves on hand than the national banks need to do.

Records we found confirm that South Dakota banks were showing significant signs of trouble very soon after the Panic of 1921. For example, the 1923 records of the South Dakota Banking Commission indicated that out of the fourteen banks listed, nine were rated as having "general conditions unsatisfactory" with Security State Bank of Dante being among them. One additional bank was ordered to comply with Commission requests for a report, another to comply with the Commission's requirements and another to levy a 75% assessment on shareholders to eliminate losses. Yet another bank was ordered to eliminate its losses on loans at the next annual meeting and still another was ordered to eliminate paper taken from the First National Bank of Webster within 60 days. (N.B. The building for the First National Bank of Webster was built in 1903, and is listed on the National Register of Historic places. It closed its doors in 1924.)

By 1925, 132 state banks and 17 national banks had failed in the state of South Dakota. National banks were not covered by the Depositors Guarantee Fund, but, according to Doane Robinson, the book resources of the failed state banks amounted to $43 million, with about $3 million having been paid to depositors from the guarantee fund. There remained a total of $38 million in unpaid deposits, leaving the state legislature to scramble, mostly unsuccessfully, for solutions to the sudden draining of the Depositors Guarantee Fund.

The first inkling of trouble for Security State Bank of Dante came with the strange agreement mentioned earlier in which then bank president James A. Wagner paid our grandfather, his son Charles and John Henzlik $1 each to accept Wagner's 175 shares of stock. This agreement was signed on May 19, 1922 and is rendered all the more curious because in her timeline of newspaper headlines, Leona Kotab reports in her book on Dante that in October of 1918, Security State Bank was prosperous. Recall that this was at a time when Rural Credits loans were providing a source of "cheap" credit, thus adding debt-money to the local money supply. This local money supply also consisted of other forms of loans (debt-money) but all of it was offset by dwindling amounts of lawful money, as Henry Loucks described it, which had debt-paying capabilities.

By September of 1919 Security State Bank had a new president by the name of E. F. Kellips. In 1920, James A. Wagner was named President of the bank. At the time Wagner was also a candidate for State Senate of Bon Homme County, where he and his family had founded and operated Tabor State Bank since 1900, along with another bank in Lesterville which had been founded in 1894. In Leona Kotab's book on Dante we find another headline for 1920 which said that Dante people were prosperous, and among several other items mentioned, we are informed that Mr. Wagner was preparing to erect a modern, all brick, two story bank building. In addition, we learn that our grandfather's son Charles had been named the new cashier and Frank Hakl, who had been one of the bank's founders, was named Vice President of the bank.

Some eighteen months later, on May 19, 1922, our grandfather, his son Charles and his brother-in-law John Henzlik would enter into an agreement with James Wagner whereby Wagner would pay the trio $1 each to accept the transfer of his 175 shares of stock in the bank to them. In exchange, our grandfather, his son Charles and his brother-in-law John Henzlik were to "guarantee the payment of all notes, bills receivable, acceptances and all other evidences of indebtedness which have *heretofore* been discounted by said Security State Bank, of Dante, S. Dakota, with the Tabor State Bank, of Tabor, S. Dakota and with the First National Bank, of Sioux City, Iowa" as well as "any notes, bills receivable, acceptances and other evidences of indebtedness which may *hereafter* be discounted by said Security Bank . . . with said Tabor State Bank. . ." Liability for the trio was capped at $100,000 for Tabor State Bank and $75,000 for the First National Bank of Sioux City, Iowa.

Essentially, the agreement allowed James Wagner to legally divest himself and his uncle Joseph Wagner, who was on the Board of Directors at Security State Bank, of all and any interest in Security State Bank. The agreement, together with the transfer of stock, also absolved both Wagners of all liability for Security State Bank, or any bank paper that had been transferred by Security State Bank to Tabor State Bank and the First National Bank of Sioux City, Iowa and any new bank paper that would in the future be discounted with Tabor State Bank. As mentioned, the liability that was assumed by our grandfather, his son Charles and his brother-in-law John Henzlik was capped at $175,000, this in exchange for 175 shares of bank stock with a 1924 stated book value of $17,500. (Frank Hakl's 25 shares would bring the total amount of shareholder equity to $20,000 at that time.)

Two questions present themselves. First, why did Wagner want to divest himself and Joseph Wagner of all and any interest in Security State Bank, when less than two years before they had built a brand-new bank building, presumably due to the citizens of Dante being so prosperous? Second, why would our grandfather, his son Charles and his brother-in-law John Henzlik enter into such an agreement, when their own liability would be ten times the book value of Wagner's stock?

Though we may never know the whole answer, evidence we have gathered indicates that both Tabor State Bank and Security State Bank were in trouble as early as May of 1922 if the above agreement is any guide. Interestingly enough, information gleaned from an online book about Czechs in banking, published in 1920, indicates that the Wagners were involved in two banks in addition to Security State Bank. One was, as previously stated, the Lesterville State Bank in Lesterville, organized by the Wagner family in 1894. The other was Tabor State Bank, organized by the Wagner family in 1900. Most certainly, the Wagners were hardly novices when it came to banking. So it would seem the Wagners clearly understood the reasons why, as Banking Commission records suggest, Joseph and James Wagner needed to return to their prior positions at Tabor State Bank in 1922. It is also quite likely that Charles (having served as County Auditor as well as Head Cashier for Security State Bank) along with John Henzlik and our grandfather likewise saw the writing on the wall.

We know from the Banking Commission minutes of 1923, mentioned above, that Security State Bank of Dante was one of several banks that was deemed to be in "general unsatisfactory condition." The examination date for Security State Bank was September 15, 1923, with the Banking Commission charging itself with the task of giving suggestions to help the new management, which may have come about, at least partially, because of the prior year's agreement. Although not conclusive, this together with other information we have, suggests but does not prove that Charles may no longer have been serving as head cashier by September 15 of 1923, with his assistant cashier F. H. Cash having possibly assumed Charles' position by that time. On September 28 of 1923 Charles died under suspicious circumstances, details of which are provided in our post-script.

Less than three months after Security State Bank was listed in "unsatisfactory condition," we find in those same Banking Commission minutes of 1923 that on December 5th, the Depositors Guarantee Fund Commission of the Banking Commission of South Dakota convened in a special session upon the call of the Superintendent of Banks. Tabor State Bank was one of the banks under discussion. At a meeting with Mr. J. A. Wagner, President of the Tabor State Bank, it was agreed that Wagner would deed 2460 acres of unencumbered real estate in Hyde County to the bank along with another 480 acres of Tripp County land "in order to protect against losses, and consequently waive an assessment of the capital stock of the bank." Deeding land over to the bank seems to have been a polite way of telling bank officers to foreclose on bad loans. This, as mentioned, was just three months after Security State Bank had been judged to be in an unsatisfactory condition.

A month after that, in January of 1924, there was a 100% assessment made on Security State Bank shareholders in order to shore up its capital. We do not know if or when the bank's shareholders had made any earlier contributions to shore up capital, but we do know that the 1924 Report from the Superintendent of Banking shows that John Henzlik together with several of his family members held 138 shares of stock. Our grandfather (or his estate) was next with 55 shares, followed by Charles (or his estate) with 32 shares and finally Frank Hakl with 25 shares. Shares were valued at $100 each, which meant that shareholder equity in the bank at that time was $25,000. The afore-mentioned 1924 Report of the Superintendent of Banks indicates that John Henzlik was President, and Frank J. Hakl (who had been one of the Bank's founders) remained in his 1920 position as Vice President. F. H. Cash, who had served as Charles' assistant Cashier was now Head Cashier.

A few months later, on October 1, 1925 Security State Bank suspended payments to its depositors and other creditors and its affairs were taken charge of by the Department of Banking and Finance. F. H. Cash, who had assumed Charles' position as lead cashier and who had just months before been elected town clerk, abruptly left town two weeks later, never to be heard from again.

By June 30, 1928 the bank's holdings were liquidated and the bank closed its doors forever. The fate of Security State Bank of Dante, like so many others of the time period, was not a result of mismanagement but rather stemmed directly from a shattered farm economy, primarily brought about by the 1920 actions of the Fed and a small handful of Congressmen.

The "unsatisfactory conditions" of Security State Bank were no doubt due to the fact that it was having trouble meeting expenses and the demands of its depositors, meaning its "cash" reserves were dipping too low. In other words, it was having trouble meeting its obligations as they fell due, this due to "lack of liquidity" or cash insolvency. One indication of this was given in the aforementioned agreement of May 19, 1922, specifically that which dealt with the loans that Security State Bank of Dante had discounted to Tabor State Bank and the First National Bank of Sioux City, Iowa.

Per standard banking practice, the solution to low cash reserves that was available to Security State Bank was to borrow funds from Tabor and First National, by "discounting" some of its own customers' loans to these banks. In exchange for lending Security State Bank funds (i.e. reserves), these banks would keep a portion of the total interest due as a loan fee, holding the loan note as collateral. So long as most borrowers kept current on their payments, this type of interbank loan would help Security State Bank to continue meeting the withdrawal demands of its customers while also allowing it to continue to make new loans. All of this was at a cost to Security State Bank that appeared to accumulate with time. From our vantage point, it appears clear that the 1922 agreement was destined to come back to haunt them all.

Another problem Security State Bank appears to have been encountering had to do with shareholder equity, which for a financially healthy bank should equal the Bank's assets minus its liabilities.

BANK BALANCE SHEET - "T" CHART
(Assets minus Liabilities = Capital)

ASSETS (Use of funds).	LIABILITIES and CAPITAL (*Source* of funds)
Reserves – cash on hand and due from other banks, plus bonds and other "liquid" assets	Customer deposits (checking & various types of customer savings accounts)
Furniture, Building, other "illiquid" tangibles, including foreclosed property	Other expenses such as supplies, utility costs, etcetera
Loans, secured by some sort of collateral	Customer deposits created at the same time the loan is created and through which loan payments are made.
	Shareholders' equity (difference between assets & liabilities) aka capital

Shareholder equity essentially provides the buffer needed by the bank to absorb losses resulting from loan defaults (up to the book value of the shareholder equity.) Whether Security State Bank had found it necessary to increase its paid-in capital prior to the 1922 agreement is unknown, but by 1924 the Banking Commission was leveling a 100% assessment on shareholder equity, meaning the shareholders had to cough up extra cash to keep bank capital where it needed to be so that it could absorb ongoing losses on defaulted loans.

In short, Security State Bank was, by early 1922, in danger of becoming insolvent due to the continual drain on its assets and reserves and the drying up of its funding sources, which funding sources includes, as our chart indicates, customer deposits (including those made simultaneously with the creation of a new loan) and shareholder equity. Put as simply as possible, there were too many borrowers deferring payments or defaulting altogether on their loans, while at the exact same time reserves and customer deposits were shrinking and thereby reducing the bank's ability to make new loans. As you can see from the chart, if too many depositors withdrew their money from Security State Bank, the bank's "source of funds" would dry up. And if too many borrowers can't make payments in a timely manner, or even worse, default on their loans, shareholder equity (and bank income) takes a hit.

Bottom line is that Security State Bank had apparently been running into problems by late 1921 or early 1922, and given the previous discussion, none of it was due to mismanagement or malfeasance.

How and why our grandfather, his son Charles and his brother-in-law John Henzlik got involved in the 1922 agreement is, from our vantage point, hard to comprehend. It's quite possible that our grandfather and the others knew and trusted the Wagner clan, especially given that the Wagners were not only of Czech descent but experienced bankers as well. It's also possible, even probable, that the Wagners and Fousek/Henzliks were employing the same "liberal policy toward borrowers" as the Rural Credits Board. After all, many of these borrowers were not just borrowers but friends as well. It's also possible, perhaps even probable, that the entire group believed things would get better; all they had to do was hang on and ride out the rough patch, something they had all done many times before.

As it happened our grandfather made a visit to a Dr. Hollingsworth on November 10, 1922. On November 23, less than six months after he, together with his son and brother-in-law, agreed to accept a transfer of 175 shares of stock in Security State Bank and less than two years after he moved his new family to Dante and purchased his grain elevator business, our grandfather was operated on for colon cancer in Sioux City, Iowa. According to an obituary appearing in the *Dante News*, and apparently written by son Charles, a postmortem autopsy revealed a cancerous growth on the lower bowel encasing the bowels and bladder, which his physicians believed to be of two years standing or possibly more. He died on March 1, 1923 (per his death certificate), after four months of nearly tortuous pain, leaving his entire family to face the remainder of the farm depression without him. He was not yet 63 years old.

Will documents show that at the time of his death our grandfather held title to 1120 acres or seven quarter sections of farmland. About 480 of these acres were under cultivation, suggesting that our grandfather was still engaged, even if only remotely, in a mixed farming operation. He also had been renting out some of this acreage and perhaps one or two buildings thereon, a side business which earned him an extra $1500 or so per year. Although very fragmented and incomplete, will documents show that his grain elevator business had earned over $27,000 in just the five months after his death alone – and this in a severely depressed economy. How much the elevator had earned in the months before or how much it could have earned had our grandfather lived we'll never know. Given what happened in the following years throughout the farm belt we can be certain it would have been a struggle to say the least.

As a reflection of these deteriorating conditions, the elevator would by 1925 be auctioned off for $3750 and the Dante house and 4 lots would, in 1924, have an assessed value of $2000, less than half what our grandfather had paid for the lots alone in December of 1920. In addition, by July of 1924, our grandfather's seven quarter sections of land had a combined assessed value of $25,050, presumably also reflecting by this time declining land values. There were four mortgages on those properties, two of which were from the Rural Credits Board, totaling $19,885. One of these had been assumed by our grandfather when he purchased the Piskule hay-land in Buffalo County from his daughter Emma and her husband Ed Piskule in August of 1920, probably because they too were experiencing financial difficulties.

In addition, will documents indicate that our grandfather had $120,000 in obligations against the elevator. We are guessing that some of these obligations involved contracts and/or advances he had made to or with area farmers for grain, and some may have been advances he had received from millers who had contracted for grain. Will documents also show that he had extended loans totaling over $8000 to his four sons and several others, which were outstanding at the time of his death.

Our grandfather also had $12,000 in loans from Security State Bank, $9,000 of which was paid off within six months after his death. A final loan from Security State Bank had been discounted with Tabor State Bank, and was never paid, possibly because the Tabor Bank too had failed. Another loan for $5000 from Farmer's State Bank of Pukwana taken out in 1922 and due June of 1923 would likewise never be paid. In his will, our grandfather said that the 15,000 bushels of grain still in the elevator would take care of his debts. This appeared to be overly optimistic.

By 1924 our grandfather's estate would be sued by Tabor State Bank for over $85,000 for the "signs of indebtedness" that Security State Bank had transferred to Tabor State Bank in exchange for cash to keep Security State Bank "in the black." As a result of this lawsuit, we have copies of the loan notes. Many of the loans had been issued to local businessmen as well as farmers and had been rolled over at least once after our grandfather's death. Apparently, the farmers and Dante businessmen who took out those loans with Security State Bank were having trouble paying them off and so were forced to roll them over multiple times, when they too were likely forced into bankruptcy.

On October 6 of 1926 the Vega Homestead was sold at a Sheriff's Sale to the State of South Dakota for the Rural Credits Board. The sale price was $6769.14. Although this was less than the 1924 appraised value of $8800, it cancelled out, on paper at least, the $5000 Rural Credits mortgage on the property. By 1928 the Lars Peterson property and the Kalsted property, along with the two parcels our grandfather had sold to his sons Otto and Milo would all be lost to foreclosure. One of the Buffalo County parcels would go for taxes, and the remaining two Buffalo County parcels would go into foreclosure. The seventh parcel would eventually be sold for taxes as well. In 1925 our great-grandmother Alzbeta (Elizabeth), who was our grandfather's mother, died. The land she had homesteaded with her husband so many years before would, in the not-too-distant future, be taken for taxes.

Family members would spend the next several decades trying to recover some of this land.

After all these years, the mysterious, often illusive – and, strangely enough given how hard it was to piece together tiny bits of information scattered hither and yon - popular and very well-known person who emerges from these pages seems to have wanted at long last to reveal his story. For whatever reason we were chosen as the vehicle through which his story could be told.

We have tried to tell the story of the exceedingly full and busy life of our grandfather as faithfully and true to the facts as we could, but of course questions remain, and the shadows need filling. Was our grandfather a one dimensional "wheeler dealer" as family lore occasionally whispered? Might he have occasionally enjoyed tipping the bottle, even when he was forbidden while serving as Vega's Postmaster? While these kinds of things may have more or less described certain elements of his personality, it falls far short of providing a complete or more nearly accurate portrayal of his character given the facts and rhythm of his life that were unfolded to us.

During his lifetime our grandfather was a farmer as well as a general merchant who sold farm implements along with general merchandise and handled repair work for farm equipment. In addition, he, together with his extended family, operated the award winning "V. Fousek Creamery" for about ten years and he dealt in cattle, hogs, grain. He also operated at least one fully equipped grain elevator, served as Vega postmaster for about seven years, was on the school board while in Vega and was, per *Brule County History,* the undisputed leader of the Democratic Party in Brule County. And as if this were not enough, he, together with his brother-in-law Wencil and his father Stephen, built the town of Vega, which served as the trade center for the area. Prior to all of this, he was active in Populist politics, having served as delegate to the state convention in Huron in 1896 and running for County Commissioner on the Populist ticket in 1898.

Details and facts we have uncovered reveal that the grandfather we never knew had to have been amazingly energetic, and hard-working – a wise, sociable and likable individual who remained to the end of his days firmly and emphatically dedicated to his family – and if his signature on the 1922 agreement is any indication, even to his friends.

He had proven himself to be resilient even in the face of seemingly insurmountable hardship, and he was quite clearly a highly intelligent individual. Up until the move to Dante he had shown himself to be a frugal businessman, utilizing credit sparingly and judiciously, and always meeting his debt obligations fully.

An obituary appearing in the *Dante News*, and apparently written by son Charles who was editor of that paper, said that there were two funeral services held for our grandfather. The first service was held in Dante at the local hall (which we believe to be the Saxophone Hall at which none other than Lawrence Welk appeared many years later). This first service was held on Friday afternoon and officiated by Rev. Frank Junek of the Choteau Creek Presbyterian Church who spoke in both the Bohemian and English languages.

On Saturday morning the body was taken by train to Kimball and from there to the Vega homestead where funeral ceremonies were held at 2pm Sunday afternoon "under the auspices of Mr. E. Thorsen of Kimball, accompanied by a fine Quartette of Pukwana." Newspaper accounts tell us that Charles and his wife Anna had the wrenching misfortune of being five hours late to this service due to car trouble. Nevertheless, the *Dante News* obituary describes the second service in Vega this way:

> Hundreds of people gathered from far and near Vega to pay their last respects to their beloved pioneer and neighbor who during 35 years of stay among them was known for his generosity, kindness, helpfulness and [?] to all. It was without question the largest attended funeral in that country since its settlement. . .

> Vaclav Fousek was born in the village of Krasnovsy, then Bohemia, on September 1, 1860 and at the age of six(sic) came to the United States with his parents who settled near Ainsworth, Iowa. Here he grew up to manhood, securing little schooling as was the usual case in the early days among foreign emigrants. Nevertheless, he acquired a liberal education through his own instinctiveness and intuition and was well read and posted on all worldly subjects. He possessed a wonderful mentality accompanied by an unusually brilliant memory that did not fail him to the end.

In short, our grandfather the Populist was, as his Brule County obituary said, "well known throughout the county, being one of the foremost leaders of his community politically and a man who was looked upon as a counselor among his neighbors." One can only wonder how many similar histories remain to be told.

Postscript: The Strange Death of Charles

Our grandfather's first-born son Charles died when he was just 38 years old, on September 23, 1923, less than seven months after his father died. Charles' death was reported as a suicide. Other than a few hushed and rather cryptic whispers while we were growing up, we originally knew nothing about Charles or his story. Yet as we delved into the strange circumstances surrounding his death, we began to have serious misgivings about the official story. These misgivings require us to begin with a brief summary of Charles' life.

Charles was born in Iowa in 1885. He came to Dakota Territory with his parents when he was between the ages of one and three. He was the oldest of eight children to grow up on the homestead his parents had laid claim to and as the oldest child, he undoubtedly was called upon to help care for his younger siblings and work beside his parents to establish the farm. News articles indicate that he frequently ran errands for his father as he grew older, and he most likely attended Populist events with his father in the 1890s.

He graduated from the College of Liberal Arts at the University of Iowa and attended law school there. During this time, he involved himself in campus activities and was "very popular" according to news articles. While in law school, he and a group of other students decided that they should run for public office. In 1909 Charles won the first of two terms as Brule County Auditor and during his first term, on October 27, 1910, he purchased the *Pukwana Press Reporter*, which is still in operation today. According to a news article appearing in the *Mitchell Capital*, Charles immediately "engaged the services of an experienced Nebraska newspaper man, who will have the active management of the paper. . ." This left Charles free to carry out his duties as County Auditor. In 1914 the Democratic Party asked him to run on their ticket for State Auditor, which he did, but the Republican ticket swept the state that year and Charles, along with nearly all others on the Democratic ticket, lost.

Will documents show that at the time of his death he and his second wife Anna owned 325 acres in Turner County, South Dakota plus a General Merchandise store in Centerville, South Dakota. When he came to Dante to assume the then prestigious position of cashier, he was already well known around the state.

Once in Dante, he immediately set about investing in the community, beginning with the purchase of Lot 12, Block 7 from the Walpole Drug Company in January of 1921. We don't know if a store was on this lot or if it was vacant at the time of purchase. This may in fact have been the location for the Farmers' Store, which seems to be a missing part to the puzzle presented by various news accounts of his death. *Brule County History* indicates that Charles and Anna had a store in Dante and we are guessing it may very well have been the Farmers Store. In any case, this lot would be sold back to the bank in January of 1923, an indication that Charles was trying to liquidate some of his holdings due to the increasingly precarious economic situation then ravaging the entire agricultural region.

In March of 1923, just days after his father's death, the *Dante News*, which was edited by Charles, ran an announcement to the effect that the Farmers Store and its stock of merchandise would be relocated to a space formerly occupied by Art Dank's Drug Store in a building owned by the Kotab's, which building was known as the Kotab Drug Store Building per the *Dante News*. According to this announcement, several thousand dollars of drugs along with additional general merchandise would be purchased in order to help fill the void left by the closure of Art Dank's Drug Store. Piecing together our own information and that gleaned from Leona Kotab's book on Dante, it seems that the Farmers Store (and its existing stock of merchandise) had been pur-

chased by M. Satin and managed by Elmer Rauch, who was one of the four businessmen present when Charles allegedly committed suicide inside the store's new location.

Will documents also indicate that at the time of his death, Charles and his wife Anna owned Lot 15, Block 7. This lot was the former home of the Square Deal Store which had been operated by Frank and Mary Barta until 1920, then sold to a Wm. A. Marin who subsequently sold the lot, and possibly the store, to Charles and Anna in January of 1921. Lot 15, Block 7 was next door to the bank. In January of 1924, Security State Bank purchased the lot from Anna, three months after Charles' death.

Charles and Anna also owned Lot 14, Block 7, which had been purchased in January of 1922 per Leona Kotab. In March of that year Charles and Anna evidently purchased the Delco Light Plant from the Cihak brothers and placed it on Lot 14, Block 7. In her petition to the court after Charles' death, Anna valued the Delco Light Plant at $600 and it later sold for $300.

Again, per will documents, Charles and Anna owned an undivided interest in Lots 14 and 15, Block 2, where the Saxophone Band/Dante Hall was located. This building was used as a dance hall, for concerts and meetings, as well as a movie hall and for church socials. Many years later, Lawrence Welk would play here. We also believe that our grandfather's Dante funeral service was held in this hall.

As mentioned in earlier chapters, Charles and Anna owned 32 shares of stock in Security State Bank. At the time of Charles' death, shares of this stock had a book value of $100, but by the time an appraisal was made on Charles' estate, shares had dropped to $50 per share, possibly necessitating the 100% assessment made by the banking commission in 1924. Years later, after the bank had suspended payment, Charles' uncle, John Henzlik, purchased these shares for 50 cents each at public auction.

Added to this long list of commitments that Charles was making not only to his own future but to the future of Dante, we have in our possession what must be the only known copy of the March 8, 1923 edition of the *Dante News*, of which Charles was the editor. Leona Kotab's book on Dante mentions the *Dante Enterprise*, which she tells us was known as the *Dante Progress* prior to 1918, and in a phone conversation with her she told us she was able to find only a few scattered issues of this paper to use for her book. However, early on in her book, Leona says that the articles she used came from a variety of local newspapers that included the *Dante News*. We take it from this that the *Dante Enterprise* more than likely at some point became the *Dante News*.

Will documents as well as Anna's later petition to the court also show that Charles, in his position as cashier, held deeds for property that was owned by the bank, for the convenience of the bank. This included lots B and F in the Hicks addition to Wagner, along with forty acres at Ravinia plus another eighty acres south of Ravinia. This was not surprising since Leona states in her book on Dante that from its inception the bank purchased and sold real estate as well as insurance.

Lastly, will documents also indicate that Charles had a $25,000 life insurance policy, with $2000 going to each of his three children from his first marriage and his first wife, and the remainder going to Anna. The last records we found said that the insurance company paid out a total of $19,000 to the family.

We found five newspaper accounts across the state of Charles' alleged suicide. These included the *Wagner Post, The Kimball Graphic, The Pukwana Press Reporter*, the *Evening Republican* of Mitchell and the *Daily Capital Journal* in Pierre. *The Pukwana Press* specifically states that it was relying on a "dispatch from Dante." Just who in Dante sent out that dispatch is a mystery.

Also a mystery is how and why all relevant editions of the *Dante Enterprise* (and/or the *Dante News*) are missing from the public record. The only reason we even found out that there was a newspaper called the *Dante Enterprise* (known prior to 1918 as the *Dante Progress*) was because Leona Kotab quoted from scattered editions in her book on Dante. To our knowledge all editions, other than our lone copy of the *Dante News*, which Charles edited, are gone. We don't even know for sure if the *Dante Enterprise* eventually became the *Dante News*, but based on information provided by Leona we believe it did. What this means to us however is that records of this rather dramatic event have for all intents and purposes been erased from Dante history, even though it made headlines in newspapers all over the state.

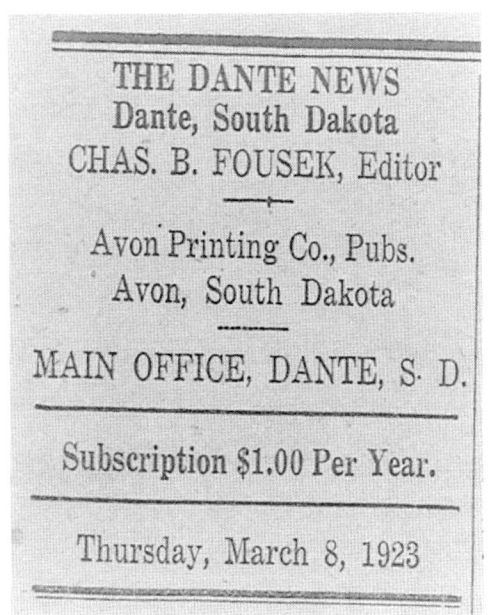

THE DANTE NEWS
Dante, South Dakota
CHAS. B. FOUSEK, Editor

Avon Printing Co., Pubs.
Avon, South Dakota

MAIN OFFICE, DANTE, S. D.

Subscription $1.00 Per Year.

Thursday, March 8, 1923

This is a section of the March 8, 1923 edition of the Dante News, which was edited and probably owned by Charles.

Family lore has it that many locals thought at the time that Charles had been murdered, but none could prove it. For us, this suspicion was bolstered by the fact that his successor and former assistant cashier F. H. Cash, who had been elected town clerk just months before the bank's suspension of payments in October of 1925, abruptly left town two weeks after the bank suspended payments, never to be heard from again. Cash it might be noted had been elected to public office several times before and could be considered a loyal and trusted member of the Dante community.

Further adding to our growing list of suspicions had to do with the fact that we were told by Ken Stewart at the Pierre Archives that bank records across the state were disposed of around 1925 by dumping said records into the Missouri River where they were to serve as a dam. Perhaps more saliently, we have the many misstatements of fact that marred those news accounts we came in possession of, even as they served to destroy Charles' reputation.

Included among these misstatements was the assertion that Charles had placed most of the stock of the state in the Collins Razor Company of Chicago "which went badly." But Charles never served in any state capacity, so how could he have placed "most of the stock in the state" anywhere? Charles did serve as a fiscal agent for the Collins Razor Company during his time in North Dakota in 1919 but his job as fiscal agent was to hire employees for the company. All told, North Dakota farmers collectively lost $200,000 due their having invested in the company, which went into receivership in January of 1921. Farmers in Iowa and elsewhere who likewise invested in the company lost similar amounts collectively. For all we know, Charles himself may have been among those who lost money due to their investment in the company. That said, the fact remains that Charles could not have invested for the state, neither the state of South Dakota nor the State of North Dakota nor any other state since he was never in a position to do so.

Similarly, we have the reports that say that Elmer Rauch was the new owner of Art Dank's Drug Store. Yet the March 8, 1923 edition of the *Dante News*, reprinted here, clearly shows that the Farmers Store was moving to the Kotab Drug Store Building into the space that had previously been occupied by Art Dank's Drug Store and further that "thousands of dollars of drugs and other merchandise" would be purchased to fill the void left by the closure of Art Dank's Drug Store. Most importantly, Leona Kotab tells us that the Farmers Store had been purchased by M. Satin and was managed by Elmer Rauch. In other words, it was Satin and not Rauch who owned the Farmers Store. It is our belief that the Farmers Store had been owned by Charles and Anna, who then sold the store to M. Satin.

News reports which said that Charles had provided a loan to Rauch for merchandise that Charles had sold to Rauch suggests two things. First, if Charles himself sold the merchandise, then he would have had to own the Farmers Store – which store it indeed seems that, as of March of 1923, Charles was in the process of liquidating. Second, if Leona is correct that Rauch only managed the Farmers Store, and was not its legal owner, then why would the bank (or Charles as cashier) give Rauch an $8000 merchandise loan and not Satin who was the legal owner of the store and its merchandise?

This is important because news reports said that Charles had been fired by his uncle from his position as cashier just two months before his death, this for supposedly pocketing the cash from the $8000 loan to Rauch, which of course meant that Charles would in effect be stealing from himself as well as his uncle and his late father's estate since all of them owned stock in the bank. Strangely, Charles did not skip town immediately after purportedly being found out by his uncle, nor was he put in jail. Instead, and apparently from the comfort of his own home, he was, at least according to some news reports, able to concoct additional illicit schemes by which to obtain money.

One of these schemes involved the insurance policy that covered the merchandise for which the loan was issued, the thinking here among reporters being that Charles decided to burn down the Art Dank's Drug Store in order to collect on the policy. Even here there was confusion, since one of the newspapers said that this policy ran to the bank, and another said it ran to Charles, indicating to us at least that if the policy ran to Charles, then it was "on behalf of the bank" in the same way that Charles' will documents indicate that certain real estate was also held by Charles on behalf of the bank. If Charles indeed thought that he could collect on this insurance, he had to be either deluded or desperate enough to believe that he would come into possession of the insurance money before anyone was the wiser, giving him time to skip town with his booty. In refutation of this theory however is the fact that a month *after* his purported firing, Security State Bank issued a loan of about $1500 to Charles for a business venture he had entered into with a local farmer. This is yet another indication that Charles had no intention of hastily leaving town.

One peculiar detail about the insurance scenario just described involved the reported visit by un-named officers of the state banking department on the Saturday and Sunday of Charles' death. This was only reported by the *Wagner Post* and read as follows: "It is understood that the officers of the state banking department who were in conversation with Charles Saturday and Sunday informed him of their intention of taking up the matter of his surity (sic) company if settlement was not made soon." The *Wagner Post* goes on to say that this strange weekend visit had to do with the money Charles had allegedly pocketed from the loan to Rauch. However, and as we understand it, state banks were not required to furnish a surety bond since they were covered by the State of South Dakota's Depositor's Guarantee Fund which had been enacted in 1915 by the state legislature.

Ultimately two diverging theories emerged from these news reports. One theory centered on providing reasons why Charles wanted to burn down the Dank's Drug Store and the other theory centered on providing reasons as to why Charles allegedly committed suicide. This second theory included the suggestion that since Charles had an $84,000 life insurance policy (grossly exaggerated as we have seen) his family would be taken care of when he was gone. So, in a rather unlikely story (if case history of arson crimes are considered), Charles as the alleged arsonist also came prepared to kill himself that Sunday night.

The scenario as collectively described by the various news accounts of that horrific night went more or less as follows. Four fellow businessmen/townsmen by the names of Sykora, Fillaus, Kloucek and Rauch had secreted themselves in the Fillaus & Sykora Hardware Store, which was located across the street from Art Danks Drug Store (really the new Farmers Store), because they feared Charles would burn down Dank's store. At Sunday midnight the men spotted Charles entering the store "with a bundle under his arm." The men surrounded the store with two of them going to the back door, while Rauch went to the front door. Where the fourth man went is not explained. However, the two men at the back door shouted to Charles to come out with his hands up. They then waited a few minutes, after which time they heard a shot. They waited "a while longer" before entering the store only to find Charles lying in a pool of blood with a gunshot wound to the head.

Might one or more of these four men have done the dastardly deed? Might the two mysterious, un-named officers of the state banking department have carried out this heinous act? Or was it Charles himself? Of course, the answer to this question has, through the passage of time, become legally moot, deprived of its practical significance.

That said, we have spent considerable time and effort in this book describing the banking and currency situation as it existed in the American West not only because it so clearly shaped the life and activities of our grandfather but also because it added a crucial dimension to the Fousek family tragedy that subsequently unfolded, beginning that fateful year of 1923.

We will probably never know whether it was really Charles or someone else who pulled the trigger that awful night, and legally speaking it matters little. Yet it seems very clear to us that the real culprit in this tragedy, as well as thousands of others that would come later, was the monetary system which, whether through errors of omission or commission, was at the root of the economic disaster that, in a familiar pattern, ravaged farm country first, before spreading nationwide. In Dante in 1923, Charles paid the ultimate price, not only because he lost his life, but also because his character and reputation were undeservedly tarnished forever.

Appendix

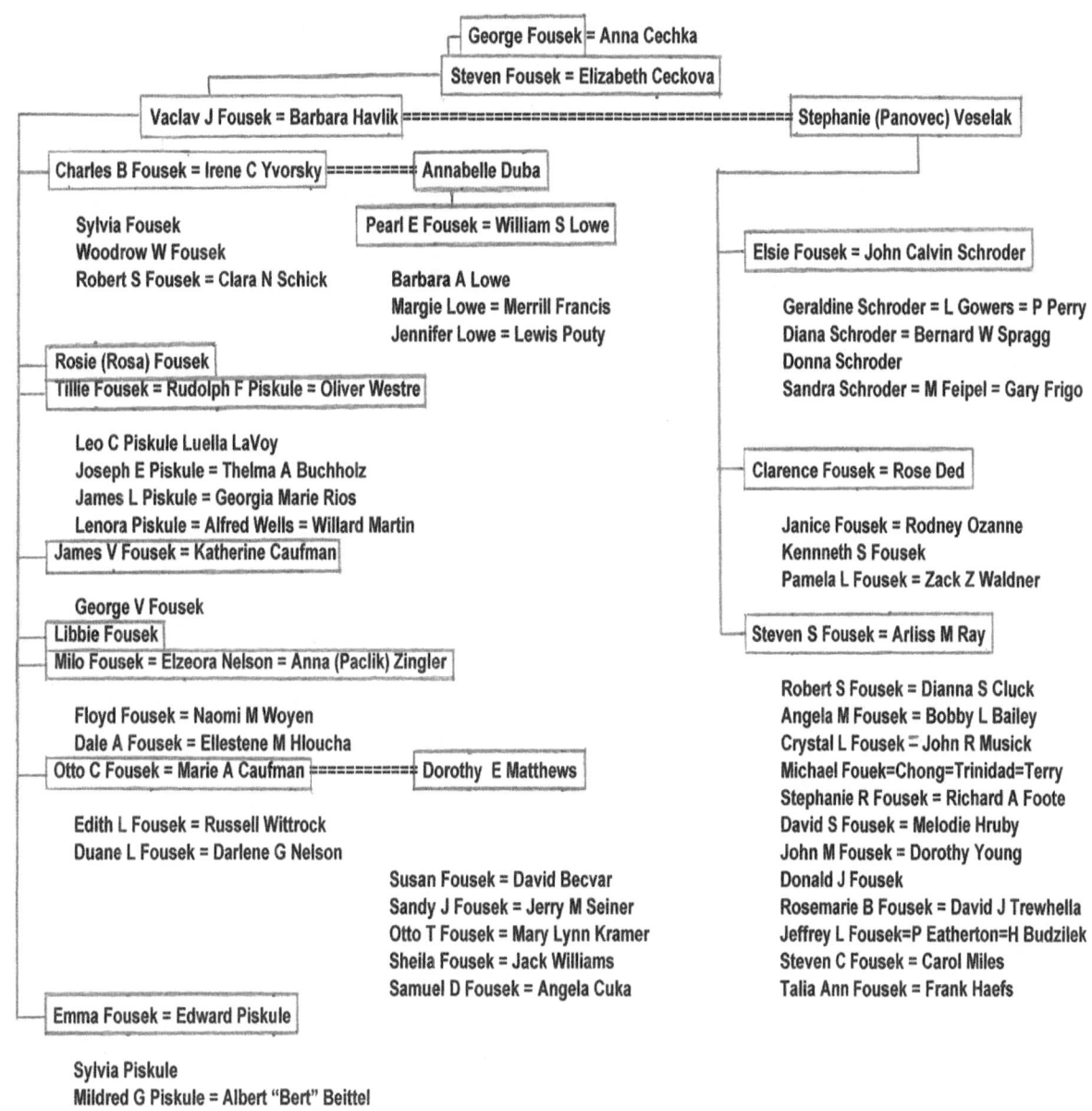

George Fousek = Anna Cechka

Steven Fousek = Elizabeth Ceckova

Vaclav J Fousek = Barbara Havlik ================================ Stephanie (Panovec) Veselak

Charles B Fousek = Irene C Yvorsky ========= Annabelle Duba

Sylvia Fousek
Woodrow W Fousek
Robert S Fousek = Clara N Schick

Pearl E Fousek = William S Lowe

Barbara A Lowe
Margie Lowe = Merrill Francis
Jennifer Lowe = Lewis Pouty

Elsie Fousek = John Calvin Schroder

Geraldine Schroder = L Gowers = P Perry
Diana Schroder = Bernard W Spragg
Donna Schroder
Sandra Schroder = M Feipel = Gary Frigo

Rosie (Rosa) Fousek
Tillie Fousek = Rudolph F Piskule = Oliver Westre

Leo C Piskule Luella LaVoy
Joseph E Piskule = Thelma A Buchholz
James L Piskule = Georgia Marie Rios
Lenora Piskule = Alfred Wells = Willard Martin
James V Fousek = Katherine Caufman

Clarence Fousek = Rose Ded

Janice Fousek = Rodney Ozanne
Kennneth S Fousek
Pamela L Fousek = Zack Z Waldner

George V Fousek
Libbie Fousek
Milo Fousek = Elzeora Nelson = Anna (Paclik) Zingler

Steven S Fousek = Arliss M Ray

Floyd Fousek = Naomi M Woyen
Dale A Fousek = Ellestene M Hloucha
Otto C Fousek = Marie A Caufman ============ Dorothy E Matthews

Edith L Fousek = Russell Wittrock
Duane L Fousek = Darlene G Nelson

Susan Fousek = David Becvar
Sandy J Fousek = Jerry M Seiner
Otto T Fousek = Mary Lynn Kramer
Sheila Fousek = Jack Williams
Samuel D Fousek = Angela Cuka

Robert S Fousek = Dianna S Cluck
Angela M Fousek = Bobby L Bailey
Crystal L Fousek = John R Musick
Michael Fouek=Chong=Trinidad=Terry
Stephanie R Fousek = Richard A Foote
David S Fousek = Melodie Hruby
John M Fousek = Dorothy Young
Donald J Fousek
Rosemarie B Fousek = David J Trewhella
Jeffrey L Fousek=P Eatherton=H Budzilek
Steven C Fousek = Carol Miles
Talia Ann Fousek = Frank Haefs

Emma Fousek = Edward Piskule

Sylvia Piskule
Mildred G Piskule = Albert "Bert" Beittel
Edwin Piskule = Eva Koss

Selected Bibliography
and List of Sources

Atherton, Lewis Eldon (1971) *Frontier Merchant in Mid-America*

Barr, Elizabeth (1918) *The Populist Uprising*, available online

Brule County Historical Society (1977) *Brule County History*

Kotab, Leona (2001) *Dante, South Dakota 1887-2000*

Bickner, Mrs. Donald W. etal. (1980) *Echoes of the Past*

Bingham, John H. and Peters, Nora V. (1947) *A Short History of Brule County*

Cerney, Jan (2004) *Images of America: Gregory and Charles Mix Counties*

DelMar, Alexander. *The Science of Money* (1885*), History of Money in America* (1899) *and A History of Monetary Crimes* (1899)

Dvorak, Josef A. (1920) *History of the Czechs in the State of South Dakota*

Glass, Orah (1970) *History of Pukwana and Vicinity*

Goodwyn, Lawrence (1978) *The Populist Moment*

Gnirk, Adeline S., editor and compiler. *Epic of the Realm of Ree.*

Gnirk, Adeline S. *Of Rails and Trails.*

Harvey, William Hope (1894) *Coin's Financial School*

Hicks, John (1931) *The Populist Revolt*

Hild, Matthew (2007) *Greenbackers, Knights of Labor and Populists*

King, S. S. (1892) *Of Bond Holders and Breadwinner: A Portrayal of Some Political Crimes Committed in the Name of Liberty*

Kohl, Edith (1938) *Land of the Burnt Thigh*

LaPointe, Ernie (2009) *Sitting Bull: His Life and Legacy*

Lee, R. Alton (2011) *Principle Over Party: The Farmers' Alliance and Populism in South Dakota 1880-1900*

Livingston. James (1989) *Origins of the Federal Reserve System: Money, Class, and Corporate Capitalism, 1890-1913*

Loucks, Henry. *The New Monetary System as Advocated by the Farmers' Alliance and Industrial Union* (1893), *The Great Conspiracy of the House of Morgan Exposed and how to defeat it* (1916), *Our Daily Bread Must be Freed from the Greed of Monopoly* (1919), *How to Restore and Maintain Our Government Bonds at Par* (1921)

Nelson, A. Dunning (1887) *A Philosophy of Price*

Postel, Charles (2009) *The Populist Vision*

Primm, James Neal (1989) *A Foregone Conclusion*, portions available online

Robinson, Doane (1901) *History of South Dakota* and *Encyclopedia of South Dakota*

Schell, Herbert Samuel (1955) *South Dakota: It's Beginnings and Growth*

Schulte, Francis J. (1895) The Little Statesmen, A Middle-of-the-Road Manual for American Voters

South Dakota State Department of History, compiler, V. VIII (1916) *South Dakota Historical Collections*, illustrated with maps and engravings.

Woodward, C. Vann (1981) *Origins of the New South, 1877 - 1913*

Wyman, Walker as told to him by Grace Fairchild (1972) *Frontier Woman: The Life of a Woman Homesteader on the Dakota Frontier.*

Wyman, Walker D. from the original notes of Bruce Siberts (1954) *Nothing But Prairie and Blue Sky: Life on the Dakota Range in the Early Days*

Zarlenga, Stephen (2002) *The Lost Science of Money: The Mythology of Money and the Story of Power*

Journals and other Literature:

Ali, Omar (May 11, 1998) *Preliminary Research for Writing a History of the Colored Farmers' Alliance,* available online

Buckhout, Dave (2004) *The Rise and Fall of Southern Populism* in three parts, available online

Demerest, Henry Lloyd (1896*) The Populists at St. Louis*, available online

Duncan, Carson Samuel, Ph.D. (1921) *Marketing: Its Problems and Methods* Available in digital format at Books.google.

Fite, Gilbert (October, 1947) *South Dakota's Rural Credit System: A Venture in State Socialism 1917-1946*

Gaither, Gerald (1976) *Blacks and the Southern Farmer's Alliance Movement.* East Texas Historical Journal, Volume 14, Issue 1, Article 7

Hansen, Mary Eschelbach, American University. *Middlemen in the Market for Grain: Changes and Comparisons* (available online)

Levy, Jonathan. *Farmers and Risk: the Fate of Landed Independence in 19*[th] *Century* America (This paper, found online, formed the basis of a book called *Freaks of Fortune: The Emerging World of Capitalism and Risk* by Jonathan Levy, published in 2012)

Lincoln, Abraham (December 3, 1861) *Annual Message to Congress*

Post, Charles. *The American Road to Capitalism*

Rothstein, Sidney, (2014) *Macune's Monopoly: Economic Law and the Legacy of Populism.* Available online

Smith, F.R. and Fossum, A.E. (1928) *Eighteenth Biennial Report of the Superintendent of Banks for the Period July 1, 1926 to June 20, 1928 to the Governor.*

Stern, Alexandra E. (2015) *War Is Cruelty: The Civil War Lessons of the Dakota War of 1862,* available online

Tweton, Jerome D. (1993) *Why Populism Succeeded in South Dakota and Failed in North Dakota.* Available online

Magazine article on Freethinkers found in Koreny, Fall 2001

Promotional brochure, circa 1901, put out by the General Passenger Department of the Chicago, Milwaukee and St. Paul Railway.

PLUS:

Newspaper articles, obituaries and advertisements obtained on microfiche at the South Dakota Archives in Pierre, in addition to online news articles through Chronicling America and Newspapers.com. Also invaluable were will documents, death certificates, marriage licenses, census data, land records from various sources.

Additional Online resources, last accessed February 27, 2017:

List of headstones at the Vega Cemetery:

http://www.lbroots.org/databases/cemeteries/cemeteries-brule/vega/

Bonanza Farms and Ranches Prove Worth of Land – Dakota Boom Explained, published in Fargo, North Dakota. May of 1890:

http://www.ndstudies.org/articles/bonanza_farms_and_ranches_prove_worth_of_land

Bibliography

Bonanza Farming by Hiram M. Drache Concordia College: http://plainshumanities.unl.edu/encyclopedia/doc/egp.ag.013

History of Iowa by Dorothy Schweider, professor of history, Iowa State University from: http://publications.iowa.gov/135/1/history/7-1.html

Personal Account of Nellie Louise Fuller Carey of Dakota Territory in the 1880s as told to her daughter: http://www.lbroots.org/databases/family-histories/chamberlain-and-me-growing-up-together/

Fort Randall: http://www.forttours.com/pages/fortrandall.asp

Financial Crisis: The Slumps that Changed American Finance. Essay in The Economist: http://www.economist.com/news/essays/21600451-finance-not-merely-prone-crises-it-shaped-them-five-historical-crises-show-how-aspects-today-s-fina

The Fed's Formative Years: 1913 – 1929 by David C. Wheelock, Federal Reserve Bank of St. Louis. http://www.federalreservehistory.org/Events/DetailView/60 (N.B. Friedman and Schwarz were more critical than this article implies.)

Federal Reserve's Role During WWI August 1914 – November 1918 by Phil Davies, Federal Reserve Bank of Minneapolis. http://www.federalreservehistory.org/Events/DetailView/17

Farm Loan Act of 1916 article in *The American Economic Review*

Four Minute Men: Volunteer Speeches During World War I
: *http://historymatters.gmu.edu/d/4970/*

Liberty Bonds: 4/19 to 9/1918 by Richard Sutch, University of California, Riverside and Berkeley. http://www.federalreservehistory.org/Events/DetailView/100

War Savings Bonds (Liberty Loans): https://sniggle.net/TPL/index5.php?entry=27Jan08

Robert Latham Owen: https://www.isnare.com/encyclopedia/Robert_Latham_Owen

U.S. Farmers During the Great Depression: U.S. Farmers Faced High Farm Mortgages and Big Debts Even Before the Great Depression Began. http://www.farmcollector.com/farm-life/u-s-farmers-during-great-depression And: http://www.ndstudies.org/articles/overview_the_1920s

U.S. Economy in World War I, by Hugh Rockoff, Rutgers University: http://eh.net/encyclopedia/u-s-economy-in-world-war-i/

The farmer in the Roaring 20s: http://www.iptv.org/iowapathways/mypath.cfm?ounid=ob_000060

The Slumps that Shaped Modern Finance: *http://www.economist.com/news/essays/21600451-finance-not-merely-prone-crises-it-shaped-them-five-historical-crises-show-how-aspects-today-s-fina*

Principles of the Well Managed Bank: http://wikibin.org/articles/principles-of-the-well-managed-bank.html

Definition of Rediscounting: http://www.investopedia.com/terms/s/shorttermdebt.asp and http://lexicon.ft.com/Term?term=rediscounting

About Freethinkers in Bohemia: http://onwardtoourpast.com/czech and http://www.archives.com/genealogy/family-heritage-czech.html

plus::http://plainshumanities.unl.edu/encyclopedia/doc/egp.ea.006

Provides a hard-to-find history of granaries, graineries and grain elevators: http://www.horizonview.net/~ihs/GrainElevators/GrainElevator_Types1.html

Political Cartoons

Political cartoon titled "The Great Race for the Western Stakes 1870 from: https://commons.wikimedia.org/wiki/File:Vanderbilt_%26_Fisk.jpg and sketch circa 1917 of a Native American Indian camp

Political cartoon "Monopoly Millionaires Dividing up the country":

https://commons.wikimedia.org/wiki/File:PUCK-
Monopoly_Millionaires_Dividing_the_Country.jpg
Drawing of Jacob Coxey and his son "Legal Tender" from
http://projects.vassar.edu/1896/depression.html)
1881 Political Cartoon "Monopoly Danger" from:
https://commons.wikimedia.org/wiki/File:Puck_monopoly.jpg
Sketch of Sitting Bull:
https://commons.wikimedia.org/wiki/File:The_American_Indian_Fig_69.jpg

Index

ABOUT THE AUTHORS

Geraldine (Schroder) Perry is the co-author of *The Two Faces of Money* and author of *Climate Change, Land Use and Monetary Policy: The New Trifecta.* She is a member of the Alliance for Just Money and is the creator and manager of three websites, including www.thetwofacesofmoney.com

Donna Schroder is the force behind this project. She is a member of Ancestry and other genealogy societies. In her spare time she volunteers for her local VFW.

Ken Fousek passed away just weeks before this book went to print. He was co-author of *The Two Faces of Money,* and served as a local historian in his home town of Excelsior Springs, Missouri for almost two decades. He had a bit of the politician in his blood having involved himself in local and national political activities for most of his life.

From left to right: Geri, Diana, Donna, Sandy. Photo taken at the conclusion of our first fact-gathering trip, just months before our sister Diana passed away.

Right photo, from left to right: Donna, Ken, Geri -taken at tne historic Alms Hotel, Excelsior Springs, Missouri 2017